The Business School and the Bottom Line

In recent decades business schools have become important components of higher education throughout the world. Surprisingly, however, they have been the subject of little serious study from a critical perspective. This book provides a sober and evidence-based corrective, charting the history and character of business schools in the light of current debates about the role of universities and the evolution of advanced economies. Previous commentators have viewed business schools as falling between two stools: lacking in academic rigour yet simultaneously derided by the corporate world as broadly irrelevant. Over-concern with criticism risks ignoring the benefits of reform, however. What business schools need is reconfiguration based on new relationships with academia and business. Such change would deliver institutions that are truly fit for purpose, allowing them to become key players in the twenty-first century's emergent knowledge societies. This timely critique should be read by academics and policy-makers concerned with the present state and future development of business education.

KEN STARKEY is Professor of Management and Organisational Learning and head of the Strategy Division at Nottingham University Business School. He is a former chair of the British Academy of Management Research Committee and a fellow of the Sunningdale Institute of the National School of Government. He is the author of ten books, including *How Organisations Learn* (2004).

NICK TIRATSOO is currently chair of a regeneration charity in East London. He was previously Visiting Research Fellow with the Business History Unit at the London School of Economics and Political Science, and Senior Research Fellow at Nottingham University Business School. He has published widely in the fields of political history, business history and planning history.

'Business schools play a key role in higher education and in the economic institutions that drive modern societies. Yet little systematic scholarship has been devoted to understanding and improving them. Starkey and Tiratsoo fill this gap admirably. They trace business schools' evolution globally; identify the diverse demands facing them today; describe their approaches to teaching and research; and provide reasonable prescriptions for their future success. This book is essential reading for all of us – administrators, faculty, students and corporate leaders alike – who want (and need) business schools to thrive.'

Thomas G. Cummings, Professor and Chair, Department of Management and Organization, Marshall School of Business, University of Southern California

'This is an important book. How academic institutions are managed so as to create strong, positive societal values is key – and this is what the book is all about. A must-read!'

Peter Lorange, President IMD and the Nestlé Professor

'This book provides critical and valuable insights into the understanding of the challenges business schools are facing in the current world as a result of globalisation trends. This thoughtful and constructive analysis will contribute to improve their leadership and governance – a top priority in making a positive impact not only in management education worldwide but also in society as a whole.'

Fernando Fragueiro, Dean, IAE Business School, Austral University, Argentina

'Increasingly influential – and increasingly criticised – there is no better gathering of facts about what's going in business schools than this work from two experienced authors who have read, probed and interviewed widely. Especially fine are their analyses of the changing relationship between town and gown; chapter 6 is a jewel. Their no-holds-barred remarks about the weaknesses of today's business school strategies, and the possibilities for tomorrow's, are simply the best available in this globalising discussion.'

J.C. Spender, Svenska Handelsbanke, Fulbright-Queen's Research Professor, Queen's University, Canada, and Lund University School of Economics and Management, Sweden

The Business School
and the Bottom Line

KEN STARKEY AND NICK TIRATSOO

CAMBRIDGE
UNIVERSITY PRESS

CAMBRIDGE UNIVERSITY PRESS

Cambridge, New York, Melbourne, Madrid, Cape Town, Singapore, São Paulo

Cambridge University Press
The Edinburgh Building, Cambridge CB2 8RU, UK

Published in the United States of America by Cambridge University Press, New York

www.cambridge.org
Information on this title: www.cambridge.org/9780521865111

First published 2007

Printed in the United Kingdom at the University Press, Cambridge

A catalogue record for this publication is available from the British Library

ISBN 978-0-521-86511-1 hardback

Contents

Tables

Acknowledgements

This book is based upon work funded by the Economic and Social Research Council (ESRC) as part of its Evolution of Business Knowledge (EBK) programme (Grant RES-334-25-0009). We are very grateful to the ESRC for its support, and also wish to thank Harry Scarbrough, the director of EBK, for his guidance and advice, and the other members of our team – Catrina Alferoff, Graeme Currie, David Knights, Andy Lockett, Laura Pearson, Alison Seymour, Sue Tempest and Mike Wright – for many stimulating conversations, and inputs of energy and ideas, without which our understanding of the business school world would have been very much the poorer.

During the course of our research we interviewed a large number of people, who agreed to talk to us on condition that they remain anonymous, and we would like to take this chance to thank every one of them again, especially because, without exception – almost! – they answered our insistent badgering thoughtfully and with good humour.

Many other people have assisted us, and we acknowledge, in particular, Lars Engwall, Guiliana Gemelli, Gerry Johnson, Andrew Pettigrew, David Tranfield, John Wilson and Vera Zamagni (who helped launch the various debates that provoked our initial interest in business schools); Armand Hatchuel and Rolv Petter Amdam (who provided important entry points into the world of non-Anglo-Saxon management); Sandra Baum, Mark Clapson, Terry Gourvish, Clive Holtham, Keri Minehart, Robert S. Sullivan, Sylvia Tiratsoo, Jim Tomlinson, Nigel Waite, Paula Parish and team at Cambridge University Press; and participants at a 2005 seminar at the Business History Unit, the London School of Economics and Political Science, especially Forest Capie and Roy Edwards.

Of course, while we have benefited greatly from the help of everyone mentioned, we alone accept responsibility for the argument that follows.

Prologue

A CAUTIONARY TALE

In May 2006 a large group of Nukak-Makú leave the Amazon jungle and arrive at San José del Guaviare in Colombia, ready to join the modern world.[1]

They are leaving the nomadic life of the hunter-gatherer, where the staples of life are killing monkeys for meat and collecting berries and nuts. Ill-adapted physically and mentally to the demands of the new life that they are seeking, and susceptible to illnesses they have not encountered before, they have no sense of how the new world in which they find themselves works. Crucially, they have no concept of money or of property. They think that the planes that they see in the sky overhead are moving on an invisible road.

It is not clear why the Nukak have acted. Perhaps the relentless struggle for existence has worn them down. It is also possible that they have been driven out by the Green Nukak, bands of Marxist guerrilla fighters, or been displaced by farmers growing coca to make cocaine. The Nukak are a peace-loving people and not prone to fight to defend their territory. Previous Nukak arrivals from the jungle have received state aid and housing and have come to enjoy the benefits of pots, pants, shoes, caps, rice, flour, sugar, oil, eggs, onions, matches, soap, housing and medical attention. This new group aims to follow suit. Having quickly learnt the value of money, their aspiration is to grow plantains and yucca, and to sell these and use the money they earn to exchange for other possessions.

Assuming an optimistic scenario, one can imagine them finding suitable land, close to town but also close to the jungle. They will learn the agricultural skills necessary for their new life. Their children will go to school to gain the benefits of an education so that they can join 'the white family', and they will also be able to retain their own traditions and the Nukak language, which is what they want. In the fullness of time, Nukak children will become fully integrated. They will receive primary and secondary education and some will go to university, where they might study for a management degree.

They might even go on to do graduate work and study for an MBA (Master of Business Administration), one of the world's most popular university qualifications! They might then become successful business people, joining one of the world's large multinationals, perhaps a forestry company or a pharmaceutical company, in which their knowledge of the jungle would prove a core competence. They might be more entrepreneurial, perhaps developing a niche eco-tourism outfit, specialising in jungle adventures for the environmentally conscious traveller.

The Nukak story encapsulates in miniature the trajectory of human history, the transition from the pre-modern to modern, the lure of civilisation and the promises it offers. The various explanations of why they have quit their jungle home are also symbolic. They have been driven out by a clash of ideologies, by the pressures of commerce, by the lure of money, property and possessions, or by a mixture of all of these. The suggestion that they might end up doing an MBA degree is, of course, fanciful – but not beyond the bounds of possibility.

If they do choose this course of development, then they will pass through one of the world's growing number of business schools, perhaps in South America, or perhaps in the North, at one of the elite schools such as Harvard, Wharton and Chicago. They might even choose to spread their wings and come to Europe to study at a leading European school – INSEAD, IMD, IESE or London Business School (LBS). They could even go the Far East, where business education is growing at an exponential rate, gaining the experience of those economies – China and India – that are predicted to challenge the economic dominance of the United States in the not too distant future. We wish the Nukak well. We wish them luck. They will need it!

NOTE

1 Juan Forero, 'Leaving the wild, and rather liking the change', *New York Times*, 11 May 2006.

I   Introduction

Our concern in this book is to examine the business school in depth, placing it in its various contexts: as part of the university system, the practice of business and, ultimately, society as a whole. We feel that this is necessary and interesting for a pair of different but interlocking reasons.

The first stems from a simple reflection on the state of the literature. It is unarguable that business schools are very significant players in today's world. One recent study talks about their 'irresistible rise', characterises their milieu as 'a sphere of immeasurable influence' and argues that they are 'among the great institutions of our age'.[1] The point is well made. Business schools have a degree of authority that stretches surprisingly far and wide. Many leading chief executives and directors, it almost goes without saying, have the schools' prime Master of Business Administration degree. Prior to its victory at the 1997 election, the United Kingdom's Labour Party sent members of its shadow Cabinet to Oxford for business school training. George W. Bush is the first American president to have an MBA, this from Harvard.[2] It may even be true that the business school and the MBA are defining characteristics of what it is for a country to have arrived at the global top table.

Yet, despite their importance, the schools have rarely attracted the serious study that they so manifestly deserve. There is, of course, a lot of coverage in the press, but much of this on closer inspection turns out to be spin. All the schools are in deadly competition, and, like universities in general, now waste few opportunities to promote themselves. With one eye on their circulation figures, newspapers and periodicals (with some honourable exceptions) largely play ball more often than is healthy, recycling public relations handout material as fact. The more we have immersed ourselves in the business school world, the more we have become aware of the fact that appearances and reality can significantly differ. At one level, therefore, what we have set out to do is simply to fill a notable gap – in other words, provide a clear-eyed, analytic and empirically informed corrective to the cacophony of claim and counter-claim, the siren voices of self-interest.

We also have more ambitious aims, however. We believe that there is an urgent need for imaginative and creative thinking about how business schools should evolve in the future. The current range of opinion about the schools and their functioning is broad and vociferous. The tenor of comment is often critical. It is obviously important, from a purely practical standpoint, to determine what is perceptive and realistic in this clamour, and what is not. We also want to go beyond current controversies, however, and believe that, if we are to do so, we must consider a raft of much wider issues, up to and including such important considerations as equality, fairness and social purpose. In the following paragraphs, we expand briefly upon these observations.

CURRENT CONTROVERSIES

It might be thought that opinions about business schools, and their place in the world, would be fairly homogeneous. After all, they are by now omnipresent, and a pretty standard part of life. But in fact there is little real consensus, even about some fairly basic questions. The business school establishment is, not surprisingly, decidedly upbeat. The sector, it asserts, has never been in better health. There are more schools, in more places, with more students, than ever before. In addition, the importance of the schools in the context of higher education as a whole has undoubtedly mushroomed. Many are at the leading edge of innovation, pioneering new methods of teaching, spearheading the growing internationalisation of student recruitment and experimenting with wholly new institutional forms – for example, overseas campuses, subsidiary operations that are closer to the heart of key markets. Most make a highly significant, perhaps crucial, financial contribution to their mother institutions. In the language of management consultancy, of the Boston Consulting portfolio matrix, business schools are often the 'cash cow', without which a significant proportion of other university activity, including the very survival of some departments, is potentially unsustainable. Beyond this, it is claimed, the schools are also greatly benefiting the economy, fuelling innovation and growth. In short, the cheerleaders maintain, the position is entirely rosy. The business school has become both vibrant and indispensable, an integral part of higher education systems and economies worldwide.[3]

Yet others are far from convinced. There are several kinds of criticism. One insistent claim is that the whole business school world has lost its educational soul, and become enthralled by money.[4] It is observed, for example, that a striking number of schools recently have been (and, in some cases, still are) embroiled in high-profile and rather unseemly altercations. In the United States, applicants to the elite MBA programmes at Harvard and Stanford were discovered hacking into confidential admissions files, thus prompting an anxious and very public debate about what such behaviour said about the prevailing business school ethos.[5] Across the Atlantic, in the United Kingdom, controversy has simmered about an equally important matter: the ways that schools finance themselves. One case in particular has provoked comment. In 2000 London University's venerable Imperial College accepted a gift of £27 million from Gary Tanaka, and used it to build and equip a new management school facility. In May 2005 Tanaka was arrested in the United States, and during the course of the next few months charged with conspiracy, securities fraud, investment adviser fraud, mail fraud, wire fraud and money laundering.[6] At the time of writing, in early 2006, all the charges against Tanaka remained entirely unproven, his good name untarnished.[7] But the whole episode has left many perplexed, a feeling that is exacerbated by a UK broadsheet's contemporaneous claim that problems with donors are 'a surprisingly common phenomenon'.[8]

Other critics, including several respected insiders, have called into question an even more elemental matter: the business schools' very reason for being. The onslaught started in 2002, when Stanford's Jeffrey Pfeffer and Christina Fong published a widely noticed article that argued vigorously that the schools were actually far less profi-cient at creating value than they habitually claimed. The usual propositions, Pfeffer and Fong noted, were that the schools provided relevant teaching for careers in business, and at the same time added greatly to the stock of management knowledge through research. Yet none of this, they believed, was actually supported by the evidence. Possession of an MBA did not correlate with career success. Most business school research had demonstrably little impact, either in the academy or – and this was really the clincher – in business. The clear conclusion, Pfeffer and Fong suggested, was that the schools were simply not delivering as promised.[9]

During the course of the next couple of years further, and harsher, criticisms were voiced. The allegation now was that business schools were not just failing to live up to their promises but also actively doing harm. In a much-trailed book entitled *Managers not MBAs*, the Cleghorn Professor of Management Studies at McGill University, Henry Mintzberg, claimed that most business school teaching had over-prioritised dry, functional disciplines, and thus pro-duced generations of managers who were largely incapable of dealing with the ingrained messiness of day-to-day business life, let alone its moral challenges.[10] During a parallel series of interviews and articles, the London Business School's Sumantra Ghoshal was even more scathing. In his view, there was a direct link between business school teaching and the spate of corporate scandals that were currently erupting in the United States, most obviously, of course, Enron. The schools had propagated pernicious ideas and techniques for the pre-vious thirty years or more, Ghoshal maintained, and these were now coming home to roost. The absolute imperative, he believed, had to be an open admission of failure, followed by no less than root and branch reform.[11]

What makes these various broadsides so noteworthy is the fact that they have often been picked up and discussed in the mainstream media. Pfeffer and Mintzberg, in particular, are not only senior and well-respected academics but accomplished public performers as well. Periodicals and newspapers, including *Business Week*, *The Economist* and the *Financial Times*, rightly take them seriously and discuss their views with interest. In no time at all, elements of the different indictments have echoed through the wider culture, chiming in with anxieties about corporate greed, globalisation and overbearing US power. A 2004 British press story about the MBA started with a telling illustration of the growing mood of disenchantment:

> A recent American television advertisement for the courier firm Fedex features . . . [a] young man on his first day at work . . . His boss tells him that there's a problem. 'We're in a bit of a jam,' he says. 'All this stuff has to get out today.'
>
> 'Yeah, er . . . I don't do dispatch,' the new recruit replies.
>
> 'Oh no, no, it's very easy,' the boss says. 'We use Fedex. Anybody can do it.'
>
> 'You don't understand. I have an MBA.'
>
> 'Oh, you have an MBA?'
>
> 'Yeah . . .'
>
> 'In that case, I'll have to show you how to do it.'
>
> The voice-over delivers the punchline: 'Fedex makes shipping so fast and easy, even an MBA can do it.'[12]

Of course, stepping back a little, it is clear that some of this opprobrium can be taken with a pinch of salt. Many business schools are well run, with educational standards fully enforced and monetary matters properly policed. In all the clamour about deficiencies in curricula and research, it is often overlooked that much of what the schools do is uncontroversial, a matter of steadily collecting, codifying and then disseminating useful knowledge about business practice, real and desired. Finally, the attempt to yoke the schools to concurrent corporate wrongdoing is not always fully convincing either. At an elementary level, as *The Economist* has observed, the evidence simply does not stack up. Enron was full of MBAs, it is true, but most other recent scandal-hit US companies were not.[13] Anyway, as contemporaneous events in Belgium, France, Germany, Italy, Japan and Sweden amply demonstrate, corporate misbehaviour is emphatically not unique to the business-school-rich Anglo-American demi-monde.[14]

Nevertheless, with such reservations accepted, the critics certainly cannot simply be dismissed. Beneath the surface there seems to be deep unease in much of the business school world, a widespread anxiety about how events are unfolding. In a column appearing in mid-2004, *Financial Times* columnist Michael Skapinker quipped: 'Most organisations have their worst enemies outside. There are small shopkeepers who detest Wal-Mart, anarchists who kick in the windows at McDonald's and environmentalists who boycott Exxon. Only at business schools are the most vociferous critics the paid employees.'[15] As we have travelled round business schools, and talked to faculty, we have become increasingly impressed by his perspicacity. Some lecturers complained to us of burgeoning workloads, and the 'industrialisation' of teaching, while others explained that they felt trapped into doing research that is essentially meaningless. A much-respected dean told us, off the record, of his belief that business schools were facing no less than a crisis of legitimacy. If his peers did not necessarily go that far, they were all in one way or another apprehensive. As for students, they worried about the real value of their degrees, and the fact that some employers' valuation of the MBA is clearly declining. Several informed journalists spoke of an impending institutional 'shake-out', which might even send some household names to the wall. We could multiply similar anecdotes many times over. Given this accrual of disquiet, it is certainly timely to ask what the future holds, and in particular how the situation might be changed for the better.

BUSINESS SCHOOL FUTURES

In thinking about the prospects for business schools, we have been struck by just how complex the issues are. The business schools are hemmed in by different but inevitably weighty pressures. Few of the key conundrums are merely technical. Many raise questions about socio-economic relationships, politics and even ethics. We can illustrate this point by looking in a little detail at two of the major challenges that the business schools will inevitably have to negotiate in the near future.

The first is the relationship between the schools and their mother institutions, the universities. We need to begin with some background about higher education systems as a whole. At one time, it was generally agreed that the university should aspire to be concerned only with knowledge and truth – that it was, in a much-repeated characterisation, an independent community of scholars, dedicated to studying and learning, and nothing else. Now, however, the position is rapidly changing. The key development has been driven from within the political economy. As governments everywhere retreat from subsidising public services, so universities, just like many other similar institutions, are forced to take commercial performance far more seriously, and this in turn has inevitable knock-on effects on the quality of education that is being offered. The new axioms are indicative. Courses are to be assessed not only in terms of their intrinsic worth but also in terms of their value for money; research must add to knowledge but also have identifiable pay-offs; each institution (and, in some cases, each constituent subunit within that institution) should not just break even but explicitly earn a surplus; and so on.

The University of California Professor of Public Policy, David Kirp, has recently charted how this trend is proceeding in the United States.[16] His analysis is at once sober and sobering. He recognises that money has always been important for universities to some extent, but believes that recent trends add up to a step change. American higher education is being 'transformed' by the power and the ethic of the marketplace. The essence of his argument is as follows:

> New educational technologies; a generation of students with different desires and faculty with different demands; a new breed of rivals that live or die by the market; the incessant demand for more funds and new revenues to replace the ever-shrinking proportion of public support; a genuinely global market in minds: taken together, these forces are remaking the university into what has variously been called the site of 'academic capitalism', the 'entrepreneurial university', and the 'enterprise university'.[17]

On the other side of the Atlantic, a variety of commentators, on both the left and the right of the political spectrum, have produced rather similar observations.[18] There is no doubt that they are describing very real trends.

The question for us is what this means for the business school. University administrators, we have already suggested, tend to view business schools as 'cash cows'. In one scenario, they may simply take their current approach and drive it to its logical conclusion, extracting the maximum commercial benefit from courses such as the MBA, regardless of what this means for pedagogy and learning. But there could be more positive outcomes. Thus, for example, deans of business schools might be encouraged to use their hard-won experiences to develop a new synthesis, say something along the lines of 'commercialisation with a human face', which would simultaneously satisfy both educational and financial imperatives, and provide a beacon of hope for those in other, harder-pressed, parts of the academy. Much depends, quite clearly, on exactly who is in charge of decision-making. Ultimately, then, how this problem is solved is less to do with educational policy as such and much more to do with bigger issues of politics.

Our second illustration concerns the question of 'Americanisation'. The business school and the MBA were, of course, initially developed in the United States, and it is unsurprising to find that, in subsequent developments all over the world, this fact has continued to cast a long shadow. Thus, when pioneers in Europe, for example, developed their own early initiatives in the 1940s, 1950s and 1960s, they often explicitly built on American foundations, using US textbooks and the case study teaching method, which was strongly identified with Harvard. Inevitably, too, they espoused, to a greater or lesser extent, similar basic values. Fairly typically, when the early champion of INSEAD, George Doriot, was selling his proposition to potential supporters in the 1950s, he emphasised that it was crucial that 'young Europeans' were 'brought up with a good conception of American ideals and the free enterprise system'.[19]

For most of the later twentieth century, little of this was very contentious. The United States economy was strong and vigorous, the powerhouse that fuelled global economic growth. It made sense to proselytise about its key constituents and secrets. In any event, there was no real alternative – the Soviet system had such obvious and crippling disadvantages. Latterly, however, an increasing number of voices, particularly in Europe, are urging a rethink. American capitalism, so their argument goes, is changing, mutating into a new and rapacious form, and in the process revealing a dark and threatening agenda of global domination. Events such as the dot.com bubble, the Enron scandal and the spectacular rise and fall of such figures as Michael Milken, Ivan Boesky, Albert Dunlap ('Chainsaw Al' or 'the Rambo in Pinstripes'), Bernard Ebbers and Kenneth Lay are taken to be deeply revealing. A system that once largely aimed to satisfy ordinary people's everyday needs is now apparently fixated on short-term financial gains for directors and shareholders, won regardless of consequences or ethics. If, in the name of profit, the environment is despoiled, communities shattered and developing countries robbed, that is just too bad. At an extreme, the most pessimistic suggest, the threat is of impending descent into 'a dog-eat-dog Mafia world of might being right'.[20] What sane person, it is quite reasonably asked, would want to teach that?

This, of course, raises the difficult question of alternatives, however. If the pace of change, as everyone agrees, is accelerating, and the current configuration of capitalism, as Will Hutton and Anthony Giddens point out, is becoming at the very least ever 'harder, more mobile, more ruthless and more certain about what it needs to make it tick',[21] how can business schools meaningfully react? One obvious step is to make the curriculum more critical, using a much broader array of linkages with the social sciences, the humanities and perhaps the natural sciences. But who is to lead this change? And will the rest of the university sector, let alone the business community, agree? Beyond this, should the non-US worlds develop general models and pedagogies of their own? Should European schools, for example, hone and promote a particularly 'European' form of management, based around alleged 'European values', principally perhaps social solidarity? Is such a thing intellectually possible and defensible? Might the Indian and Chinese schools follow suit? What would be the implications for the newly emerging schools in Latin America and Africa? So, once more, as we approach the nub of the issue, it becomes bewilderingly complex, and leads us back to fundamentals. A concern with one problem has opened up a Pandora's box of others. Ultimately, in this case, at least, it appears that we must in the end confront the basic question: exactly who or what are the business schools for?

THE CHAPTERS THAT FOLLOW

The thrust of what ensues takes it shape from these remarks. We do not – and cannot – provide full answers to all the questions that we believe are germane, but we do hope at least to sketch in what we see as the main agenda. We begin with a group of five chapters that trace the rise of the business school, follow its diffusion and then analyse in detail how it functions today, exploring in particular the institutional pressures that are present, the prevalent kinds of education and research, and some contemporary innovations. We then turn to the future. Chapter 7 is written in a rather different register from the rest of the book, and takes the reader though an imaginary MBA class. Our purpose, here, is to highlight some of the fundamental dilemmas that business education now faces. In chapter 8 we review some of the practical choices facing the schools over the coming years, and make some suggestions of our own about what, we believe, the fruitful way forward is.

Finally, we need to be frank in acknowledging our own limitations. Many readers will no doubt assume that researching business schools is fairly easy, essentially a matter of collating and processing widely available existing evidence. After all, as has already been noted, the schools have been, and continue to be, highly newsworthy, perhaps more remarked upon than any other part of the academy. The actual situation is a good deal less propitious than it appears, however. Press coverage of business schools is – we repeat – often unsatisfactory. There is in general much more information available in the public sphere about big, famous schools than their smaller, but very much more numerous, counterparts. The same is true, *mutatis mutandis*, of the MBA as opposed to other kinds of business school degree. In addition, there is the awkward but unavoidable fact that those who work in the sector often have their own particular agendas, and respond to outside investigators accordingly. MBA students are aware that publicly criticising a course can have a negative impact on their school's reputation, and thus possibly damage how they themselves are later perceived in the job market. Faculty may be protective of their teaching methods, afraid that they will be copied or unfairly criticised by outsiders. An elemental solidarity – that 'we are all in this together' or that 'we've got to go on working with these people' – sometimes inhibits criticism of other institutions and courses. The fact that this remains a profession in which demand exceeds supply – and in which, therefore, poaching is a fact of life – is a further reason for reticence. No one, understandably, wants to jeopardise a lucrative career move in the future. At the apex, those who lead business schools are forever worrying about protecting themselves against competitors. Over a meal one day we chatted with a leading dean about how difficult we had found it to uncover hard data about business school finances. He scoffed, and asked why we thought such material either would, or should, be in the public domain; to him, our expectation of transparency was simply naive. In short, establishing the truth about business schools is a rather more difficult task than might be imagined.

In working on this book, we have been acutely aware of all these problems. Our approach has been to research sources as exhaustively as possible, supplementing printed and archival material with interviews, and then to subject our findings to critical scrutiny. But we freely acknowledge that further analysis needs to be carried out on many of the more detailed points that we touch upon. Our aim has been to fashion a general overview, designed to introduce the key issues and stimulate better-informed debate inside and outside the sector. We certainly do not claim to have written the final word.

NOTES

1 Stuart Crainer and Des Dearlove, *Gravy Training: Inside the Shadowy World of Business Schools* (Oxford: Capstone, 1998), xi, 2.

2 For President Bush, see Kim Clark, 'Grading the M.B.A. president', *U.S. News and World Report*, 3 April 2006.

3 For such broadly upbeat assessments, see, for example, Della Bradshaw, 'Darden's dean finds inspiration in Socrates', *Financial Times*, 16 July 2006, and Glenn Hubbard, 'Do not undervalue the impact of business education', *Financial Times*, 28 July 2006.

4 For classic statements of this view, see Crainer and Dearlove, *Gravy Training*.

5 Philip Delves Broughton, 'A lesson in moral leadership', *Financial Times*, 25 April 2005.

6 Imperial College London press releases, dated 25 October 2000 and 24 June 2004; anon., 'Amerindo's Vilar charged with stealing from client', *Bloomberg.com*, 27 May 2005; Paul Palmer, 'Billionaire benefactors who fell to earth (and why the Royal Opera House and Imperial College are left feeling rather embarrassed)', *Evening Standard*, 23 June 2005; Edward Simpkins, 'School for scoundrels? How should universities react when their benefactors are accused of malpractice?', *Sunday Telegraph*, 26 June 2005;

and anon., 'Amerindo's Vilar, Tanaka plead not guilty to new charges', *AP Worldstream*, 9 February 2006.

7 A spokesperson for Imperial College commented: 'The charges against Mr Tanaka are a matter for him and not Imperial College. Given that there are legal proceedings pending, we don't wish to say anything further at this stage that may prejudice a fair hearing of the matter in the US courts. We should also remember that Mr Tanaka is innocent of any charges unless convicted by a court of law.' See Simpkins, 'School for scoundrels?'.

8 Simpkins, 'School for scoundrels?'. See also, for particular cases, Jonathan Pryn, 'Cambridge University row takes place over Tyco donation', *Evening Standard*, 5 November 2002, and anon., 'Mitte Foundation withdraws gift to U. of Texas', *Chronicle of Higher Education*, 13 June 2003.

9 Jeffrey Pfeffer and Christina T. Fong, 'The end of business schools? Less success than meets the eye', *Academy of Management Learning and Education*, 1(1) (2002), 78–95.

10 Henry Mintzberg, *Managers not MBAs* (Harlow: Pearson Education, 2004). See also Simon Caulkin, 'Masterclasses they're not', *Observer*, 27 June 2004.

11 Sumantra Ghoshal, 'Business schools share Enron blame', *Financial Times*, 17 July 2003; Simon Caulkin, 'Business schools for scandal', *Observer*, 28 March 2004; Sumantra Ghoshal, 'Bad management theories are destroying good management practice', *Academy of Management Learning and Education*, 4(1) (2005), 75–91.

12 Stefan Stern, 'Can MBA graduates deliver in the real world?', *Daily Telegraph*, 6 September 2004.

13 Anon., 'Bad for business?', *Economist*, 17 February 2005.

14 Indeed, work by the anti-corruption campaigners Transparency International shows that countries with long-standing MBA programmes are generally perceived to be rather less dishonest than their neighbours. See, for, example, Transparency International, *Report on the Transparency International Global Corruption Barometer 2005* (Berlin: Transparency International, 2005), 18–19.

15 Michael Skapinker, 'Schools have responsibilities', *Financial Times*, 13 July 2004.

16 David L. Kirp, *Shakespeare, Einstein and the Bottom Line: The Marketing of Higher Education* (Cambridge, MA: Harvard University Press, 2003).

17 Kirp, *Shakespeare, Einstein and the Bottom Line*, 2, 6. For other analyses of US higher education that explore the same broad point, see Eric Gould,

The University in a Corporate Culture (New Haven, CT, and London: Yale University Press, 2003), and Jennifer Washburn, *University Inc.: The Corporate Corruption of American Higher Education* (New York: Basic Books, 2005).

18 As regards the United Kingdom, for example, see Gordon Graham, *Universities: The Recovery of an Idea* (Thorverton: Imprint Academic, 2002); Duke Maskell and Ian Robinson, *The New Idea of a University* (Thorverton: Imprint Academic, 2002); and Mary Evans, *Killing Thinking: The Death of the Universities* (London and New York: Continuum, 2004).

19 Jean-Louis Barsoux, *INSEAD: From Intuition to Institution* (London: Macmillan, 2000), 54.

20 Will Hutton and Anthony Giddens, 'In conversation', in Will Hutton and Anthony Giddens (eds.), *On the Edge: Living with Global Capitalism* (London: Vintage, 2001), 35.

21 Hutton and Giddens, 'In conversation', in Hutton and Giddens (eds.), *On the Edge*, 9.

2   The development and diffusion of the business school

It is tempting to assume that business schools – and the MBA qualification that is their touchstone – must always have been much as they are today, an integral component of modern life. The schools seem to have such permanence and ubiquity that it is difficult to think of the world without them. Everywhere, it seems, with the possible exception of parts of Africa, they thrive. They are woven into higher education, the business system and the culture. In short, they just seem to be part of the furniture. Yet there is much more of a story here than meets the eye. The classic business school is of surprisingly recent origin. It emerged in the United States at the end of the nineteenth century, and then only started to be copied in the rest of the world several decades later. Moreover, wherever business schools appeared they tended to be accompanied by controversy. Some believed that there were better ways of developing business and management skills; more doubted whether such skills either could or should actually be taught at all. In this environment, the whole sector developed awkwardly, and was prone to periodic bouts of soul-searching and crisis. In this chapter, we examine this rather chequered history in detail, attempt to uncover its basic dynamics, and then look briefly at some aspects of its legacy.

THE MARCH OF BUSINESS SCHOOLS

The early rise of the business school in the United States was in many respects astonishing. The pioneering Wharton School was founded in 1881. By the turn of the twentieth century there were two other similar institutions. Thereafter, the numbers increased dramatically, from about a dozen in 1910 to 100 in 1929 and around 120 by the beginning of the Second World War. From virtually nowhere, business degrees rapidly came to make up a very significant fraction of all those awarded – no less than 9.1 per cent in 1939/40. As yet, the focus was largely on the undergraduate level, and the development of largely vocational competencies. But the position was also evolving. Those gaining master's degrees in business numbered a mere 110 in 1919, but 1,139 ten years later. In addition, the curriculum was everywhere becoming more academic. By the late 1930s most schools taught accounting, economics, banking and finance, marketing, statistics and management, while many also offered business organisation and law. Peripheral courses, such as secretarial skills and journalism, were on the wane.[1] Reflecting on the totality of these developments in his book on the first 100 years of the MBA, the historian Carter A. Daniel emphasised their 'unprecedentedness', and observed: 'No parallel exists in academic history for a subject that grew in only four decades from small and random beginnings to one of the largest components of a university. It was unique, and it was by far the most significant development in American higher education in the twentieth century.'[2]

After 1945 the US embrace of business education was perhaps even more remarkable. The number of institutions offering business degrees continued to grow rapidly, and gradually encompassed a whole gamut of different subsets, from university departments to free-standing institutions and for-profits providers. By the end of the twentieth century it was estimated that at least 900 different players offered a master's degree in business, while 1,292 or 92 per cent of all mainstream colleges and universities offered the subject as an undergraduate major.[3] Students signed up for such courses in ever greater volumes, as the figures in table 2.1 demonstrate. There were periods of quite astounding growth, such as in the 1970s. The master's degree also came of age, constituting about a third of the total by the 1990s. Altogether, business education began to dominate the educational landscape. In 2002/3 bachelor's degrees and master's degrees in business made up an extraordinary 22 per cent and 25 per cent respectively of all those awarded.[4]

Table 2.1 *US-earned degrees in business by degree-granting institutions, selected years 1955/6 to 2002/3*

Year	Bachelor's degrees	Master's degrees
1955/6	42,813	3,280
1965/6	62,721	12,959
1975/6	143,171	42,592
1985/6	236,700	66,676
1995/6	226,623	93,554
2002/3	293,545	127,545

Source: National Center for Educational Statistics, *Digest of Educational Statistics* (Washington, DC: National Center for Educational Statistics, 2004), table 278.

Meanwhile, US proselytisers were also promoting the need for business schools in many other parts of the world. Their efforts started in Europe at the end of the Second World War. Of necessity, many Americans were forced into close proximity with European managers and entrepreneurs during these years, and this tended to produce disdain. The Europeans seemed autocratic and amateurish, wedded to long-outdated methods of production, marketing, human relations and accountancy. Poor management in turn presaged low productivity and modest living standards. The threat that socialists and communists might capitalise on popular discontent with austerity was ever present. If Europe was to rebuild itself, the Americans concluded, then the 'management gap' had to be swiftly closed. One key objective, therefore, became the creation of a modernised cadre of managers, trained and proficient, that could spearhead reconstruction. A drive to improve business education inevitably followed.[5] At first US government agencies linked to Marshall Aid provided the lead, but later European surrogates together with the Ford Foundation substituted. The individual initiatives ranged across a broad spectrum. It was believed that first-hand exposure to American institutions would be revelatory, and so study visits were one enduring feature. The tone was set in 1951, when a high-profile UK team crossed the Atlantic and concluded emphatically that education for management and high productivity were 'closely related'.[6] More conventionally, there were generous grants, sometimes worth hundreds of thousands of dollars, for projects that were judged worthwhile, with individual beneficiaries including universities, particular faculties, networks, and organisations promoting conference series. And alongside all this came a constant stream of exhortation: Europe had to change, and should expand its business and management education facilities forthwith.

In subsequent decades similar arguments and admonitions were deployed in many other parts of the world. American government programmes remained prominent, but as time passed, and the US business education sector itself reached maturity, there was increasing activity by individual schools, with the likes of Harvard being particularly active in finding and then promoting overseas partners. Hundreds of links were created – involving everything from staff swaps, student placements, mentoring and help with curriculum development to more direct forms of financial assistance. From the 1980s onwards American missionaries were joined by many others. To name but a few, the European Union was involved in promoting developments in China; the Catholic organisation Opus Dei supported individual institutions in, amongst other places, Nigeria and Argentina; the Word Bank's International Finance Corporation arm began a programme to encourage business education in Africa; and a raft of European schools established their own particular partnerships, whether in the newly capitalist east of the continent, north Africa, the Middle East, Asia or Latin America. Everywhere, it seemed, those who had been won to the cause were in turn attempting to convert others.[7]

All this activity produced some obvious and substantial results.[8] In the 1950s and 1960s the expansion of business schools was largely limited to Europe. Thereafter, country after country in the developing world followed the same road, sometimes purposefully, sometimes fit-fully. The subsequent collapse of communism and the intensification of globalisation provided further momentum. By 1998 an informed commentator could claim: 'Finally, the MBA has conquered the world. Like cola drink, you can find an MBA programme almost anywhere. From Argentina to Zimbabwe and from Ankara to Zeist there are pro-grammes for those who seek the world's most recognised and envied academic qualification. Whatever the language or culture, an MBA means something wherever you are.'[9] As the twenty-first century dawned there was especially strong growth across Asia. In 1991 there had been about 130 approved management education institutions in India, with an annual intake of 12,000 students; by 2005 the compar-ative figures were, respectively, about 1,000 and 75,000.[10] In China the Ministry of Education licensed nine universities to teach master's business programmes in 1991, but ninety-five fourteen years later.[11] Even quite small countries were caught up in the expansion. In 2003 Nepal, with a population of 23 million, had four universities and four private management institutes providing degree-level business educa-tion. Two years later it was reported that Singaporeans could choose to enrol on courses run by no fewer than ten leading international providers, three of whom had dedicated local campuses.[12]

In each of these different phases, American influence remained strong. Some countries, it is true, modified the original model. The British, for example, famously rejected the US insistence that the MBA be taught over two years, and shaped it to the twelve-month format that they used for every other kind of master's degree. Different countries produced their own hybrids. But almost everyone adopted American teaching methods and textbooks to some extent or other,[13] American faculty were universally recognised and respected as the leading lights of the profession, while the MBA itself retained a distinctively American twang. Significantly, when eastern Europe was forced to grapple with a return of capitalism in the early 1990s, a rash of different schools suddenly appeared offering what they point-edly referred to as 'U.S. MBA education'.[14]

AMERICAN CONTROVERSIES

At first sight, this history looks unproblematic – the triumphant development and diffusion of what appeared to be a highly successful model. Yet closer inspection reveals a much more complicated story, shot through with debate and conflict, in which progress was rarely automatic and a happy ending never assured. To illustrate this point, we look first at the situation in the United States, and then turn to the rest of the world.

The basic fact about the business school in America is that it was always subject to criticism, and sometimes intense criticism at that. A couple of examples will give a flavour. In the late 1950s two academics, Robert Aaron Gordon and James Edwin Howell, were hired by the Ford Foundation to report on the state of US collegiate business education. After toiling for three years, and interviewing 'more than a thousand businessmen and educators', they published their findings in 1959. The tone was decidedly gloomy. Business education, Gordon and Howell conceded, *looked* healthy, 'a giant in the halls of higher education', supremely successful in attracting students and funds. Beneath the surface glitz, however, unease reigned. Their conclusion could hardly have been less reassuring. Under the subheading 'Business education adrift', they wrote:

> [Collegiate business education] is an uncertain giant, gnawed by doubt and harassed by the barbs of unfriendly critics. It seeks to serve several masters and is assured by its critics that it serves none well. The business world takes its students but deprecates the value of their training, extolling instead the virtues of science and the liberal arts. It finds itself at the foot of the academic table, uncomfortably nudging those other two stepchildren, Education and Agriculture. It is aware of its ungainly size and views apprehensively the prospect of still further growth, knowing that even now it lacks the resources to teach well the horde of students who come swarming in search of a practical education.[15]

What made this all the more convincing was that a second report, this time sponsored by the Carnegie Foundation, which by chance had been issued concurrently, made a series of almost identical observations.[16]

Nearly thirty years later the American Assembly of Collegiate Schools of Business (AACSB), the main representative body, began to consider what business education should look like in the twenty-first century. The upshot was a report by another pair of business school insiders, Lyman Porter and Lawrence McKibbin, which was again based upon thousands of interviews and questionnaires, garnered from all the different interested parties. The conclusions drawn featured some disturbing echoes. Porter and McKibbin believed that most business schools were caught in a rut, and had begun to drift. They argued: 'The most descriptive operative word in the mid-1980s in business schools has been *complacency*. The over-riding concern seems to be how to get more resources to "keep on doing what we're doing". The pervasive attitude might be described as "I'm all right, Jack".'[17] What made matters worse, Porter and McKibbin continued, was the fact that few believed ' "what we're doing" ' actually had much merit. This extended, crucially, to business itself:

> [I]n the course of our investigations we encountered some well-reasoned concern, particularly among senior executives in the business world, that business school students tend to be rather more narrowly educated than they ought to be if they are to cope effectively in a rapidly changing and increasingly complex world. From this perspective, business schools seem to be turning out focused analysts, albeit highly sophisticated ones, but, at the same time, graduates who often are unwittingly insensitive to the impact of these outcomes on factors other than 'the bottom line'. This is a view with which we ourselves strongly concur.[18]

Clearly, such assessments were a far cry from the happy picture that was a staple of so much business school self-promotion.

If, as these episodes show, criticism of business schools could be trenchant, it could also be extremely wide-ranging. Indeed, at one time or another, just about every aspect of business school life was subject to some degree of opprobrium.[19] One persistent set of allegations focused on the curriculum. There were continuing claims that the standard of business education was poor, that, in effect, second-rate students were being given a second-rate education. It was vocally insisted, by turns, that courses were either too vocational or (as we have seen) too theoretical – either over-concerned with functional detail or so abstract as to be useless in the hurly-burly of everyday business interactions. Faculty were berated for their lack of practical experience. Their research was portrayed as largely immaterial, nit-picking and out of touch. A typical judgement, dating from the mid-1980s, was that 'the research in business administration during the past 20 years would fail any reasonable test of applicability or relevance to consequential management problems or policy issues concerning the role of business nationally or internationally'.[20] The charge, in short, was that the schools were not fulfilling their real educational purpose, and thus making minimal difference to US economic life. As Herman Krooss and Peter Drucker encapsulated it in 1969: 'Altogether the business schools in America have tended to react rather than act. They have codified rather than initiated. The new concepts, ideas, and tools of business have originated largely outside the business school and practically without benefit of academicians.'[21]

Alongside all this there was anxiety about the wider ramifications of continued business school growth. Some portrayed the schools as bastions of a voracious capitalism, which were undermining the academy's traditional mission of free enquiry. More usually, argument raged over the very practical matter of whether the pattern of endless expansion could be sustained. Pundits alternatively forecast boom and bust. Much energy was spent on analysing morsels fed by recruiters, and debating what salary increment MBAs were enjoying. Opinions fluctuated, even in the very short term. On 14 January 1992 the *New York Times* published a story headlined 'For MBAs dim outlook this spring', yet just three months later the *Wall Street Journal* proclaimed: 'They're back! MBAs are rediscovering Wall Street.'[22] There was never a time when the future appeared fully secure. In summary, though the schools were succeeding in attracting students and making money for themselves and their parent universities, for the most part they remained insecure and unloved. The same charges were repeated again and again, in what Carter A. Daniel identified as 'an endless cycle', which had begun in the early years of the twentieth century and then echoed remorselessly on down the following decades.[23]

THE COURSE OF DIFFUSION

We now turn to the question of the transfer of the American model to the rest of the world. Looked at from the perspective of the twenty-first century, it perhaps appears as if diffusion proceeded at an insistent pace, inexorably encompassing more and more developed and then developing countries. In reality, however, the process tended to be convoluted and contested. Those on the receiving end of US advances were by no means passive, and the proffered solutions were often argued over, and sometimes even rejected, leaving a footprint that is still very much observable today. We begin by examining some facts about diffusion, and then try to explain its dynamics.

The figures in table 2.2 give an indication of how some major countries responded to the American admonitions. Some quite clearly remained relatively unenthusiastic. Germany, France and Japan were all in this group, though each to some extent made up ground from the 1990s onwards. The Federal Republic, for example, had just 500 MBA students in 1990, but about 5,500 in 2004.[24] Elsewhere there was no such reconciliation. The case of Italy is telling. In the 1950s and 1960s both the US government and the Ford Foundation were very eager to boost Italian business education, not least because they feared that economic backwardness and poverty, especially in the south, might open the door to communism. Many

Table 2.2 *MBA programmes and institutions delivering MBA programmes, selected countries, January 2006*

Country	Number of programmes	Number of institutions delivering MBAs
United States	1,138	562
United Kingdom	367	160
Canada	104	53
France	100	67
Australia	92	46
Spain	87	50
Germany	86	60
Italy	27	18
Russia	27	20
Japan	24	22

Source: www.mbainfo.com.

millions of dollars were spent on different initiatives.[25] All that was achieved for several decades, however, was a series of 'mushrooms', which came and went but left little trace.[26] Thus, an investigation of Italian schools and courses in the 1980s concluded as follows.

- They are few . . .
- They are mostly concentrated in the north . . .
- Very few of them are rooted in the educational establishment . . .
- They have a weak background of theoretical and applied research and a weak community of management scholars . . .
- Many programmes are crude transplantations of managerial concepts and tools generated elsewhere and inappropriate to the Italian environment.
- The 'management education industry' is plagued by too many profit-orientated organisations with short-term objectives . . .
- There is a lack of adequate recognition of the role of management education by opinion leaders, entrepreneurs and politicians . . .[27]

As table 2.2 demonstrates, in 2005 Italy still had far fewer schools and programmes than many of its similarly sized neighbours.

Unsurprisingly, the Anglo-Saxon countries seem to have been the most willing to follow the American lead. Yet, even here, the position was sometimes rather more problematic than it appeared. The United Kingdom provides a good example. At first sight, the British look to have been particularly responsive to the missionaries' zeal. There was certainly an enormous expansion of provision. The number of business schools increased from none in the early 1960s to more than 100 in 2004, while during the same period the output of MBAs rose from about fifty per year to some 10,900 per year, and the number of full-time students studying business studies and associated subjects at undergraduate level grew from about 1,000 to 149,965 (compared to, for example, 47,440 studying the physical sciences and 32,565 studying 'mass communication and documentation').[28] Moreover, much of this expansion was straightforward emulation. Many British academics and university administrators crossed the Atlantic on study visits in the 1950s and 1960s, while several prominent schools received big Ford Foundation subventions, and so a desire to copy American pedagogy, in particular, was inevitable. Thus, for example, almost all British business schools chose to use the case study method, and, to some extent, American textbooks.[29]

On closer inspection, however, it is apparent that such observations are only part of the story. Two points are germane. First, it is notable that the British uptake of American ideas was never a smooth process, but in fact waxed and waned considerably. Progress was initially rather slow: indeed, in 1963 the British Institute of Management (BIM) could state regretfully: 'As a nation we have not yet started on the task of providing trained and capable managers in sufficient numbers at the right time.'[30] Then, when growth occurred, there were considerable swings of fortune. A frenzy of activity in the mid-1960s, which produced the first dedicated business schools in London and Manchester, was followed by a considerable downturn. Commenting on the situation in mid-1971, the journal *Management*

Decision observed: 'The great euphoria with which management education was ushered on to the British tertiary education scene has faded.'[31] Four years later, according to a correspondent in the *Director*, the business schools were still going through 'a period of circumspection, not to say acute introspection'.[32] The 1990s were equally tumultuous. The number of MBAs awarded each year more than doubled over the course of the decade, but, in 1993, the situation was thought so dispiriting that a *Management Today* survey began with the strapline 'MBA: chic in the '80s, sick in the '90s'.[33]

Second, and related to this, is the fact that the pursuit of the American model in Britain was always to some extent controversial. Practitioners frequently squabbled over precise ends and means – about everything from who constituted the target market to how they should be taught. Institutions jostled for space, and offered a bewildering and rather unstructured array of slightly different qualifications. At times the atmosphere grew almost hysterical, with strongly worded and sometimes vitriolic manifestos being launched in quick succession. Press coverage amplified the divisions.[34] In addition, there were continual and more disturbing allegations about standards, with many fearing what one authority referred to as the ' "depreciation of the currency" of the MBA'.[35] Business schools and other university providers of management courses were shown to differ considerably in their competencies.[36] Some institutions, such as London Business School, were believed to be beyond reproach, and enjoyed an enviable international standing, but others, as a survey of 1988 put it, were 'no more than marking – or killing – time'.[37] Critics pointed to the poor quality of some courses; the lack of rigour in admission policies and final grading;[38] the low number of faculty doing research;[39] the indifference of their output;[40] and the apparently high incidence of unfortunate internal altercations.[41] Viewed in its entirety, therefore, this was hardly a sector that appeared at ease, either with itself or with its surroundings. The constant stream of laments from business school luminaries throughout the period spoke for itself.

EXPLAINING DIFFUSION: 'RETARDANTS' AND 'ACCELERATORS'

The pattern described in the previous paragraphs is, at first sight, puzzling. The United States was of course an economic superpower throughout this period, and so represented a powerful exemplar to the rest of the world. Many of the initiatives to export business schools were well crafted and funded. It is also true that most big countries in Europe, at least, worried that they were falling behind the Americans in the race for growth, and accepted that this was something to do with an observable 'management gap'.[42] In the light of these factors, it seems odd that doubts about business education seem to have persisted for so long. Why were so many countries initially so unenthusiastic? And, even more perplexing, why did most later soften their attitudes and to a greater or lesser extent adopt American solutions? The best way of understanding these trends is to explore the range of 'retardants' and 'accelerators' that shaped the diffusion process, and trace the way that these changed over time. We begin by looking at the former, first on the supply side and then on the demand side.[43]

On the supply side, it is clear that governments in the host countries sometimes proved less helpful to American missionaries than they might have done. Politics could play a part. There were eddies of anti-Americanism and anxieties about US strategic intentions. The cause of industrial modernisation rose and fell. In the United Kingdom the post-1945 Labour administration headed by Clement Attlee was interested in productivity issues and thus management, its three Conservative successors less so.[44] More usually, the crux of the problem was the way that the higher education system had come to be regulated over the preceding decades, or, in some cases, centuries. In many countries governments had legal powers over what did or did not constitute a degree, and perhaps how postgraduate studies were organised, and so it was by no means easy to slot in a new qualification such as the MBA simply because some outsider had suggested it.[45] Higher education institutions themselves constituted a further source of impediment. Beyond the Anglo-Saxon world, the three-year undergraduate/one- or two-year master's progression was largely unknown, and nor were universities – in the American sense – necessarily the only providers anyway.[46] To make matters worse, there were basic problems of cultural incompatibility. In Europe and much of the rest of the developed world most universities had traditionally concentrated on medicine, the sciences, the humanities and law, and there was a widespread view that business and management were inferior subjects without real substance that had no place in the halls of learning.[47] Thus, when the suggestion was made that the latter should be added to the curriculum, hackles were invariably raised. During the 1950s and the 1960s US agencies persistently tried to convince the University of Cambridge to take up 'industrial management', believing that this would send a powerful signal to the rest of the European educational establishment. The response was a story of prevarication, aloofness and prejudice. When the university finally accepted a Ford Foundation grant of $93,000 in 1968, American hopes were briefly rekindled, but in the end the results were again disappointing, with a Ford functionary reporting: 'I can't say that our grant . . . did much to change their ways. The grant funds were used as prescribed but not much of any permanent impact can be discerned . . . it was worth a try, but did not succeed.' Interestingly, when a proposal was subsequently made to introduce business education at the ultra-traditional Tokyo University, it ran into almost exactly the same trouble, with 'factions in the senior common room' said to be anxious that 'a grubby commercial course might cheapen their . . . academic reputation'.[48]

On the demand side, there were also strong retardants. Much of the corporate world outside the United States remained wary of business education in any guise. Many countries had, unsurprisingly, perfected their own arrangements for developing managers, and these rarely bore much resemblance to the American prescriptions. In Japan, for example, the process was organised through the 'lifetime employment system':

> Under this . . . employees were recruited straight from graduation
> by companies, and developed internally through on-the-job
> training, and later off-the-job training programmes, which were
> tailored to provide the employees with required company-specific
> skills and capabilities at each major landmark in their career as
> they climbed the internal promotion ladder . . . As there was
> little inter-firm mobility, there was scarce need for the employees
> to obtain external management education/training credentials as
> proof of their capabilities . . .[49]

More fundamentally, there was a deeply entrenched and widely
shared belief in many countries that managers were 'born, not bred'.
Germany's characteristic and influential *Unternehmer* (individual
entrepreneurs) asserted that 'innate qualities or an inner calling'
rather than training were the essential prerequisites of business leadership.[50] French executives accepted that it was important to be proficient in certain academic subjects, but they were dubious about the
existence of management principles, never mind the possibility of
their transmission. An authoritative enquiry recorded: 'They argue
that the technical knowledge acquired in such schools as the School
of Mines and the *École Centrale*, or the precise mathematical or legal
training in which the law schools . . . specialised, are all that is
needed before the business executive acquires practical experience in
the firm.'[51] In the United Kingdom the generally accepted maxim was
that management was best learnt 'sitting at Nellie's knee' or attend-
ing 'the school of hard knocks' – that is, in the workplace. In 1963 the
main employers' association, the Federation of British Industries,
published a report that neatly demonstrated how traditionally
inclined business communities and the new breed of business education enthusiasts differed over the most basic of concepts and assumptions. Their contrasting convictions are shown in table 2.3 over the
page.

In addition, business in Europe and Asia was, needless to say, not
without its prejudices, and sometimes these also impacted on how

Table 2.3 *Federation of British Industries: varying definitions of key concepts, 1963*

Concept	In the university	In industry
Knowledge	As an end in itself	To be used for action
Education	As an end in itself	Viewed with some prejudice
Business as a profession	Some prejudice	As an end
Time factor	Of relative importance	Scheduled
Decision-making	Only on full and tested information	On best information available
Work	Individualistic	In framework of organisation

Source: Federation of British Industries, *Management Education and Training Needs of Industry: A Report by an FBI Working Party* (London: Federation of British Industries, 1963), 4.

American ideas were received. There was a lurking feeling in some quarters that the United States was intent on trying to take over the world, using institutions such as business schools as advanced bridgeheads. Substantial numbers read books such as David Riesman's *The Lonely Crowd* and William Whyte's *The Organization Man* and wondered whether America really had the right to hector anyone about anything.[52] Barely conscious apprehensions or jealousies fuelled intransigence, and sometimes outright hostility.

Finally, students, too, were by no means necessarily enthusiastic about what the Americans proposed. Several influences shaped opinions. At a pragmatic level, those in countries where there was already an established pathway into management were naturally wary about opting for a still largely untested alternative, one that was, moreover, usually perceived as relatively expensive. Doubts about exactly what was going on in the United States reinforced caution. Some early pioneers from Europe who crossed the Atlantic to study in US schools were distinctly underwhelmed, and reported so on their return. The son of a former Shell managing director, who had spent a year at Stanford, was typically sceptical:

> It is clear that business education in the States, though phenomenally successful in terms of enrollment, still occupies a position of considerable academic uncertainty. Overcrowded classrooms neutralising the benefits of the case method, a generally indifferent faculty, poor quality text books, fundamental disagreement on policy – these can be found in even the best of the U.S. graduate schools. And is the value of an M.B.A. so much greater than that of two years of experience within an organisation?[53]

Entrenched status anxieties added a further dimension of inertia and doubt. Some British students felt that studying to go into 'trade' was a second-best option, which promised a life of tedium and grime, and entrapment in the rat race. Similar feelings were observable elsewhere. Indian business schools had begun life entangled in the British Raj, typically producing graduates for the colonial bureaucracy, usually of clerical (or 'babu') rank. After independence in 1947 the taint of 'babuism' lived on. The preferred route into management for anyone who was intellectually or socially up to it was through the engineering stream at an Indian institute of technology or university. Business education was for the lower orders.[54] In short, the embryonic MBA market in many parts of the world was notable not for its vitality but for its conspicuous hesitancy and doubt.

During the 1980s and 1990s most of the factors that have been touched upon began to change. 'Accelerators' existed across the spectrum. On the supply side, first of all, a variety of governments introduced reforms that made the provision of American-style business education very much easier. The range of legislation differed case by case. Some countries, such as China, intervened directly to encourage business schools. Elsewhere the measures were essentially permissive, though no less important for that. In 1988 the Japanese Ministry of Education began to reshape postgraduate education as a whole, removing the stipulation that courses be taught full-time, and moderating the traditionally onerous entry requirements. Ten years later the German parliament passed a law that enabled higher education institutions to introduce bachelor's and master's degrees.[55] In each case, business education was the prime beneficiary. Meanwhile, attitudes in universities were also mutating. The catalyst was a burgeoning anxiety about funding, fuelled by escalating inflation, wider public expenditure cuts and resurgent interest across the world in market-led solutions. In the new and tougher conditions, vice-chancellors and presidents had to look to their mettle, and there was growing concern with developing fresh income flows. Some concentrated on increasing fee income, others looked to diversify into science parks and conference facilities, but almost all began to take a far more hard-headed approach to the question of programme provision. In this re-evaluation, business and management studies seemed to be a particularly attractive option. The American precedent suggested that such courses could be relatively lucrative in their own right; but closer association with the corporate world also promised all kinds of other pecuniary opportunities, from direct subventions to bespoke research projects and the sponsorship of chairs. As a consequence, it was not long before university administrators in many countries were beginning to perceive that expanding this kind of provision might be a relatively straightforward way of generating extra income.

In turn, the expanding ranks of business schools also grew more commercially minded and aggressive about chasing recruits. Some of the early pioneers were largely uninterested in financial performance, in line with academia's tradition of high-mindedness. Few tried to develop the market. From the 1980s onwards, however, a more professional approach permeated almost every level. Writing in 1990, after interviewing a group of UK MBA directors, Patrick Miller and Arthur Money commented:

> A decade of change has coincided with a decade of Thatcherism in which British business schools have focussed increasingly on their raison d'etre and have come to the conclusion . . . that they have got to go out to meet more clearly defined market needs. What this has meant is that the new focus has transformed the whole mentality of business schools so that short and long courses have to be seen to be profitable.[56]

Demand now began to be seen as something that could be actively shaped. Advertising budgets increased, recruitment fairs and ever more glamorous prospectuses proliferated. There were continuing attempts to draw in previously neglected market segments – for example, in many Western countries it was often foreign students, who could be charged premium fees. New attention was given to pedagogy, and in particular to the question of how to make courses as attractive as possible. In both France and Japan leading schools took the – to some – unpalatable decision to start teaching exclusively in English, and thereby boosted their roles.[57]

Finally, as regards the supply side, a miscellany of pressure groups also contributed to the process of change. The key players varied over time, encompassing both the international (for example, the Association Internationale des Etudiants en Sciences Economiques et Commerciales – better known by its acronym, AIESEC – and the European Foundation for Management Development) and the country-specific (for example, in the United Kingdom the Business Graduates Association (BGA), the Association of Business Schools (ABS) and the Association of MBAs (AMBA)), but their cumulative effect was impressive. For what they did, albeit in slightly different ways, was both promote the general idea that business education was 'a good thing' and provide practical help for those who wanted to make it happen. Thus, to give a couple of examples from either end of the period, the BGA produced its first guides to British business schools in the 1970s, and introduced a scheme, in partnership with the banks, to help students finance their studies;[58] while the ABS's periodic serial, *Pillars of the*

Economy, launched in the 1990s, did much to popularise the idea that business education made an important contribution to a nation's general well-being.

Turning to the demand side, there is no doubt that changes here, too, were of considerable significance. Corporate attitudes to business education unarguably became more positive. Older antipathies, of course, did not disappear overnight. In 2002 it was reported that '[a] common complaint among Japanese MBA graduates is that they go back to work empowered and motivated – only to run up against a seniority system that ranks people according to age and status, not skill'.[59] At about the same time, surveys in Britain revealed that some companies and even sectors still remained very unenthusiastic about MBAs.[60] There were occasional broadsides in the press. Interviewed in 2004 about his forthcoming reality TV series judging a cohort of aspirant entrepreneurs, the self-made multi-millionaire Sir Alan Sugar was characteristically forthright:

> I'm not going to be impressed by people with professional and academic qualifications . . . That don't mean nothing to me. All that is, in the business world, is a nonsense . . . [MBAs are] all a load of bollocks, quite frankly. That just tells me you're clever. If you want to be in business, then come along and we'll see if you've got any business acumen. It's as simple as that really.[61]

Nevertheless, it was clear that doubters and critics were increasingly in the minority.[62] Broad trends in the wider political economy often proved irresistible. The 1980s and 1990s were notable for the rise of financial service providers and consultants worldwide, and both quickly gained a reputation for recruiting MBAs. Reporting in 1990, the executive search specialists Saxton Bampfylde International noted that the qualification formed 'a better fit' in such firms than in 'mainstream business, manufacturing in particular', and explained: '[Their] cultures are attuned to the more individualistic ethos and "deal-making" expectations of elite graduate schools.'[63] The subsequent growth of interest in entrepreneurs and entrepreneurship acted in the same direction, particularly since the business schools were by now so attentive to market signals that they were able to respond quickly with their own specially developed programmes. More generally, globalisation also played its part. As companies diversified abroad, there was an obvious demand for English-speaking graduates who were conversant not only with the local business culture but also with the international scene as a whole.

Meanwhile, student attitudes were also mutating. Previous antipathies to 'working in trade' rapidly melted away even in the more straight-laced countries, and by the early 1980s seemed nothing more than a puzzling anachronism. The worlds of finance and international business took on a new glamour. More specifically, the reputation of the MBA, too, improved dramatically. Detailed research suggested that those who had gained the qualification were usually happy with their courses and subsequently enjoyed enhanced salaries, and such findings rapidly percolated into the popular press. Indeed, by the late 1990s the MBA had come to be touted worldwide as the essential key to a better lifestyle, the 'yuppie's union card', or, as an Indian commentator suggested, the 'educational equivalent of a BMW'.[64]

The world's reaction to the American proselytising about business schools was, therefore, far from straightforward. Rational debate and assessment were conspicuous by their absence. On the other hand, prejudice and self-interest – whether pro or contra – were often crucial. The US missionaries initially hoped that their work would proceed smoothly, but this rapidly proved illusory. Dissemination ebbed and flowed, was moulded by an unpredictable array of national and international factors, and inevitably bore the scars to prove it.

SEEKING LEGITIMACY: THE RISE OF ACCREDITATION

In the previous paragraphs, we have looked at the development and diffusion of the American business school model, and observed that what is most striking about both these processes is the fact that they were so unassured. Despite the surface bluster, the bottom line was that the business education sector grew up almost everywhere in troubling circumstances, and emerged – to repeat Gordon and Howell's wonderfully apt phrase – 'an uncertain giant, gnawed by doubt and harassed by the barbs of unfriendly critics'. When we recently put this interpretation to a prominent dean, by and large he assented. Business schools, he agreed, had long struggled to establish their bona fides, and even their legitimacy. He also insisted, however, that in the past ten or fifteen years the position had much improved, because the schools had at last embraced accreditation – that is, a methodology for enforcing fully robust quality standards. Others have argued similarly. To round out our story, we clearly need to ask whether this view is justified. We begin by briefly tracing how and why accreditation has recently become of such import, and then evaluate its overall significance.

The history of accreditation is intimately bound up with the history of the institutions that were at its heart – the gatekeepers of standards. These comprised a small group of dedicated, non-commercial operations that, in exchange for a fee, provided certification, usually recognition of conformity to certain criteria. Their story is worth reprising. Until the late 1980s the whole business of accreditation was fairly low-key. In the United States the AACSB had promulgated standards in fits and starts from 1919 onwards, but it was really more of a membership organisation than an enforcer of quality. Significantly, even as late as 1986 nearly two-thirds of the AACSB's affiliated members remained unaccredited. Porter and McKibbin, here as in relation to other issues, were struck by the sense of inertia, reporting that '[i]n general, we found the deans we interviewed to have more burning issues on their minds than accreditation'.[65] Across the Atlantic the situation was, predictably, far less developed. Indeed, Europe had no serious accrediting body until AMBA emerged out of the Business Graduates Association in the late 1980s, and began offering to certify individual MBA courses.[66] From the early 1990s, however, the situation everywhere changed swiftly. Two events proved particularly catalytic. In 1995 the AACSB took the decision to start operating in Europe, allegedly because 'American business schools were demanding more information about their peers in order to set up cross-border programmes and alliances which were becoming increasingly fashionable'. Then, early the following year, and largely in response, the European Foundation for Management Development (EFMD), which had previously been a rather moribund trade body, created what became known as EQUIS – the European Quality Improvement System.[67] The upshot was that all those involved in accreditation were now pitched into what became an increasingly naked battle for market share.

In the new conditions, brand and reputation became ever more crucial. The AACSB made much of the fact that it already accredited schools in Canada, Mexico and Latin America, and could therefore claim to be a proven international operator. It stressed that it had no intention of striding into Europe 'like some sort of Yankee invasion', and promised to respect local cultures. As a sign of its good intentions, it immediately began employing local assessors, and shortly afterwards set up a 'blue-ribbon committee' to instigate 'a thorough review of . . . [its] international accreditation standards and propose changes appropriate for global quality leadership in the next decade'.[68] On the other hand, the AACSB certainly did not shrink from periodically playing on the cachet of its American roots. Thus, when *The Financial Times* interviewed Roy Herberger, AACSB president-elect, in 1997, he stated emphatically that 'US norms . . . predominate', and continued: 'The American MBA is . . . a standard that people aspire to. It still is a standard that holds high value.'[69] The EFMD responded in kind, underlining that both its heritage and its core values were firmly European. It took care to involve some of the Continent's most prominent deans, such as Antonio Borges of INSEAD, Carlos Cavalle of Spain's IESE, and Wil Foppen of the Rotterdam School of Management, and cultivated a cerebral and sophisticated image. But here, again, there was a steely edge, with Cavalle, for example, telling the press, in relation to American schools, 'We only need time . . . Then I think we can beat them.'[70] For its part, AMBA stressed its integrity and its commitment to the highest standards. In 1999 one of the organisation's senior figures explained: 'Basically our accreditation criteria represent what a good quality MBA should be. You can be quite sure then that, for the money you're spending, you're getting a good quality product.' On its website, AMBA described itself as no less than 'the guardian of MBA quality'.[71]

Beyond the rhetoric, all three organisations of course needed clients, and there was a simultaneous scramble to sign up as many schools – preferably prestigious schools – as speedily as possible. The AACSB accredited ESSEC in 1997, and Warwick and Rotterdam in 1998. The EFMD made even faster progress, accrediting LBS, ESADE, SDA Bocconi, INSEAD, ESCP and HEC Paris in 1998, and eleven others during the following year, while at the same time persuading a further thirty-odd schools (including Monash and HEC Montreal) to put their names down for future candidacy. Meanwhile, AMBA was also active, and by 2000 had accredited courses at a total of thirty-five institutions in the United Kingdom and about the same number elsewhere, including IMD, SDA Bocconi and the Helsinki School of Economics and Business Administration.[72] Of course, such vigorous rivalry was not to everyone's liking, and there were periodic calls for an end to hostilities and greater collaboration. Each of the big three made occasional noises about wanting to form alliances, and there were several more serious if short-lived flirtations. But actual examples of collaboration were few and far between. When the AACSB and AMBA agreed to visit Warwick together in order to carry out their separate investigations simultaneously in 1999, the story was novel enough to be reported in the national press.[73]

In subsequent years the expansion continued unabated. By 2004 the AACSB (now formally renamed AACSB International) had 466 accredited members worldwide, including fifty-four outside the United States and eight in the United Kingdom (Ashridge, Aston, Cranfield, Henley, LBS, Manchester, Strathclyde and Warwick); the EFMD had awarded the European Quality Label to sixty-four schools, including two in the United States (Thunderbird and Warrington at the University of Florida) and fourteen in the United Kingdom

(Ashridge, Aston, Bradford, Cambridge Judge, Cass, Cranfield, Henley, Lancaster, LBS, Leeds, Manchester, Open University, Strathclyde and Warwick); while, for its part, AMBA now accredited courses in thirty-eight UK schools and forty-four others, mostly in Europe or the white Commonwealth.[74] Commentators continued to wonder whether this situation was sustainable, and in particular whether there was really room for three players in the European market. Nevertheless, the impetus towards cooperation remained weak. In June 2002 the AACSB and EFMD announced a strategic alliance, though this did not appear to produce much in the way of tangible results. Indeed, within little more than a year the press was once again referring to 'a battle for survival'. According to *The Guardian*, the AACSB's strategy was 'to move closer to the European Foundation for Management Development . . . and eventually take it over; and to try to make accreditation from . . . [AMBA] irrelevant'. The organisation's director was quoted as saying: 'As AACSB grows we will be able to say that we accredit in all countries and all continents and you can rely solely on us.'[75] In 2004/5 competition continued, with both the EFMD and AMBA moving to accredit a wider array of master's courses beyond the MBA, and a surge of interest in forming wholly new accreditation bodies for the burgeoning providers of Asia and Latin America.[76]

This gives some idea of accreditation's rise. But what about its impact? Had it – as our informant suggested – brought the business school sector a new measure of credibility and status? There were certainly some positives. The accrediting bodies provided a degree of reliable information in an increasingly complex market, and thereby acted to curtail confusion and abuse. They also to some extent provoked quality improvement. Porter and McKibbin examined the AACSB's assessment activities in particular, and were generally impressed. As they reported, 'the imposition of specific Standards together with a systematic audit review process [had] indeed pushed many schools beyond where they might have gone voluntarily'.[77] Other commentators subsequently made similar claims.[78] With this accepted, however, there were also some important drawbacks and limitations.

First, the accreditors' public engagement was actually rather more circumscribed than it at first sight appeared. Each of the bodies was good at cultivating selected groups of deans and administrators, to be sure, but their work outside these circles could be patchy. As has already been noted, the majority of schools anyway remained unaccredited. Second, the way that accreditation operated tended to be rather opaque. Important details were sometimes hidden in the small print. The proliferation of Kitemarks threatened further confusion. It was even difficult to ascertain exactly how the main players differed substantively. As has been noted, the EFMD emphasised its bedrock of 'European values'. It apparently believed that 'Europeanness' equated to 'a rejection of standardisation'. But its claim to originality here was partly undermined by the fact that the AACSB had some years before also distanced itself from a 'one size fits all approach', and subsequently often reiterated that 'diversity is a positive characteristic to be fostered'.[79]

Third, the accreditors' impact on quality was probably more questionable than it seemed. Critics argued that, as the three main bodies were forced to compete for market share, so their original interest in promoting standards had given way to a narrowly defined obsession with self-promotion. Put crudely, the public good was being sacrificed for private gain. In this scenario, they alleged, accreditation had become 'more like membership . . . [of] a country club than . . . anything to do with improving the quality and practicality of education'.[80] Nailing down such claims was difficult, because much of what the accrediting bodies did remained private, a matter between them and their clients. There was without doubt a prima facie case to answer, however. The main accreditors were all unashamed empire builders. They did not behave exactly like commercial ventures, of course, because, as has been noted, they shared a 'not-for-profit' constitutional status; but, that said, they did undoubtedly cherish size, simply because this brought status, power and, of course, the resources to upgrade internal pay and conditions. A key question, therefore, was how the bodies balanced their missions – in other words, how they simultaneously tried to increase membership and protect, or even enhance, standards. The evidence was not always reassuring. To begin with, it appeared that, on particular occasions, narrow organisational needs had indeed come to dominate. For example, when some informed American academics examined the AACSB's adoption of what it termed a 'mission linked approach' in the early 1990s, their conclusions were as follows:

> The creation of the Accreditation Project Task Force [the first step in the reorientation] grew from the disaffection of the deans/directors of the majority of US business schools which could not acquire the resources to achieve accreditation under the existing AACSB standards. Those dissatisfied administrators had formed a competing accrediting body called the Association of Collegiate Business Schools and Programs . . . This organization still exists and has accredited a number of programs, some of them at community or junior colleges. While no AACSB official has admitted as much, to some degree the AACSB's standards were made more flexible in an attempt to create AACSB accreditation opportunities for a larger and more diverse group of schools.[81]

In addition, it was unclear how far the accrediting bodies really enforced their stated standards. All reported that they turned down a proportion of applicants, but, on the other hand, some of the procedures that they adopted over the years seemed surprisingly liberal. A good example was the way that AMBA choreographed its evaluation procedure in the early 2000s. At this time, the organisation required candidate institutions to complete a self-certification document, and then undergo an assessment visit. The latter was scheduled to take as much as one and a half days. This approach was in itself unremarkable, similar to that used, for example, by the UK government's quality watchdog. But what was striking was the way that AMBA sought to regulate the process. Its list of stipulations included the following points.

- A pre-assessment visit to the institution [applying for accreditation] may be undertaken . . . to advise on the preparation of the self-audit document . . .
- The on-site assessment visit . . . [follows] a pre-arranged agenda . . .
- The accreditation panel that undertakes the on-site assessment is composed of four or five members; typically, two or three senior academics from Schools offering accredited MBA programmes, specialists from the Association and possibly one corporate representative who holds an accredited MBA . . .
- The assessment panel is always mutually agreed with the institution.[82]

The emphasis on avoiding awkwardness and controversy was certainly marked. What AMBA envisaged – at least to the outside eye – appeared to have more in common with an induction process than a searching and critical examination.

At the dawn of the twenty-first century, therefore, the business education sector was still marked by the same pathologies that had plagued it since its inception. A small group of elite business schools appeared to offer good-quality and useful education. In the surrounding penumbra, however, standards varied considerably. The continued rumbling of criticism about providers in many parts of the world was indicative,[83] as was an American expert's observation that 'the MBA is one of the most popular degrees to fake, because it is widely regarded as a ticket to a better paying job'.[84] The sector as a whole still certainly had much ground to make up. We now turn to look at how it has fared in the past few years.

NOTES

1 Robert Aaron Gordon and James Edwin Howell, *Higher Education for Business* (New York: Columbia University Press, 1959), 20–1, and Carter

A. Daniel, *MBA: The First Century* (Lewisburg, PA: Bucknell University Press, 1998), 144–8.

2 Daniel, *MBA: The First Century*, 148.

3 Pfeffer and Fong, 'The end of business schools?', 78.

4 National Center for Educational Statistics, *Digest of Educational Statistics* (Washington, DC: National Center for Educational Statistics, 2004), tables 250, 251.

5 Robert R. Locke, *The Collapse of the American Management Mystique* (Oxford: Oxford University Press, 1996), 17–54; Steven Schlossman, Michael Sedlak and Harold Wechsler, 'The "new look": the Ford Foundation and the revolution in business education', *Selections*, 14(3) (1998), 8–28; T. R. Gourvish and N. Tiratsoo (eds.), *Missionaries and Managers: American Influences on European Management Education 1945–60* (Manchester: Manchester University Press, 1998); and Giuliana Gemelli (ed.), *The Ford Foundation and Europe (1950s–1970s)* (Brussels: European Interuniversity Press, 1998).

6 Anglo-American Council on Productivity, *Management Education* (London: Anglo-American Council on Productivity, 1951), 20.

7 For 'missionary activities' of one kind or another in this period, see, *inter alia*, James W. Schmotter, 'Business schools after the Cold War', *Chronicle of Higher Education*, 25 March 1992; Burton Bollag, 'Business schools flourish in post-communist eastern Europe', *Chronicle of Higher Education*, 17 January 1997; Sarah Murray, 'Schools on a mission to teach', *Financial Times*, 13 December 2004; Linda Anderson, 'Training tomorrow's lecturers', *Financial Times*, 24 January 2005; Adam Thompson, 'Catholic tinge to academic rigour', *Financial Times*, 16 May 2005; Michael Peel, 'A beacon of light in a land of tumult', *Financial Times*, 5 June 2005; Priscilla S. Rogers and Irene F. H. Wong, 'The MBA in Singapore', *Business Communication Quarterly*, 68(2) (2005), 180–96; John R. McIntyre and Ilan Alon (eds.), *Business and Management Education in Transitioning and Developing Countries* (Armonk, NY: Sharpe, 2005); and Peng Zhou, *Development of MBA Education in China: Opportunities and Challenges for Western Universities* (Toowoomba, Queensland: University of Southern Queensland, n.d.).

8 For a detailed examination of the chronology of change, see Rolv Petter Amdam, 'Business education', in Geoffrey Jones and Jonathan Zeitlin, *Oxford Handbook of Business History* (Oxford: Oxford University Press, 2006), and Haldor Byrkjeflot, CEMP Report no. 8, *The Structure of*

Management Education in Europe (Bergen: University of Bergen, Norwegian Research Center in Management and Organization, 2001).

9 Ray Wild, 'The MBA world – a view from the UK', at www.mbainfo.com.

10 Vipin Gupta, Kamala Gollakota and Ancheri Sreekumar, 'Quality in business education: a study of the Indian context', in McIntyre and Alon (eds.), *Business and Management Education*, 15.

11 Della Bradshaw, 'China's lust for business learning', *Financial Times*, 31 July 2005.

12 Alfred Rosenbloom and K. C. Bijay, 'Management education in Nepal: a view from the high country', in McIntyre and Alon (eds.), *Business and Management Education*, 71; Rogers and Wong, 'The MBA in Singapore', 184.

13 For a perceptive exploration of the American influence in one geographical context, see Lars Engwall, 'The Americanization of Nordic management education', *Journal of Management Inquiry*, 13(2) (2004), 109–17.

14 Kirsteb Gallagher, 'European educators are wary of overseas MBA programs', *Chronicle of Higher Education*, 1 December 1993.

15 Gordon and Howell, *Higher Education for Business*, 4.

16 F. C. Pierson, *The Education of American Businessmen* (New York: McGraw-Hill, 1959).

17 Lyman W. Porter and Lawrence E. McKibbin, *Management Education and Development: Drift or Thrust into the 21st Century?* (New York: McGraw-Hill, 1988), 310–11.

18 Porter and McKibbin, *Management Education and Development*, 316.

19 Daniel, *MBA: The First Century*, 235–42.

20 Jack N. Berman and Richard I. Levin, 'Are business schools doing their job?', *Harvard Business Review*, 62(1) (1984), 141.

21 Herman E. Krooss and Peter F. Drucker, 'How we got here: fifty years of structural change in the business system and the business school, 1918–1968', in Peter F. Drucker (ed.), *Preparing Tomorrow's Business Leaders Today* (Englewood Cliffs, NJ: Prentice-Hall, 1969), 21–2.

22 Gail Tyson, 'Management and the media', *Selections*, 4(1) (2004), 24.

23 Daniel, *MBA: The First Century*, 288.

24 Detlev Kran, *Quality Improvement of Business Education in Germany, Austria and Switzerland* (Bonn: Foundation for International Business Administration Accreditation, 2005), 3.

25 Giuliana Gemelli, 'The "enclosure" effect: innovation without standardization in Italian postwar management education', in Lars Engwall and

Vera Zamagni (eds.), *Management Education in Historical Perspective* (Manchester: Manchester University Press, 1998), 127–44.

26 Ian McNay, 'European management education: history, typologies and national structures', *Management Education and Development*, 4(1) (1973), 9.

27 Claudio Dematté, 'Notes on Italian management', *International Management Development* (Autumn 1983), 39–40.

28 Council for Excellence in Management and Leadership, *The Contribution of the UK Business Schools to Developing Managers and Leaders: Report of the Business Schools Advisory Group* (London: Council for Excellence in Management and Leadership, 2002), 37; Phil Baty, 'Newcomer's stocks rise in bull market', *Times Higher Education Supplement*, 15 August 1997; Higher Education Statistics Agency, 'Student tables', table 2e, at www.hesa.ac.uk/holisdocs/pubinfo/student/subject0304.htm.

29 Gerry Smith, 'Key books in business and management studies: an analysis of heavily used literature in UK business schools', *Management Education and Development*, 8(3) (1977), 119–30; Gareth Smith, 'The use and effectiveness of the case study method in management education: a critical review', *Management Education and Development*, 18(1) (1987), 51–61.

30 British Institute of Management, *The Making of Managers* (London: British Institute of Management, 1963), 2.

31 Anon., 'The recession in management education', *Management Decision*, 9(2) (1971), 108.

32 Michael Simmons, 'The business schools pause for thought', *Director* (December 1974), 507.

33 Council for Excellence in Management and Leadership, *The Contribution of the UK Business Schools*, 37; Judith Oliver, 'A degree of uncertainty', *Management Today* (June 1993), 26.

34 See, for example, Andrew Robertson, 'Business schools: is the backlash justified?', *Management Decision*, 4(3) (1970), 12–15, and Mick Silver (ed.), *Competent to Manage* (London: Routledge, 1991).

35 Peter G. Forrester, *The British MBA* (Cranfield: Cranfield Press, 1986), 2.

36 Higher Education Funding Council for England and Wales, *Quality Assessment of Business and Management Studies* (Bristol: Higher Education Funding Council for England and Wales, 1994).

37 Jane Rogers, *MBA: The Best Business Tool? A Guide to British and European Business Schools* (London: Economist, 1988), 2.

38 Kate Ascher, *Masters of Business? The MBA and British Industry* (n.p.: Harbridge House Europe, 1984).

39 Council for Excellence in Management and Leadership, *The Contribution of the UK Business Schools*, 26.

40 Commission on Management Research, *Building Partnerships: Enhancing the Quality of Management Research* (Swindon: Economic and Social Research Council, 1994).

41 See, for example, Phil Baty, 'Hull files revisited as questions continue', *Times Higher Education Supplement*, 5 May 2000.

42 For a classic rumination on this phenomenon, see Jean-Jacques Servan-Schreiber, *The American Challenge* (Harmondsworth: Penguin Books, 1968).

43 The approach used in what follows borrows from and extends that developed in Nick Tiratsoo, 'The "Americanization" of management education in Britain', *Journal of Management Inquiry*, 13(2) (2004), 118–26.

44 Nick Tiratsoo and Jim Tomlinson, *Industrial Efficiency and State Intervention: Labour 1939–51* (London: London School of Economics/Routledge, 1993); Nick Tiratsoo and Jim Tomlinson, *The Conservatives and Industrial Efficiency, 1951–64: Thirteen Wasted Years?* (London: London School of Economics/Routledge, 1998).

45 For one example, see L. I. Okazaki-Ward, 'MBA education in Japan: its current state and future direction', *Journal of Management Development*, 20(3) (2001), 197–235.

46 For an insightful analysis of the difficulties of introducing US educational forms into France and Germany, see Robert R. Locke and Katja E. Schöne, *The Entrepreneurial Shift: Americanization in European High-Technology Management Education* (Cambridge: Cambridge University Press, 2004), 82–107.

47 See, for example, Robert R. Locke, *Management and Higher Education since 1940: The Influence of America and Japan on West Germany, Great Britain, and France* (Cambridge: Cambridge University Press, 1989).

48 Tiratsoo and Tomlinson, *The Conservatives and Industrial Efficiency*, 71; Mariam Chamberlain, 'Final grant evaluation', 8 September 1977, Grant 68-498, Reel 1510, Ford Foundation Archive, New York; anon., 'Back to school', *Economist*, 11 November 1999.

49 Okazaki-Ward, 'MBA education in Japan', 198.

50 Heinz Hartmann, *Authority and Organization in German Management* (Princeton, NJ: Princeton University Press, 1959), 166.

51 Henry W. Ehrmann, *Organized Business in France* (Princeton, NJ: Princeton University Press, 1957), 297.

52 David Riesman, *The Lonely Crowd: A Study of the Changing American Character* (New Haven, CT: Yale University Press, 1951), and William Whyte, *The Organization Man* (New York: Simon and Schuster, 1956). For a comprehensive discussion of attitudes to the United States in one country, see Richard Kuisel, *Seducing the French: The Dilemma of Americanization* (Berkeley: University of California Press, 1993).

53 D. C. St M. Platt, 'The perils of American business education', *Director*, 12(8) (1960), 296.

54 Cyril Sofer, *Students and Industry* (Cambridge: Heffer and Sons, 1966); Gupta, Gollakota and Sreekumar, 'Quality in business education', 4–5.

55 Okazaki-Ward, 'MBA education in Japan'; Kran, *Quality Improvement of Business Education*, 3–4.

56 Patrick Miller and Arthur Money, *A Working Note on Recent Developments in the Design of the British MBA* (Henley: Henley Management College, 1990), 1.

57 See, for example, Michiyo Nakamoto, 'Big effort under way to achieve world-class status', *Financial Times*, 13 December 2003, and Steve McCormack, 'Strengthening the French connection', *Independent*, 13 October 2005.

58 Stuart Thom, 'The Business Graduates Association – the first ten years', *Business Graduate*, 8(1) (1978), 4–6.

59 Setsuko Kamiya, 'Which way with an MBA', *Japan Times*, 6 October 2002.

60 See, for example, J. Mayhead and T. Ambler, 'Why companies shun MBAs', *Market Leader* (Autumn 2002), 49–53.

61 Sholto Byrnes, 'Alan Sugar: let's get down to business', *Independent*, 19 July 2004.

62 See, for example, for the United Kingdom, Christopher Mabey and Andrew Thompson, *Achieving Management Excellence* (London: Institute of Management, 2000).

63 Saxton Bampfylde International, *The MBA Question: Perceptions and Reality in the UK* (London: Saxton Bampfylde International, 1990), 7.

64 Sathnam Sanghera, 'When MBA beats GSoH in the lonely hearts ads', *Financial Times*, 4 February 2005.

65 Porter and McKibbin, *Management Education and Development*, 199, 202.

66 Andrew Lock, 'Accreditation in business education', *Quality Assurance in Education*, 7(2) (1999), 68–76.

67 Della Bradshaw, 'Credit where credit is due', *Financial Times*, 18 March 1996; Della Bradshaw, 'Getting to grips with quality', *Financial Times*, 5 April 1999.

68 Bradshaw, 'Credit where credit is due'; Della Bradshaw, 'Order gives way to muddle', *Financial Times*, 21 July 1997.

69 Bradshaw, 'Order gives way to muddle'.

70 Bradshaw, 'Getting to grips with quality'.

71 Anon., 'Accreditation is key to quality', *Independent*, 9 September 1999; statement at www.mbaworld.com.

72 Crainer and Dearlove, *Gravy Training*, 176–7; Bradshaw, 'Getting to grips with quality'.

73 Della Bradshaw, 'Rivals join forces to meet needs of the global market', *Financial Times*, 15 February 1999.

74 Figures from organisations' own websites.

75 Des Dearlove, 'Fly the kitemark that makes an MBA matter', *TimesOnline*, 27 January 2003; Francis Beckett, 'Takeover bid', *Guardian*, 17 September 2003.

76 See, for example, Della Bradshaw, 'Bumpy ride on the road to harmony', *Financial Times*, 11 September 2005, and William Barnes, 'Asia aspires to monitor its own', *Financial Times*, 6 November 2005.

77 Porter and McKibbin, *Management Education and Development*, 206.

78 See, for example, Emma Haughton, 'Accreditation is less an inspection than a real exchange of ideas, vigour and energy', *Independent*, 16 October 2003.

79 European Foundation for Management Development, *EQUIS: The European Quality Improvement System* (Brussels: European Foundation for Management Development, n.d.), 1; AACSB International, *Eligibility Procedures and Standards for Business Accreditation* (St Louis, MO: AACSB International, 2004), 4.

80 John L. Stanton, 'What's that MBA really worth?', *Food Processing*, 9 September 2001.

81 John F. McKenna, Chester C. Cotton and Stuart Van Auken, 'Business school emphasis on teaching, research and service to industry. Does where you sit determine where you stand?', *Journal of Organizational Change Management*, 8(2) (1995), 4–5.

82 Association of MBAs, *Ambassadors for MBA Quality* (London: Association of MBAs, 2002), 3.

83 For some recent examples, see Renée Beasley Jones, 'MBA program probe draws puzzled response: official wonders if state regulations within CSU system are arcane', *San Diego Business Journal*, 29 July 2002; Locke and Schöne, *The Entrepreneurial Shift*, 190–3; Henk Rossouw, 'S. Africa council raps M.B.A. programs', *Chronicle of Higher Education*, 4 June 2004; anon., 'N.Y. reins in for-profit colleges', *Insidehighered.com*, 23 January 2006; and pp. 64–70 below.

84 Quoted in anon., 'Faking it', *Economist Global Executive*, 6 August 2004. See also Allen Ezell and John Bear, *Degree Mills* (Amherst, MA: Prometheus Books, 2005).

3   Business schools in the era of hyper-competition: 'more "business" and less "school"'

In the previous chapter we have described how the business school sector developed wordwide, underlining, amongst other things, the recent extraordinary growth of provision. Next, we turn to look in more detail at what is occurring today. We begin by observing that schools are currently having to compete as never before, and then go on to explore how they are reacting, taking in both short-term and medium-term strategies. Our argument in a nutshell is that competition is forcing schools everywhere to become very much more hard-nosed: in the memorable formulation of one anonymous dean, 'more "business" and less "school"'.[1]

INCREASING COMPETITION

The basic fact nowadays is that few if any business schools can take their continued existence wholly for granted. The sheer number of schools in itself breeds competition, of course. Nottingham is a medium-sized city in the English Midlands. It has two well-rated business schools offering a wide variety of programmes. But it is also in close proximity to three other cities that have notable business schools, while prestigious institutions such as London Business School, Cranfield and the Said Business School at Oxford are only a couple of hours away by car or train. In Los Angeles no fewer than fifteen large graduate business programmes run side by side. The Australian case is even more extreme: the country has a total population of only 19.5 million, but thirty-four different MBA degrees. The fact is that, everywhere, schools find themselves pitted against each other. The scale of this competition has been magnified by some recent changes in the wider economic and institutional environments, however, and these are worth exploring in a little detail.

To begin with, it is clear that business school budgets are coming under increasing pressure from several different angles. One major problem is that the relatively sudden growth of the whole sector has led to a general shortage of faculty, which in turn has tended to inflate costs significantly. The exact figures here are difficult to pin down. In most schools, staff account for at least a half to two-thirds of the overall budget. One estimate in the United States is that faculty pay has been increasing at 2 to 3 per cent per annum, partly driven by salary inversion – the fact that new hires have to be offered the same as or more than their established colleagues.[2] Comparative figures for other parts of the world are not available. Nevertheless, the general trend is indisputable. A recent AACSB International task force report concludes of the United States that '[f]undamental market imbalances' are leading to 'a continuing cycle of rapidly escalating salaries, especially among new faculty, that has removed many schools from the market for doctorally qualified talent', and then adds: 'Dealing with salary increases may be even more challenging for non-U.S. schools, which historically have had relatively lower salaries and fewer funding sources.'[3] Indeed, when we talked to deans in Europe, this was usually their number one concern. Interviewed in the spring of 2004, the head of a medium-sized British institution was in despair because he simply could not offer the kind of rewards packages that the market dictated: 'We went out last summer . . . and . . . I think we had . . . six or eight posts, and I think we made three appointments.'[4]

At the same time, many schools are experiencing difficulties with some of their established sources of income.[5] The recent stock market downturn has tended to depress the value of endowments and savings.[6] Moreover, the general trend for governments across the developed world to cut back whenever they can on subsidies to higher education has also hit hard. The problem here is not just the loss of resources but the uncertainty that has frequently accompanied the changes. Taking part in a question and answer session for the Graduate Management Admission Council (GMAC) magazine *Selections* during 2003, Dennis Logue, the dean of the Price College of Business at the University of Oklahoma, provided an arresting description of his school's recent travails. Successive state deficits meant that Price's budget had fallen by between 6 and 7 per cent over the past two years, he explained. Creative use of the university's reserves and the fortuitous arrival of some external funding had to some extent mitigated the blows. But the school was not unscathed. Its research budget had been reined in, and less use was being made of adjunct professors, even though this sometimes resulted in fewer classes being offered. As Logue saw it, he was involved in a never-ending juggling act, forever having 'to borrow from Peter to pay Paul'.[7] Occasionally, government interference has been even more pronounced. For instance, in March 2004 the Ministry of Human Resources in India suddenly and unilaterally declared that the country's six elite business schools had to cut their fees sharply, from figures such as Rs 100,000–150,000 per year to a standard Rs 30,000 per year. The objective was to increase access, but for the schools it seemed to be a threat to their very autonomy, and one that they bitterly resented.[8]

To make matters worse, these pressures have coincided with fresh fluctuations on the demand side. Many business schools initially developed in something of a bull market, when a regular rise in annual student applications could be reasonably predicted. In recent years, however, the situation has changed, and become very much less propitious. The popularity of different types of business degrees has varied tremendously. The MBA programmes that were once the bread and butter staple increasingly struggle, however. One estimate is that applications to the top MBA programmes across the world have in fact dropped by as much as 30 per cent since 1998, with some schools even seeing declines of 50 per cent or more.[9] In addition, the whole way that the market works seems to have become far more complicated and erratic. Demand is shaped by general career issues, as always, but equally by a range of other factors, sometimes geo-political or international in scope. Analysing the recent stall in MBA enrolments at Australian business schools, a *Financial Times* correspondent cited, amongst other things, full employment, 'a strengthening local dollar', which had eroded the country's competitiveness in the region, and higher living costs caused by 'a one-in-100-year drought'.[10] Elsewhere, it is the 9/11 atrocity that has caused the turbulence. In the years immediately after 2001 the US government tightened up on visa regulations, and students from all over the Middle East and Asia began to be turned away. American schools suffered, while their British, Australian and European competitors capitalised.[11] Fairly typically, an experienced German recruiter told the *International Herald Tribune* in 2004: 'I've been to a couple of education fairs this year, especially in the Arab world, and people are complaining about the procedures to get into the U.S. and the U.K. and they're looking for alternatives . . . We have to take advantage.'[12] Subsequently, however, the situation changed again. A concerted American government and university campaign was put in place, and recruitment, particularly from China, started rising. Ironically, in 2005 it was the turn of the British schools to complain about 'government unhelpfulness'.[13]

The general mood of nervousness about recruitment is further amplified by the fact that players outside the established university sector are eyeing up some of the business schools' prime markets. Many management consultancies have begun offering executive education programmes, playing on their alleged proficiency in practical knowledge.[14] Meanwhile, new 'for-profit' providers, such as the Capella University, Kaplan University, Strayer University, Sylvan Learning System's National Technological University and the University of Phoenix, are moving into the business master's degree arena, offering a wide range of Web-based or distance learning courses. What appears to be particularly threatening is the fact that, although these institutions have relatively low entry requirements, remain unaccredited by the main sector bodies and sometimes are not even particularly cheap, they nevertheless appear to be capturing market share, enrolling approximately 10 per cent of all US MBAs in 2003/4, up from 2 per cent ten years beforehand.[15]

Finally, it is important to underline that the sense and scale of competition have also increased because business schools everywhere are now very much in the public limelight. Comment has particularly accelerated in the last ten years, with growing coverage in the press and on the Web.[16] In addition, there has been a marked growth in the number of published league tables, ranking business schools against each other in terms of their faculty, research record, diversity, impact on student income, reputation amongst recruiters, alumni evaluation or whatever other criteria are felt to be most appropriate.[17] Indeed, in 2004/5 *BusinessWeek*, *The Economist*, the *Financial Times*, *Forbes*, the *International Herald Tribune*, *US News and World Report*, the *Wall Street Journal* and the UK Treasury[18] – to name only the most well regarded – all produced their own particular annual versions of this format. Of course, such endeavours remain controversial, and it is periodically argued that the tables are essentially ephemeral, and have little real impact on either school or student perceptions. The evidence suggests otherwise. Authoritative research by the GMAC demonstrates that 'published rankings' are by some way 'the single most influential source of communication' that graduate students use in forming their impression of a school.[19] Faculty insiders are invariably aware of this and behave accordingly. Deans know that poor performance in an important league table can lead to trouble, and perhaps put their job on the line.[20] Much effort is invested in avoiding obvious pitfalls. A deputy dean at Wharton acknowledges: 'You want to figure out any problems before the *Financial Times* does.'[21] If bad news comes, schools go into overdrive to reassure students, staff and alumni, and then often form working parties to institute change.[22] The fact is, as one of those journalists most closely involved concedes, that the rankings are taken not just 'seriously' but 'disturbingly' so.[23]

As things stand, therefore, business schools are increasingly having to look to their mettle. Even the most prestigious are feeling financially exposed. Student recruitment is difficult. Other sources of income are becoming less dependable. The glare of publicity remains relentless and unforgiving. Rumours of 'a meltdown' or 'a shakeout' are repeated in common rooms and the press.[24] We now turn to look at what schools are doing to protect themselves.

STRATEGIES: (1) THE BOTTOM LINE

For many, the prime (and almost automatic) response to these changing events has been to concentrate on the bottom line. At the top of schools, governors, boards, advisers and deans set the tone. The evolution of the latter is particularly significant. Forty years ago running a business school was something that a senior professor might well take on as a matter of duty shortly before retirement. Nowadays deans almost constitute a profession in their own right, a cohort with unique and specialist skills. An increasing number are appointed from outside the academy, mainly from business; all have to spend a high proportion of their time raising money. Turnover is fast, with many moving on after little more than a handful of years.[25] *The Economist* recently likened deans to sports coaches, hired to improve performance, fired at will, but with one eye always on building their own careers.[26] Others see a likeness to corporate CEOs. Whichever image is more apposite, the truth is that financial performance now largely makes or breaks a dean's reputation. The practical strategies that flow from this are entirely predictable.

One obvious step that many schools have taken is to increase fees. *BusinessWeek* estimates that US tuition fees are currently rising at an average rate of between 4 and 7 per cent per annum, though this disguises some much bigger individual cases – such as the recent 17 per cent hike at the Haas School or the 26 per cent hike at the Paul Merage School of Business.[27] In other parts of the world the figures tend to be, as always, less readily available, but there are various straws in the wind. Table 3.1 presents some data on the 'estimated cost of full-time MBA programmes' to home students at a selection of well-known Australian, Canadian and European schools. It suggests that between 2002 and 2004 there was an average increase of 51 per cent – with individual figures ranging from Cranfield's relatively

Table 3.1 *Estimated total cost of full-time MBA programmes, dollars, 2002–4*

School	2002	2003	2004	% change 2002/2004
Australian GSM	24,990	29,900	35,078	+ 40
Cranfield	34,500	38,844	45,000	+ 30
Erasmus	31,500	39,000	64,575	+ 105
ESADE	37,844	48,072	54,600	+ 44
Essen	15,000	17,089	20,731	+ 38
Helsinki	16,000	20,000	24,000	+ 50
McGill	5,400	8,470	9,050	+ 68
SDA Bocconi	26,500	32,500	35,150	+ 33

Source: BusinessWeek Online; all figures refer to home students.

modest 30 per cent to Erasmus's massive 105 per cent. As well as raising their fees, schools have also sought to boost their other traditional sources of income, primarily endowments and gifts. Not unexpectedly, the Americans have shown the way. One survey itemised fourteen major donations to US business schools between 1997 and 2003, ranging in size from $23 million to $62 million.[28] More recently, the sums have been getting even bigger. In late 2004, for example, Stephen M. Ross, the developer of the $1.7 billion Time Warner Center at Manhattan's Columbus Circle, donated no less than $100 million to the business school at the University of Michigan.[29] In Europe, independent fund-raising has historically tended to be something of a Cinderella activity because of the ubiquity of state financing, but, even here, the new pressures are making themselves felt. Many schools are currently scrambling to create and nourish more effective alumni networks. An administrator at a top UK institution told us: 'We've had an alumni office with one or two members of staff in it probably for twelve years, but it's only in the last four years that we've really started to invest in it.' In fact, she added, alumni were now seen as 'absolutely vital to . . . [our] business model'.[30] As yet, only one or two of the very biggest European schools are active on anything like an American scale. INSEAD is probably the most successful: it raised $145 million between 1995 and 2000 (80 per cent from corporates), and is currently involved in a fresh campaign that aims to bring in $240 million by the end of the decade.[31] Nevertheless, the competition – particularly in the United Kingdom – is certainly catching up rapidly. In the past few years, for example, Lancaster University Management School won a grant worth £4.5 million from the Northwest Development Agency, while Imperial College, as we have noted, was gifted £27 million by the entrepreneur Gary Tanaka.[32]

As well as trying to boost their income, most schools have tried to restrain or even cut their costs. Quite understandably, such retrenchment is rarely discussed much in public; indeed, considerable effort is often expended in disguising whatever changes are being made. No one wants to be labelled a 'lame duck', incapable of sustaining a full portfolio of relevant activities. But, in more than a few cases, faculty have been trimmed, the balance between high and low wage earners altered and uneconomic courses jettisoned, perhaps under the camouflage of 'restructuring'.[33] In addition, schools have begun re-examining the annual tariff that most pay to their parent universities, as a contribution towards essential budgetary items such as central charges, contingencies and future development costs. The traditional view of such outflows was that they were unavoidable, the price that had to be paid for being part of a wider liberal and collaborative endeavour. As competition has increased, however, so attitudes seem to have hardened. One of the deans that we spoke with commented:

> I think part of what I am now trying to do (having got the idea
> over to the university that we're a pretty profitable department –
> in fact, we're the most profitable department in the university;
> we're also the biggest as well by student numbers, anyway, if not
> by staff) I think the next stage is to say: 'Well, hang on, this isn't

really a very good thing for us to do; what we really need to be doing is to have a better match between our income and our expenditure, because there's no point in making vast surpluses which disappear into the ether.'[34]

In cases where this approach has been pushed hard, there have sometimes been notable changes. Thus, Warwick University's Business School currently enjoys 'semi-autonomous' status, with a devolved budget and considerable scope for financial manoeuvre – a contrast to its early years, when it was just one amongst a host of other roughly equal academic departments.[35]

STRATEGIES: (II) MARKETS

To complement the focus on the bottom line, business schools have also become increasingly concerned with their markets, seeking to solidify existing demand, attract fresh segments of the population and, more generally, respond meaningfully to the broader social changes that are occurring in the home and at the office. One central strategy, which has been pursued almost everywhere, is to try to make the MBA student body more diverse – that is, move it away from its alleged traditional 'middle-class, white, male' fulcrum. An obvious way of doing this has been to target women. The policy instruments used here have evolved over time. Amongst other things, schools have been concerned to rid their programmes of any 'boy's club' elements (for example, alcoholic 'bonding sessions'); boost female staff numbers; introduce flexibility for those with childcare responsibilities; provide tailored scholarships; and make campuses as safe as possible, particularly at night. The results have been variable. The broad percentage of women on Anglo-Saxon MBA courses has increased from about 20 per cent in the late 1980s to about 30 per cent today, but the evidence suggests that the rate of change has become increasingly sluggish. Accordingly, many deans are once again turning to examine the problem in detail – for instance, by setting up task forces with outside partners such as women's lobbying groups (one example is Chicago's influential Committee of 200) to recommend prescriptions.[36]

Meanwhile, schools have also been trying to tap into another obvious potential reservoir: overseas students. The dynamics here are complicated, governed by factors as diverse as ex-imperial connections, language and (as has been noted) current international security concerns. But the basic impetus is everywhere very noticeable. Anglophone schools target India, Pakistan, China, Hong Kong, Singapore, ex-communist eastern Europe, the Baltic states, Russia and – most recently – the Middle East. The French look to north and sub-Saharan Africa, while Spanish schools try to recruit in Latin America. The results have been fairly spectacular. In the United States foreign students currently account for 20 to 30 per cent of the total on many MBA programmes, while in the United Kingdom and parts of continental Europe, though no exactly comparable figures are available, the average proportion is almost certainly much higher.[37] One credible estimate is that three-quarters of full-time UK MBAs are currently awarded to overseas students.[38] Looking at individual cases makes the point graphically. Of London Business School's 2004 MBA class, for instance, 31 per cent came from western Europe; 25 per cent from North America; 22 per cent from Asia; 10 per cent from Latin America and the Caribbean; 6 per cent from eastern Europe, central Europe and central Asia; and 2 per cent each from Africa and Oceania.[39] Little wonder that a few business schools have taken the next logical step and begun building campuses abroad, in direct proximity to their most important target markets.[40]

In parallel with these initiatives, schools have re-examined the structure of the MBA degree itself, with a view to making it more user-friendly, and therefore attractive. Some offer a plethora of different variants – for example, 'full-time', 'part-time', 'modular', 'evening' and 'weekend' – and are increasingly willing to allow students the freedom to switch between them.[41] Others have started to deliver the degree online. In 2003 BusinessWeek estimated that there were about ninety schools running distance learning MBAs, and the number has undoubtedly grown since then. Moreover, some of these programmes are clearly quite large: for example, in the United Kingdom the Open University, the Edinburgh Business School (part of Herriot-Watt University) and Henley Management College claim to have, respectively, about 15,000, 9,000 and 6,000 students currently enrolled.[42] Certainly, the old model, in which faculty delivered what they wanted, when they wanted, how they wanted, has fewer and fewer supporters. In North America the conventional wisdom has always dictated that the full-time, classic MBA takes two years of study, and not a day less, but even this is now being questioned, and there are moves to introduce the shorter one-year format that is usual in parts of Europe.[43] At Donald Trump's Wall Street TrumpU, it is now even possible to enrol in 'An MBA in a Day' – a distillation of the conventional MBA programme into four one-hour sessions![44] As the seasoned business school watcher Stuart Crainer recently observed, when it comes to MBA provision in the twenty-first century, '[c]hoice is the name of the game'.[45]

Finally, as regards markets, it is important to stress that, for most schools today, the MBA is, in any event, only one of several 'product lines', and that wherever possible a measure of diversification has been pursued in order to generate extra income flows. The new qualifications and types of programme take on a bewildering number of forms. Provision aimed specifically at executives really took off in the 1990s, and has subsequently become almost ubiquitous. The market is competitive, but demand shows little sign of slowing. Indeed, here as elsewhere, there is mushrooming specialisation. A few top schools offer senior executives the chance to take highly customised MBAs, playing on their reputation and charging commensurately high fees.[46] The growing importance of the *Financial Times'* Executive MBA ranking, introduced in 2000, reflects the trend. For the majority, the popular option is to forge ongoing relationships with particular companies, in order to provide them with their own dedicated programmes.[47] Alongside these initiatives, most schools have moved to reassess the traditional student market. The gradual expansion of higher education in the past decade or two has offered many opportunities. Few schools at present do not offer some sort of undergraduate programme, perhaps in collaboration with colleagues from other parts of their universities. There are also a growing number of tailored master's degrees, such as MScs in particular financial disciplines, which can be delivered relatively cheaply, and thus attract those priced out of the MBA.[48] In all these cases the key driver is economic – in essence, the desire to provide an immediate comfort zone in an environment that is ever more turbulent and troublesome.

STRATEGIES: (III) IDENTITY

The third way that schools have responded to the growth of competition is a good deal more considered, and revolves around attempting to create a lasting identity. The starting point here is recognition that measures such as cutting staff costs or tweaking the MBA will only go so far, because they are easily mimicked. What a school really needs if it is to prosper in the longer term, the argument goes, is a unique selling point, something that sets it off decisively from the pack. Accordingly, almost across the board, there is a fresh concern with image and positioning.[49] At present, four different (though overlapping) strategies are being explored.

First, many schools are seeking to tighten their focus – that is, hone in on something that they feel gives them a specific and perhaps decisive edge. A couple of examples are illustrative. The United Kingdom's Cass Business School is a few minutes' walk from London's main financial district, the City. When it recently received a big private donation, enough to contemplate a major expansion, Cass decided to rethink its mission completely. The proposition that it has come up with is basically all about its ever more vibrant neighbour. Interviewed in the press, the dean explains: 'Cass has the distinct advantage of being in the heart of the City, which attracts students. It has also helped us develop an important aspect of our pedagogy, in that [City] practitioners can be drawn into programmes.

That is much harder for other business schools.' Based upon this logic, Cass currently projects itself as aspiring to become no less than 'the intellectual heart of the City of London'. At the Swiss school St Gallen there is also a promotion of place, though this time in a rather different sense. The school has always taught business and economics, but in January 2005 it decided to launch a new MBA. An obvious requirement was to create a formula that was somehow original. In the end, the school has opted to emphasise its roots in the surrounding region. Neighbouring schools, St Gallen maintains, are largely international in outlook, essentially orientated to London, New York or Beijing. By contrast, its programme is very much more targeted: a German MBA, 'rooted' in a German-speaking context, and catering for those who wish to work in German or central European firms. It is this quality, the school hopes, that will ultimately allow it to prosper.[50]

Alongside tighter focus, a number of the more affluent schools are attempting to gain advantage by constructing new buildings or campuses. As an American insider has observed, 'It's like an arms race . . . There are a lot of very good business-school programs, and it can be hard to distinguish among them. Facilities are one tangible way to do that.'[51] Part of the objective here is, without doubt, to impress by sheer size and opulence; to say, in effect, 'We are here, we mean business, and we are going to crush the opposition.' Press handouts and websites obsessively itemise the names of the eminent architects who have been involved, the enormous amounts of money that have been spent and the lavish facilities that have been provided. For example, the BI school in Oslo notes of its recently opened building that it is 'designed like an open town . . . [with] terraces, galleries, small nooks and quiet areas, which have been created as special meeting places and to add life'; it has 50,000 square metres of rooms, including twenty auditoriums, twenty-eight classrooms and 1,200 work stations, and can cope with up to 8,000 students and 600 staff at any one time.[52] Alongside the hyperbole, there are occasionally less strident messages about mission and stance. In the planning process, school committees have mined history for apposite metaphors – for example, the medieval monastery.[53] One popular aim is to create a 'meeting place', somewhere where people will want to interact, but also where there will be chance encounters, fruitful contact between strangers. Thus, at the IEDC-Bled School of Management in Slovakia, the new building is, according to its dean, 'designed around an open atrium leading to other rooms, reflecting its philosophy of not only being a regional leader but also open to the world'.[54]

Third, schools are looking with ever more vigour at how they can benefit from relationships with other players in the same field. Hardly a week goes by without one school or another announcing that it is in partnership. Networks, alliances and associations, too, are proliferating.[55] But perhaps the best example is accreditation. In the 1980s and 1990s seeking to be accredited was a minority activity, viewed as something that only the elite could contemplate. Currently, any school with even modest ambition has either achieved such recognition or is trying to obtain it. The figures speak for themselves. At the turn of the century it was estimated that 517 schools worldwide had programmes accredited by one or other of the three main agencies (the AACSB, the EFMD's EQUIS arm and the Association of MBAs). In 2005 the total was 693, an increase of 34 per cent.[56] The point is that accreditation – like all the other forms of collaborative endeavour – has come to be seen as yet another potent way of trying to trump the competition. Fairly typically, when the School of Business Administration at the University of Houston Victoria received AACSB accreditation in May 2005, its president stressed that it had joined an exclusive club: 'Less than 15 per cent of the world's business schools obtain accreditation . . . it sends a message . . . that we met certain standards.'[57]

Finally, it is notable that a number of schools are attempting to bind all or some of the foregoing elements together by gradually reinventing themselves explicitly as brands. Of course, the more affluent and active have always been involved in branding of one kind or another. What has changed is the scale and intensity of activity. The

United States, not unexpectedly, again leads the way.[58] The rest of the world is rapidly catching up, however. A 2005 survey of thirty-three UK schools found that as many as a half had rebranded in the past five years, and almost the same proportion reported an increase in spending on marketing in the past two years.[59] Similar trends are occurring elsewhere. Spain's ESADE recently went through a comprehensive branding exercise, amongst other things adopting a new logo, a combination of old and modern lettering that, the manager responsible explained, signified the school's 'pride in its traditions' as well as its 'forward-looking and innovative' nature. It was rewarded with a sharp climb up the league tables. In the summer of 2005 INSEAD followed suit, appointing the leading consultancy NB Studio to redesign its identity for the first time in over a decade, and simultaneously beginning a search for an advertising agency and a Web designer. A spokesman commented that the objective was to capture and then use 'the basic intellectual DNA of the school'.[60] Brands and branding are clearly moving centre stage.

STRATEGIES: (IV) 'NAKED GAMESMANSHIP'[61]

The final group of strategies encompasses activities that revolve around playing the system. Some are harmless, others seemingly less so. Clearly, business schools, like all higher education institutions, are supposed to behave in line with accepted rules and norms. Many no doubt do. On the other hand, there is also some evidence to suggest that, as competition has increased, some have been tempted to take short cuts, using subterfuge and spin to cover their tracks. The major areas of concern are about standards, and the compilation of the data that is used in the various rankings.

Judged by their public pronouncements, business schools make enormous effort to safeguard the integrity of their programmes. During the past few years, however, there have been many claims that, in reality, this commitment is sometimes rather less clear-cut and pervasive than it seems. Specific anxieties relate to, amongst other things, lax admission procedures; spoon-feeding in classes; lack of vigilance in the face of obvious cheating; grade inflation; and inadequate, perhaps insufficiently demanding, overall appraisal procedures.[62] The truth is difficult to establish. For obvious reasons, schools tend to keep problems of any kind firmly under wraps. Anyway, some of the issues at stake may well be quite complex, since variation in 'quality' or 'standard' is never easy to measure over time. It is unarguably true that few schools actually ever fail MBA students, but in their view, at least, this is simply because they are good at screening applicants effectively in the first place. Nevertheless, with all these points accepted, there are a number of recent cases that certainly give pause for thought.

In May 2003 the United Kingdom's Quality Assurance Agency reported on a routine investigation into LBS. The findings were generally positive, and the agency confirmed that it had 'broad confidence' in the school's 'current management of the quality of its programmes'. There were one or two passages that raised eyebrows, however. The discussion of how the 'economics subject area' functioned, for example, suggested a surprising degree of insouciance about assessment:

> It is the School's expectation that all student work which contributes to the final award should be double-marked . . . The audit team noted expressions of concern, in a report from the external examiner for economics, that double-marking of students' work did not appear to be taking place. The team's own scrutiny of the student work . . . led it to the view that the external examiner's comments had been helpful to the School, which had responded to them . . . The external examiner . . . had also commented in successive years on the character of the Management Reports which are produced by second-year MBA full-time students . . . [referring to] 'grade inflation' or 'grade drift'.[63]

For a school with a worldwide reputation, which prided itself on being the crème de la crème, this was, to say the least, rather unexpected.

At the end of the following year, and at the other pole of the business school pecking order, there was a second revealing episode. *The Times Higher Education Supplement* had been interested in allegations of 'dumbing down' for some years, and now produced a long analysis of the University of Luton, which it introduced with the headline 'Caught in vicious cycle of declining standards'. This examined a range of issues, but at one point cited a '2002 Business School report' which allegedly read as follows: 'Over the past five years, numbers of . . . students have changed little in total, but their level of entry qualification has declined . . . [A] major issue for the School is the increasing number of business and management students (mostly but not entirely from overseas) who appear to face difficulties with academic English.' Such comments appeared remarkable, and were made more so by a Luton spokesperson's reported response that 'most business schools had similar problems at the time'.[64]

The final example comes from Australia. In 2003 a lecturer teaching at the University of Newcastle's Graduate School reported fifteen MBA students at an 'offshore' campus in Malaysia for gross plagiarism. His expectation was naturally that disciplinary action of one kind or another would follow, but in fact the university simply swept the whole matter under the carpet. Controversy followed, and, in the end, the New South Wales government's Independent Commission Against Corruption was asked to investigate. What it discovered was fairly devastating. Senior figures in the Graduate School, it recounted, had been 'motivated by a desire to avoid any potential adverse consequences that the allegations may have had to damage the University's offshore program', and as a result had engaged in 'corrupt practices'. Moreover, those responsible for the wider mechanisms in place to safeguard quality had simply failed to act. Even outsiders were implicated. For example, the commission concluded of one, who had been brought in to assess the complaint, that he 'lacked independence and relevant experience and should not have been appointed', and added in a damning coda: 'His inquiry was flawed by his failure to examine pertinent issues, including whether there had been any plagiarism.' All in all, this was not a pretty picture, and it reinforced the view in some people's minds that – amongst other things – business schools' overseas franchise operations were to some extent out of control, and required far closer policing.[65]

Turning to the issue of data compilation, the issue is very straightforwardly whether schools report on their performance to ranking agencies and others in a way that is truthful, or not. Needless to say, most senior business school officials continue to insist that they always act honestly. Yet doubters are more numerous and vocal than ever before. In 2002 no less a figure than the Academy of Management president, Jone Pearce, publicly referred to the 'widespread concern' that some schools were 'cooking their books'. Three years later the American academics Harry DeAngelo, Linda DeAngelo and Jerold Zimmerman were even less circumspect, stating bluntly: 'To influence the rankings, some schools adopt behaviors that are reasonably questioned as unethical, and informed insiders suggest that there are (as yet undisclosed) examples where such behavior has inarguably crossed the line.'[66] Even deans are beginning publicly to express cynicism. One told the *St Louis Post-Dispatch*: 'My comment about the rankings is they are biased, bogus, and misguided – and I accept them without reservation.'[67] Clearly, there is some kind of case to answer.

Unsurprisingly, those who compile the rankings for journals such as *BusinessWeek* and the *Financial Times* have always been aware that there is potential for deception. Questioned by *Selections* in 2001, one experienced practitioner openly declared: 'I can tell you . . . schools lie.'[68] What such people also underline, however, is that they have gradually introduced a variety of safeguards (ranging from the employment of outside auditors to the common formatting of data),[69] and that these have by and large greatly diminished the problem. Thus, a prominent member of the 'ranking corps' who we interviewed estimated that schools got about 8 to 10 per cent of the questions on monitoring forms wrong, but added that this was usually the consequence of plain carelessness, illustrated by the fact that the mistakes were frequently to the detriment of the institutions themselves.[70]

Such reassurances deserve to be taken seriously. Nonetheless, there are still obvious grounds for concern. First, there is little doubt that many schools expend substantial energy in trying to 'game the system' – that is, accrue advantage in virtually any way possible that is not blatantly illegal. Some hire public relations advisers to soften up key journalists. A *BusinessWeek* staffer reported as long ago as 1990: 'Not a week goes by when I don't receive a package of videos or a visit . . . I feel like a politician being lobbied by special-interest groups.'[71] More try to manipulate the required data, in order to depict themselves in the best possible light. In 2002 two American business school faculty, Dennis Gioia and Kevin Corley, published a paper, based upon interviews with senior figures at sixteen different institutions, that described 'a whole litany of actions designed to circumvent or take advantage of the rankings criteria'. Examples included:

> Putting some incoming students (especially international or minority students) into special 'preadmission class' so their number do not count toward the final numbers tabulated and reported for the autumn MBA 'entering class', admitting lower quality candidates into a master of science program first and then transferring them to the MBA class after their first year, only reporting the average bonus for those receiving bonuses instead of reporting the average bonus for the whole class . . . as well as encouraging students to rank their own school highly or 'risk lowering the value of their own degree' . . . thus shooting themselves in the foot.[72]

Subsequently, ever more elaborate techniques have become commonplace. One recent development is a concentration on 'placement'. Schools recognise that the MBA job market continues to be tight, but they are also acutely aware that they will be judged in part on how their students fare after graduating, and specifically on how much they earn, a staple of several much-consulted rankings.

Accordingly, many have begun trying to do whatever they can to massage the figures upwards. Some quietly bring in high-powered career search firms or outside consultants, often at considerable cost, while others wring whatever advantages they can from alumni networks and corporate contacts. Cornell University's Johnson Graduate School recently came up with a particularly novel solution, using its major benefactor's private jets to fly in extra recruiters to meet the graduating class.[73]

In addition, and despite all the rankers' assurances, there is occasional covert manoeuvring that touches upon the boundaries of probity. In June 2004 the *Daily Texan* journalist Lomi Kriel published a long article exploring how the Mays Business School had been able to jump twenty-eight places up the *U.S. News and World Report* rankings in the previous year. The basic facts were clear-cut. The school's performance rested upon extraordinary achievements in two particular measurement categories, 'job placement at graduation' and 'job placement three months later', in which rises of 61 and 73 places respectively had been registered. What remained at issue was the explanation. The *U.S. News and World Report* emphasised that it stood by the integrity of its data. A senior analyst conceded, 'It's very rare, very rare that schools jump that much,' but then added, 'I challenged them . . . I said everybody would be wondering if their placement data was that great, especially not in the greatest year . . . It would be very, very embarrassing for them . . . especially if I had challenged them on it.' For its part, the school cited 'a famously tight knit alumni network' and 'a new focus on students' responsibility to find their own jobs'. Others were puzzled, however. The recently departed director of Mays' graduate business career services department commented, 'I wasn't expecting it . . . it's quite a big jump,' and then added, somewhat alarmingly, 'There's a lot of pressure on people to do what's right or to do what's keeping [their] job safe . . . People are constantly being fired based on a drop in the rankings . . . They have to make sure they meet some number, so that the school continues to move up or maintain where they're at.' Confusing matters further, there were also differences of opinion about whether the relevant raw data actually still existed or not. Kriel reported that she had applied to see the files, but been told 'it's not a requirement, and there is no such information'. In reply, the school disputed whether this was true, and claimed that in any event its priority was always to safeguard graduates' privacy, an apparently eminently reasonable explanation. The row rumbled on. In July 2004 the *Daily Texan*'s editor publicly insisted that he stood by the story.[74] Subsequently, Mays returned to a somewhat lower position in the *U.S. News and World Report* rankings. Outside observers were left wondering. Had Kriel simply misunderstood what was going on, or was this a case where a school had – in DeAngelo, DeAngelo and Zimmerman's phrase – 'inarguably crossed the line'?

Business schools have always competed against each other to a certain extent, but the situation today is unprecedented. A surge in the number of providers has coincided with growing market turbulence, and ratcheted the pressure up all round. In such conditions, it is unsurprising to find that the whole ethos of business schools has begun to alter. As the preceding paragraphs have documented, the emphasis today is everywhere on commercial values – on maximising revenue, cutting costs, exploiting new markets and, perhaps, surreptitiously bending the rules in ways that are sometimes questionable. In the following chapters, we turn to content issues, and explore in detail what the new realities mean on the ground, looking first at teaching, and then at research and knowledge transfer.

NOTES

1 Quoted in Dennis A. Gioia and Kevin G. Corley, 'Being good versus looking good: business school rankings and the Circean transformation from substance to image', *Academy of Management Learning and Education*, 1(1) (2002), 109.

2 Katherine S. Mangan, 'The Great Divide: concerns grow over pay gaps between professional-school professors and everyone else', *Chronicle of Higher Education*, 30 May 2003, and Dan LeClair, 'The professor's paycheck', *BizEd* (March/April 2004), 58–60.

3 AACSB International Management Education Task Force, *Management Education at Risk* (Tampa, FL: AACSB International, 2002). See also AACSB International Doctoral Faculty Commission, *Sustaining Scholarship in Business Schools* (St Louis, MO: AACSB International, 2003).

4 Interview, 1 April 2004. See also Sadie Williams, *Management and Leadership Teaching: Present Trends and Future Demand* (Lancaster: Lancaster University Management School, 2000).

5 Gail Tyson, 'Deans talk dollars', *Selections*, 3(1) (2003), 24–8.

6 Tyson, 'Deans talk dollars', 24–5.

7 Carlotta Mast, 'Different contexts, different challenges', at www.gmac. com/selections/spring2003/different/logue. See also Kirp, *Shakespeare, Einstein, and the Bottom Line*, 130–45.

8 Anon., 'A strange battle', *Business India Intelligence*, 11(8) (2004), 1–2.

9 Jennifer Merritt, 'MBA applicants are MIA', *BusinessWeek*, 18 April 2005.

10 Tim Elliot, 'Australian schools struggle to fill desks. So why study for an MBA in Australia?', *Financial Times*, 23 May 2005.

11 Paul Mooney and Shailaja Neelakantan, 'No longer dreaming of America', *Chronicle of Higher Education*, 8 October 2004.

12 Gill Plimmer, 'Turning their backs on US schools', *Financial Times*, 6 September 2004, and Jennifer Joan Lee, 'International education: Europe lures students once more', *International Herald Tribune*, 19 October 2004.

13 Polly Curtis, 'Ministers "hampering" overseas student recruitment', *EducationGuardian.co.uk*, 2 August 2005.

14 Lisa Wood, 'Bringing practicality to the table: management consultants', *Financial Times*, 23 May 2000.

15 AACSB International Task Force, *Management Education at Risk*, 7–8; William C. Symonds, 'Cash-cow universities', *BusinessWeek Online*, 17 November 2003; and Reuben Kyle and Troy A. Festervand, 'An update on high-tech MBA', *Journal of Education for Business*, 3 January 2005.

16 See, generally, Linda Wedlin, *Playing the Ranking Game: Field Formation and Boundary-Work in European Management Education* (Uppsala, Sweden: Uppsala University, Department of Business Studies, 2004), and Tyson, 'Management and the media', 17–21.

17 Nicholas Thompson, 'The best, the top, the most', *New York Times*, 3 August 2003. See also the special 'rankings' issue' of *Selections*, 1(2) (2001); Andrew J. Policano, 'What price rankings?', *BizEd* (September/

October 2005), 26–32; and AACSB International Committee on Issues in Management Education, *The Business School Rankings Dilemma* (Tampa, FL: AACSB International, 2005).

18 The involvement of a government department in this kind of activity is an entirely new departure, and one that has attracted considerable attention: see, for example, Des Dearlove, 'Treasury rankings put UK schools in the shade', *Times*, 16 May 2005.

19 Graduate Management Admission Council, *Global MBA Graduate Survey* (McLean, VA: Graduate Management Admission Council, 2005), 3.

20 C. Edward Fee, Charles Hadlock and Joshua Pierce, 'Business school rankings and business school deans: a study of nonprofit governance', *Financial Management*, 34(1) (2005), 143–66; and Katherine S. Mangan, 'Rankings may push business deans out', *Chronicle of Higher Education*, 3 June 2005.

21 Quoted in Thompson, 'The best, the top, the most'.

22 Jerold L. Zimmerman, Working Paper FR 01-16, *Can American Business Schools Survive?* Rochester, NY: University of Rochester, Bradley Policy Research Center, 2001, 12–13, and Gioia and Corley, 'Being good versus looking good', 112–13.

23 Interview, 11 February 2005.

24 See, for example, Della Bradshaw, 'The MBA industry may be facing a shakeout', *Financial Times*, 28 April 2005.

25 Linda Anderson, 'Improbable mix of talents sought', *Financial Times*, 23 October 2000; anon., 'Meet Joe Dean', *BizEd* (May/June 2002), 36–9; and Simon Hoare, 'The university fat cats', *Guardian*, 25 January 2005.

26 Anon., 'Light on their feet', *Economist*, 27 April 2006.

27 Mica Schneider, 'The ever-costlier MBA degree', *BusinessWeek Online*, 28 October 2004.

28 Tyson, 'Deans talk dollars', 24–8.

29 Mica Schneider, 'A $100 million thanks for Michigan', *BusinessWeek Online*, 9 September 2004; and Doron Levin, 'Price climbs for B-school naming', *Los Angeles Business Journal*, 17 January 2005.

30 Interview, 8 March 2004.

31 Aisha Labi, 'Across Europe, chasing the money', *Chronicle of Higher Education*, 30 April 2004.

32 Association of Business Schools, *Media Bulletin*, 14 (n.d.), 1–4; Linda Anderson, 'Imperial College receives £27m gift from alumnus', *Financial Times*, 6 November 2000; and see p. 3 above.

33 See, for example, anon., 'Lecturers face axe in cash crisis', *Birmingham Post*, 17 April 2002; and Francesca di Meglio, 'Thunderbird endures shrinking pains', *BusinessWeek Online*, 22 November 2005.

34 Interview, 29 April 2004.

35 Francis Beckett, 'Standing alone in business', *EducationGuardian.co.uk*, 15 July 2004; and interview 8 March 2004. See also, for an American example, Kirp, *Shakespeare, Einstein, and the Bottom Line*, 130–45.

36 See, for example, Tricia Bisoux, 'Thirty percent', *BizEd* (July/August 2002), 22–6; anon., 'Men's work?', *Economist*, 12 June 2003; and Francesca di Meglio, 'Breaking B-school gender barriers', *BusinessWeek*, 8 December 2004.

37 Anon., 'But can you teach it?', *Economist*, 22 May 2004; Higher Education Statistics Agency data, at www.hesa.org.uk; and material from www.businessweek.com.

38 Council for Excellence in Management and Leadership Business Schools Advisory Group, *The Contribution of the UK Business Schools*, 17.

39 See the MBA rankings at www.businessweek.com.

40 See, for example, Thomas Crampton, 'Setting up a business school in Asia', *International Herald Tribune*, 18 February 2003, and Rogers and Wong, 'The MBA in Singapore', 180–96.

41 Kathy Harvey, 'Time to work, learn and play; you don't have to put your career on hold with the new MBAs business schools are offering', *Independent on Sunday*, 20 March 2005.

42 Mica Schneider, 'Distance learning closes the gap', *BusinessWeek Online*, 19 August 2004; and Steve McCormack, 'Study at the click of a mouse', *Independent*, 23 June 2005.

43 Anon., 'Definitely shorter, maybe sweeter too', *Economist Global Executive*, 4 May 2003; and Stuart Crainer, 'Flexibility is the name of the game', *TimesOnline*, 16 May 2005.

44 Stuart Crainer, 'TrumpU, where an MBA can be done in a day', *TimesOnline*, 6 October 2005.

45 Crainer, 'Flexibility is the name of the game'.

46 Jodi Schneider, 'Back to B-school: CEOs are turning to custom-designed programs at top schools to educate the senior ranks', *Chief Executive*, 7 January 2004.

47 Anon., 'But can you teach it?'; and Della Bradshaw, 'Specialisation is the key in a growing market', *Financial Times*, 16 May 2005.

48 AACSB International Management Education Task Force, *Management*

Education at Risk, 8; and Caitlin Davies, 'Degrees of profit', *Independent*, 20 November 2003.

49 Tricia Bisoux, 'A matter of reputation', *BizEd* (March/April 2003), 46–9.

50 Della Bradshaw, 'Deans vie for the world stage', *Financial Times*, 20 September 2004; anon., 'Swiss, please', *Economist Global Executive*, 5 May 2005.

51 Quoted in Katherine S. Mangan, 'The new "arms" race in business-school buildings', *Chronicle of Higher Education*, 7 June 2002.

52 Details at www.bi.no/templates/ArticleColor____33884.aspx. See also, for example, Adam Thompson, 'Catholic tinge to academic rigour', *Financial Times*, 16 May 2005.

53 Clive Holtham, 'Building for business knowledge: constructing a new business school in the heart of London', *Business Information Review*, 20(4) (2003), 215–25.

54 George Bickerstaff, 'Thoroughly modern monasteries', *Financial Times*, 10 January 2005.

55 Anon., 'Designing the successful alliance', *BizEd* (March/April 2005), 9–10.

56 Linda Anderson, 'Consensus the ideal', *Financial Times*, 11 September 2000; and material from accreditors' websites.

57 Tracy Simmons, 'Business school wins international accreditation', *Victoria Advocate*, 12 May 2005.

58 Tricia Bisoux, 'The Zen of B-school branding', *BizEd* (November/December 2003), 24–9.

59 The Association of Business Schools and Carrington Crisp, *The Business of Branding Survey 2005* (London: Association of Business Schools, 2005). See also Nicholas Pyke, 'Where the brand is everything', *Independent*, 8 May 2003; Steve Coomber, 'Branding makes a big difference for schools', *TimesOnline*, 16 May 2005; and Martin Thompson, 'Determined to make their mark', *Independent*, 13 October 2005.

60 Steve Coomber, 'Esade reveals the logic behind its new logo', *TimesOnline*, 16 May 2005; and Sarah Balmond, 'NB Studio at business end of school identity design', *Design Week*, 20(20) (2005), 4.

61 We have borrowed this phrase from one of Della Bradshaw's excellent articles in the *Financial Times*: see 'Plenty of room for naked gamesmanship', *Financial Times*, 17 January 2003.

62 See, for various different instances and allegations, *inter alia*, Phil Baty, 'QAA to target "failing" MBAs', *Times Higher Education Supplement*, 8 November 2002; anon., 'Doctored résumés, poisoned applicants',

BusinessWeek Online, 12 March 2003; Tim Elliot, 'Top in enterprise, bottom in integrity', *Financial Times*, 2 June 2003; Polly Curtis, 'Cheating MBA student faces course expulsion', *EducationGuardian.co.uk*, 24 July 2003; Jeffrey Pfeffer and Christina T. Fong, 'The business school "business": some lessons from the US experience', *Journal of Management*, 41(8) (2004), 1504–5; Francesca di Meglio, 'Grade inflation: devaluing B-schools' currency', *BusinessWeek Online*, 19 April 2005; and Della Bradshaw, 'Double trouble as students hire impersonators', *Financial Times*, 20 June 2005.

63 Quality Assurance Agency, *London Business School: Institutional Audit* (London: Quality Assurance Agency, 2003), 25. See also Phil Baty, 'Watchdog mauls LBS and Cambridge quality', *Times Higher Education Supplement*, 24 October 2003.

64 Phil Baty, 'Caught in vicious cycle of declining standards', *Times Higher Education Supplement*, 19 November 2004.

65 Independent Commission Against Corruption, *Report on Investigation into the University of Newcastle's Handling of Plagiarism Allegations* (Sydney: Independent Commission Against Corruption, 2004), 6. See also David Cohen, 'Inquiry faults 2 Australian university officials in plagiarism case', *Chronicle of Higher Education*, 5 July 2005.

66 Anon., 'Do business schools cook their books?', *Ascribe Higher Education News Service*, 2 October 2002; and Harry DeAngelo, Linda DeAngelo, and Jerold L. Zimmerman, *What's Really Wrong with U.S. Business Schools* (n.p., 2005), 12.

67 Martin Van Der Werf, 'Olin School dean gives ideas on upgrading MBA', *St Louis Post-Dispatch*, 13 May 2005.

68 Carlotta Mast, 'The people behind the rankings', *Selections*, 1(2) (2001), 23.

69 Anon., '*BusinessWeek* foils attempt to inflate business school's rankings', *Chronicle of Higher Education*, 6 November 1998; Della Bradshaw, 'Growing enthusiasm for scrutiny', *Financial Times*, 17 January 2003; and Della Bradshaw, 'Business schools bite back at proliferation of surveys', *Financial Times*, 26 January 2004.

70 Interview, 11 February 2005.

71 Claudia H. Deutsch, 'The M.B.A. rat race', *New York Times*, 4 November 1990.

72 Gioia and Corley, 'Being good versus looking good', 113.

73 Amy Joyce, 'A new degree of competition: in a tough job market, placement wars spur business schools to give MBAs an extra push', *Washington Post*, 12 May 2003.

74 Lomi Kriel, 'High A&M MBA rankings lacking supporting data', *Daily Texan*, 16 June 2004; Shawn Millender, 'Daily Texan questions A&M business school rank', *Battalion*, 22 July 2004; and Clint Johnson and Zein Basravi, 'A&M rankings under review', *Daily Texan*, 23 July 2004.

4 Business school education

Business schools have always prided themselves on the quality of their education, their ability to fashion successive generations of students who are thoroughly prepared for the rigours of the outside world, whether in business, government or elsewhere. In the light of the previous chapters, it is obviously pertinent to ask how this much-toted mission is currently bearing up. To be specific, is the recent spate of negative publicity, allied to the strong growth of competition, forcing the schools to sharpen up their acts, and perhaps respond constructively? Or is it instilling into them a fear of failure and reluctance to experiment, and so ultimately producing nothing but stultifying conformity?

Comment on these matters is certainly plentiful at present, and, in fact, hardly a week goes by without a story appearing in the press about business school teaching and curricula. Reading this material indicates no obvious consensus, however. The schools themselves, unsurprisingly, almost always stress their dynamism. The standard line is that they are alive to the challenges and ready to embrace fundamental changes – that is, if they have not embraced them already. In a much-trailed article published in late 2004, no less a figure than Laura D'Andrea Tyson, dean of London Business School, announced a bout of soul-searching, designed to determine her institution's 'role in the education of the next generation of business leaders'. The impetus, she explained, was a growing suspicion that 'our customers "had issues" with our products', and a recognition that '[w]e needed to understand why, and whether we were offering what they, and other employers throughout the world, needed'. Many of Tyson's peers have reported similar epiphanies and reassessments. A recent *BusinessWeek* article referred to a 'slew of curriculum changes [that]

B-schools are implementing in hopes of making their programs more effective and competitive in a tightening environment'.[1] Yet substantial doubts remain. Schools have trumpeted fundamental changes before, while actually engaged only in tinkering.[2] There is an obvious temptation to see the latest bout of introspection as purely cosmetic, perhaps even a calculated sleight of hand designed to distract attention from worrying truths about the MBA's declining value. Interviewed in 2005, the retiring dean of Yale, Jeffrey E. Garten, regretted that business schools were prone to 'fads', and accepted that curricula innovations were often 'more sizzle than steak'.[3] Indeed, some believe that the real trend at present is not reform at all but a far less attractive retrenchment. In 2003 Darden professor Mark Haskins wrote a personal commentary for *BizEd* denouncing what he felt was a depressing convergence around a very stale norm. In his view, the seat of the problem was what he called the 'great homogenization process', which increasingly mired schools in 'an expanding arena of similar practices, philosophies, and purposes', and ultimately produced only 'a widespread, indistinguishable sameness'. Interestingly, an April 2005 *Financial Times* editorial largely concurred, observing that 'too many schools' were offering 'me-too products', before tartly concluding: 'Institutions have to differentiate their offerings and create brands, something only a few have succeeded in doing.'[4] Clearly, given such divergence of opinion, it is prudent to re-examine the evidence carefully.

CURRICULUM DEVELOPMENTS

The optimists' case is certainly not hard to make. Each year *Business-Week* publishes detailed profiles of nearly 300 schools, and includes a good deal of material on their programmes and teaching methods.[5] This shows that, in 2004, for instance, 56 per cent of schools had 'revised' their 'core MBA curriculum' in the last two years, while 69 per cent had introduced at least one new elective in the last twelve months.[6] Of course, such data is self-reported, and also a little imprecise, most obviously because words such as 'revise' can be understood in very different ways. Nevertheless, the general picture that emerges is reasonably clear. This is a sector that appears alive to the need for change. Delving a little deeper, into both curriculum content and basic pedagogy, provides a wealth of apparently significant illustrations.[7]

It is clear, to begin with, that some schools are energetic in trying to keep their courses as up to date as possible. They are conscious of emerging business priorities and problems, and believe that these should be dealt with in the curriculum. In 2003 the *New York Times* noted that US programmes had begun featuring Wal-Mart, while, a year later, the same newspaper recorded the arrival of outsourcing as 'a prime subject for business students'.[8] More generally, there has been growing interest in important new topics such as globalisation, the knowledge society, entrepreneurialism, 'soft skills' and the qualities necessary for good leadership. Indicatively, in 2002 an AACSB-International-appointed task force noted that there were currently 400 international business programmes running in the United States – double the number a decade before.[9] A further revealing example concerns the business schools' developing concern with ethics.

In the 1980s and 1990s business schools certainly claimed that they taught ethics, but the coverage was in fact for the most part uneven, irregular and ill-considered. In the United States, one expert remarked, the subject of ethics at business schools was like the weather: 'Everybody talks about it but nobody does anything about it.'[10] In their comprehensive report on American management education and development of 1988, Porter and McKibbin reached analogous conclusions, noting, essentially in passing, that deans and other faculty who they had questioned listed ethics more frequently than anything else as a response to the 'other areas needing more emphasis' section of their survey.[11] Across the Atlantic the situation was little better. For example, an investigation of ethics teaching at British business schools reported, amongst other things, that past initiatives had occurred mainly as a result of 'individual lecturer enthusiasm'; there was a 'low level of support' from programme managers;

and the available course materials were 'inadequate'.[12] The incontrovertible – if somewhat awkward – fact was that ethical perspectives of whatever kind remained largely relegated to the margins. Even senior faculty and administrators appeared confused about the fundamentals. In the mid-1990s a team of researchers questioned 291 business school deans (three-quarters from the United States) about five hypothetical ethically ambiguous situations, and came up with some extraordinary conclusions. In one of the scenarios, the sample was asked to comment on an imaginary dean who had admitted an unqualified applicant to an MBA programme under pressure from the candidate's father, a large contributor to the school. Astonishingly, 10 per cent actually considered this behaviour to be ethical, while no less than 48 per cent admitted that they would have done exactly the same. Nor was this an unrepresentative case, since similar kinds of reaction were observable throughout the study.[13]

From the turn of the century, however, the situation began to change. Corporate scandals on both sides of the Atlantic – from Marconi to Enron – provoked much negative comment, and led to the charge (already noted) that business schools were somehow complicit. Accordingly, it was not long before there was a flurry of activity to examine what had gone wrong and if possible promote reform. In the United States the Aspen Institute created the Beyond Grey Pinstripes initiative to encourage socially and environmentally aware programmes, and this generated considerable publicity, not least because of its annual 'alternative' rankings. Across the Atlantic the newly launched European Academy of Business in Society – a collaboration between government departments, corporates and universities – provided a similar focus.[14] All three main accreditation agencies also became involved. For example, in 2003 AACSB International simultaneously amended its curriculum content criteria, in part to encourage the study of ethical and legal issues, and set up a special task force to examine what else might be done to encourage the further advancement of such provision.[15] Everywhere the issue was rapidly moving up the agenda.

Over the next few years change began to ripple out through the sector. The precise extent of what was occurring remained hard to assess. For one thing, definitions tended to vary. Thus, the new courses were called everything from the fairly straightforward 'business ethics' through 'corporate citizenship' to the more esoteric 'stakeholder management'. In addition, while some schools opted to introduce specialist modules on their own, others took a more holistic view, and attempted to integrate ethical concerns of one kind or another into their programmes as a whole.[16] Isolated surveys provided valuable snapshots. Dirk Matten and Jeremy Moon contacted 166 European schools in 2003, and found that about one-third had optional corporate social responsibility modules on their MBA programmes, with the United Kingdom and Ireland particularly well represented. In the United States an informal AACSB International poll discovered that 35 per cent of members required students to take at least one ethics course.[17] Perhaps predictably, some more radical voices were disappointed that progress was not quicker. In early 2005 the University of Kansas's Diane Swanson repeated her charge of previous years that 'many if not most business schools continue to be complicit in corporate neglect of social responsibilities', and highlighted the recent finding that only a half of the BusinessWeek top fifty MBAs had 'a required course specifically devoted to the study of business ethics'. She was especially critical of AACSB International, arguing that it should forthwith change its accreditation criteria to make the study of ethics mandatory.[18] Many faculty in both the United States and Europe certainly sympathised.[19] Nevertheless, such criticism accepted, it was clear that the mood across business schools worldwide had unarguably changed, and that ethics was now almost everywhere considered to be a matter of both importance and relevance.[20] Significantly, surveys of key senior personnel underlined the point. For example, in 2003 Fred Evans and Leah Marcal asked a sample of 295 deans to respond to the statement 'I believe that business ethics ought to be an important part of the educational mission of AACSB-accredited business programs', and discovered that 55 per cent 'strongly agreed' and 34 per cent 'somewhat agreed'.[21]

Turning to basic pedagogy, there is no doubt that here, too, the situation is evolving. Many business school faculty – like their peers elsewhere in the academy – are steadily moving away from reliance on the traditional menu of set piece lecture, seminar and written assignment. More and more are introducing methods such as interactive debate, group work, role play, simulation, field studies and periods of outplacement. In addition, there is increasing use of technology to improve delivery or help achieve desired outcomes. A recent survey commented:

> The comparison between the classroom and a theatre is nothing new. But the comparison is now going beyond analogy. Increasingly, a business school classroom is taking on the accoutrements of a professional theatre, complete with lights, cameras, microphones, and acoustic panels. Many schools are paying close attention to light, wall color, and sound quality in anticipation of digitally recording classes for replay via DVD and online streaming video.[22]

Underpinning all this, at least in some institutions, is a philosophical shift in approach that places the student much more firmly at the heart of the learning experience; values interaction as opposed to passive consumption; and attempts to develop character and outlook rather than simply impart particular skills or competencies. Thus, the University of Bath School of Management notes on its website that its 'culture' is one that 'looks beyond business processes and techniques to emphasise the importance of self-awareness, intuition, [and] cross-cultural sensitivity'. The watchwords here as elsewhere are 'critical thinking', 'teamwork', 'creativity' and – above all – 'personal development'.[23]

THE EXTENT OF CHANGE: (I) CASE STUDIES

In the light of this evidence, it is incontrovertible that business schools *are* to some extent developing their curricula, and trying to keep abreast of the times. Nevertheless, in our view, the extent of this change can easily be greatly exaggerated.[24] Deans and university administrators of course like to put the best possible gloss on things. New ethics courses or teaching methods attract attention. When programmes are looked at in the round, however, it is their conservatism and conformity that is in fact often most striking. To discover what is really going on, it is necessary to move away from the headlines, sales pitches and press releases, and look at some of the more everyday aspects of business school pedagogy – and, in particular, at what actually occurs in the average classroom.[25]

We begin by examining one particular course component that has become almost synonymous with MBA education: the case study. Some background is in order. The case study method was honed at Harvard in the 1920s and thereafter spread widely, reaching Europe in the 1950s, and subsequently the rest of the world.[26] The attraction was that cases appeared to introduce 'real life' into the classroom: they allowed students to get a feel for situations as they actually were, rather than as theorists painted them. Today, case study work is a ubiquitous part of many types of course, taking up about one-third of the average MBA, for example.[27] The cases in circulation cover an enormous variety of different industries and situations. Some are quite long, others rather short. The big distributors of cases, such as Harvard and the European Case Clearing House (ECCH), do significant business; indeed, it is claimed that the former sells 7 million cases a year, grossing some £20 million.[28] Quite obviously, saying anything sensible about such an enormous mass of material is rather difficult, so what we have done is isolate a small but indicative sample. The ECCH awards annual prizes to the best-selling cases in a number of different categories. In what follows, we look at the overall winners for the years 1995 to 2004. This is certainly not perfect, but, on the other hand, it does give us at least some kind of handle on the type of cases that the ordinary business school student is likely to experience.[29]

We need to underline straightaway that all our sample cases make arresting reading and demonstrate important points. Nevertheless, that said, having examined them closely we also think that they share some debilitating weaknesses, which bear on the wider issues being considered. Three stand out. First, there is a pervasive problem about research quality. The literature suggests that case studies should always be based on exhaustive enquiry.[30] It appears, however, that our authors' sources are in general rather restricted. The majority rely to a surprising extent simply on material supplied by the companies being studied. Indeed, of the 210 direct quotations from people or documents that are featured in the ten texts, only a fifth come from elsewhere. Moreover, it is also true that our authors are drawn to management voices rather than those of others. There are 183 quotes specifically from individuals in these texts, and they can be broken down as follows:

> Quotes from senior managers (CEOs, directors, VPs, etc.) 107
> Quotes from other managers 50
> Quotes from employees 1
> Quotes from customers 2
> Quotes from 'others' 23

An obvious retort here is that such bias is simply unavoidable. Most case studies deal with crises or turning points, when those at the helm have to deal with challenging circumstances, and so some emphasis on the management view is entirely understandable. This argument certainly has a degree of validity, yet it is by no means wholly persuasive. In passing, we note that adopting such an unbalanced research approach sets a poor example to students, who might well be persuaded that interviewing the CEO is sufficient to understand an entire organisation. More seriously, however, we also believe that the predominant focus too often promotes self-serving subjectivity at the expense of neutral observation. The following example is illustrative.

In the ECCH 2002 winner *easyJet: The Web's Favorite Airline*, the authors, Brian Rogers and Nirmalya Kumar, describe their sources as follows: 'The case was written using interviews and material provided by the company. Among the materials provided were a case study from the February 1999 issue of the *European Management*

Journal written by Don Sull, and an article on easyJet from the November 1999 issue of *Bilan* magazine written by Giuseppe Mellilo.'[31] In fact, this list is even more restricted than it appears, because Sull's analysis of easyJet also only uses internally generated material.[32] What this means in practice is well illustrated by the fact that, of the twenty-one direct quotations in Rogers and Kumar's text, fourteen come from easyJet's owner, Stelios Haji-Ioannou, and six come from other easyJet sources, with the sole exception attributed to an unidentified 'commentator'. In this situation, there are, predictably, instances in which Rogers and Kumar offer judgements that appear to be based solely upon Haji-Ioannou's claims. Surprisingly, this is true even of quite fundamental issues. Thus, for example, at the very outset of the case, Rogers and Kumar state that easyJet had maintained 'high levels of customer satisfaction',[33] but it later transpires that they are merely repeating Haji-Ioannou's own opinion, with the hard facts as they are presented in the case confined to a short, unsourced and, in fact, curiously inconclusive table about punctuality.[34]

The second problem with our cases concerns the question of context. Case studies are by their very nature compressed, and cannot of course deal adequately with absolutely everything that may be relevant. Most focus, to repeat, on managers and firms at particular moments, but provide some background information on the wider political economy. Nevertheless, the balance here is, in our view, by no means always well struck. Many cases depict managers as authors of their own destinies, powerful actors who really are masters and mistresses of the future. Far fewer admit that wider factors may in fact also be highly influential. The point can be made by reference to Sumantra Ghoshal et al.'s *Lufthansa: The Challenge of Globalisation*, the ECCH winner in 2003.[35]

This case revolves around Lufthansa's early 1990s journey from alleged 'state-run basket case' to private enterprise dynamo. Much is made of the management strategies – first cost cutting and then the quest for globalisation – that are said to have made this transformation possible. On the other hand, although the story is fundamentally about a privatisation, there is a surprising reticence about some aspects of what this process meant and how it unfolded. The case study begins with a brief general statement noting that Lufthansa passed into private hands between 1991 and 1994, and shortly afterwards a few further details are added: 'At the outset of Phase 2 of the turnaround . . . [Lufthansa] embarked on negotiations with the German government to become a private company and to withdraw from the government pension fund which further tied it to the State. In 1994, the government diluted its holdings to 36% and a new organisational structure was announced.'[36] As it happens, however, this is considerably less than the full story.

The German government's intention to sell its 51.2 per cent share in Lufthansa was, in fact, reported as early as at least February 1992.[37] Thereafter, one of Lufthansa management's prime aims was quite clearly to make the airline as attractive as possible to future private investors. Shortly after the 1994 sell-off the company's annual report boasted: 'At the time the annual accounts were being prepared, Lufthansa shares were trading at DM 250. That was nearly 40 per cent higher than at the time of privatisation. An investment in Lufthansa equity thus yielded a distinctly higher return than the German share index Dax as a whole.' Similar comments appeared in the press at the time of a second sale of shares in 1997.[38] In addition, the pension fund issue concerned rather more than just a straightforward disentanglement from the state scheme. The real problem was money – specifically, the question of who was going to cover the sums owed to the airline's retirees. Some hard bargaining obviously occurred over this issue, but, in the end, the government apparently decided that the matter had to be resolved or privatisation would be jeopardised, and as a result it provided DM 1.55 billion to buy out, in effect, all current liabilities.[39] Lufthansa's trajectory at this time, therefore, occurred in a particular context. Managers played their part in reshaping the business, but so did the government. Privatisation was a multifaceted phenomenon, which incentivised executives and also set the parameters for what was strategically possible. Without adequate recognition of such realities, the story of how the airline evolved in the early to mid-1990s remains misleadingly incomplete.

Finally, the way that our case studies deal with labour issues also leaves something to be desired. If, as the evidence already quoted demonstrates, ordinary workers' voices in our sample are conspicuous by their absence, this does not mean that the cases necessarily ignore industrial relations as a whole. In fact, most say at least something about work and the workforce. It is also noticeable, however, that there is a widespread tendency to depict situations in terms of recent managerialist perspectives, and ignore issues that do not fit. The 1995 ECCH winner, IMD's *Federal Express Quality Improvement Programme*,[40] illustrates some of the problems.

The case begins by quoting FedEx's founder and chair, Frederick W. Smith, on his company's credo: 'Federal Express, from its inception, has put its people first, both because it is right to do so and because it is good business as well. Our corporate philosophy is succinctly stated: People–Service–Profits (P–S–P).' It then explains that great importance is placed on 'leading and motivating employees', and describes in detail the tools that are used, such as FXTV (a dedicated television channel), a variety of awards for outstanding customer care and the Survey Feedback Action (SFA) Index, which systematically and regularly measures rank and file assessments of twenty-six statements regarding pay, working conditions, senior management, and so on. Throughout, it is underlined that FedEx's particular approach colours all its operations. For example, it is noted that FedEx had chosen to work with the consulting firm ODI over the quality issue because '[the latter] paid little attention to statistical techniques but a lot more to the thought processes and involvement of people within the company in developing quality programs'.[41]

Closer examination of these passages, however, reveals that some of the discussion about FedEx's alleged leading-edge practices is decidedly thin. For example, it is stated that, though other firms used the SFA Index, FedEx had 'consistently obtained above average ratings',[42] but it is noticeable that no actual numbers are cited. Likewise, the FedEx boast that in 1989 the SFA Leadership Index (which was derived from the SFA Index) had reached 76, the 'largest single jump' ever,[43] is unsubstantiated. Overall, there is an imbalance between descriptions of FedEx's consultative machinery and hard evidence documenting outcomes – for example, what the SFA Index actually revealed about employee attitudes. Moreover, the case's basic characterisation of FedEx's industrial relations approach as humane and liberal is also open to question. Smith himself remained hostile to trade unions because he believed that 'neither traditional "management" nor traditional "labor relations" was suited to a service business whose success depends on people wanting to go all out for the enterprise'.[44] It is true that Smith spent a high proportion of his time on workforce matters, and that every FedEx employee had the guaranteed right to appeal any management decision right up to a board sub-committee, under a system called the 'guaranteed fair treatment procedure', but a portrait of the final appeals committee in 1991 demonstrated that it was essentially dominated by management. A small group of very senior executives reviewed cases summarised for them by the company's personnel department. They discussed the issues on their merits, and, clearly, sometimes understood the pressures that ordinary FedEx workers could be under. On the other hand, there was no place for any independent voice in the proceedings. Little wonder that, in 'about 85 percent' of the appeals that came before it, the board upheld the decisions of lower management.[45]

Taken as a whole, therefore, these observations are not encouraging. We have been discussing a number of very high-selling cases. We conclude that they do not seem to demonstrate any strikingly inquisitive intent. In fact, in our view, many simply recycle a number of rather dated assumptions about how business – and, indeed, society – should be run. There is little here about reflecting on sources or grappling with complexities. We are back in a familiar world in which, straightforwardly and with almost no hint of reservation or scepticism, the CEO is king, the workforce is subservient and success is a function purely of inspirational leadership. Our point about con-servatism in the curricula seems to hold.

At this point, however, we need to consider a significant poten-tial qualification. Case studies are artefacts, and can, of course, be deployed in many different ways. It is entirely possible that faculty react to them as we do, and compensate for their deficiencies when they actually use them in the classroom. To nail down our argument, therefore, we clearly need to look closely not just at the cases them-selves but also at how they are commonly taught.

THE EXTENT OF CHANGE: (II) CLASSROOM TEACHING

It is worth noting, to start with, that many authors of case studies rou-tinely offer their peers an accompanying document called a teaching note,[46] which typically explains in some detail both the case itself and how it can best be put over to an audience.[47] The knock-on effect of this convention is that class instructors often have the option of being able to teach cases straight off the shelf, with the choreography fully detailed, the questions and issues dissected, the conclusions drawn and little or no extra work required. What we need to ascertain, obvi-ously, is whether this kind of thing is actually normal.

It is certainly true that the pundits who write about the case study method almost all strongly caution against their formulaic deployment.[48] Case studies, the mantra runs, do not have 'correct' answers. The data, as in real life, is messy and incomplete. Analysing it may produce contrasting but equally valid conclusions. The impor-tant point in looking at case studies, then, is not to learn their alleged 'lessons' by rote but to explore all the various different possibilities that they throw up, and gain deeper knowledge by doing so. The case study session leader is seen as pivotal in this process, akin to the con-ductor of an orchestra and, above all, responsible for bringing out the best in the class. At a recent colloquium of eminent faculty in India, one of the contributors declared: 'The instructor is neither in posses-sion of the universally applicable "Truth" nor is he [sic] impelled by an inner voice to win everyone over to the "Truth". The instructor is a facilitator who creates the learning conditions in the classroom.'[49] There is little in this approach that resembles the traditional Socratic method, with its relatively fixed notions of right and wrong, teacher and taught. Case studies, the pundits emphasise, are about expanding minds, not rigidly following someone else's recipes.

Whether the majority of faculty actively apply such nostrums, however, is self-evidently quite another matter. Clearly, some institutions do currently use the case study method with notable imagination. In his 1987 book on Harvard Business School, *The Empire Builders*, J. Paul Mark reported: 'With few exceptions, instructors follow the guidelines set forth in the teaching note when one is available.'[50] Today, both Harvard and other top-ranked schools unarguably employ a much more flexible and innovative approach.[51] In our own conversations with staff, however, we discovered that such creativity is probably far less pervasive than might be imagined. Some of those who we talked to observed that, with sharply increasing class sizes and bigger administrative loads, never mind the pressure to research and publish, their hands were essentially tied. They simply did not have the time, as one put it, 'to act like Fancy Dans'. Others underlined that leading an open-ended discussion required considerable mental dexterity and abundant self-confidence, and lamented that training opportunities to hone such aptitudes were few and far between.[52] All told, it appeared to us that many found reliance on the teaching note, perhaps with one or two minor embellishments, largely unavoidable.

In order to reach a fuller and more independent view on the realities of case study use, we decided to see for ourselves, and sat in on a number of programmes, carefully recording how they evolved. What we discovered, unfortunately, only reinforced our wider anxieties. To give a flavour of our findings, we reproduce one of our research reports, which concerns an MBA module taught at a business school with an international reputation for innovative research. Needless to say, all the names and some identifying details have been changed, but otherwise the piece stands largely as it was originally written.

Report on Grapefruit Business School Full-Time MBA Elective on 'The Consultant's Mind'

This is a report on the Grapefruit Business School Full-Time MBA Elective on 'The Consultant's Mind'. It is based on the distributed course material; our own observation of the course sessions; and informal conversations with a variety of interested parties.

The course structure The distributed documentation referred to the course as a learning laboratory, which would help students move from a phase in which they had concentrated on tools and techniques to a phase in which they would begin to embrace practical concerns, in preparation for their emergence into 'the real world'.

In specific terms, the course objective was to help students develop the outlook of a strategy consultant, and thus skills such as 'the art of enquiry, the art of listening, the art of strategic thinking and the art of thinking about thinking'.

The course was delivered over one semester. All the sessions mixed short expositions by the tutor with detailed discussion of different case studies, presented in either written or video form.

The assessment was an assignment on a further case study, to be handed in a short time after the course had ended.

The distributed material consisted of a course outline, including a short reading list; a folder of cases; some handouts summarising relevant questions or approaches; and the tutor's notes (which were placed on the school's intranet).

The tutor The course tutor was Kentaro Wiggens (hereafter KW), a professor of management, Harvard MBA and international consultant.

KW stated that he was a great believer in the case study method, particularly if it involved forthright debate. As he advised the class at the beginning of session one: 'You get at least one year's worth of experience from a case . . . You get about four years' worth from discussing it.'

KW's style was directive. He started session one by underlining to the class that he would be fully in charge, declaring: 'There is a flow in my mind . . . in order to maintain the flow, I have to manage discussion . . . I need to get to where I want to go.' Subsequently he was true to his word, encouraging students in certain directions, but firmly (if politely) rebuffing comments or questions that he felt were out of place. As he put it to a student during a break: 'I'm walking you down a path.'

On the other hand, KW was certainly sympathetic as well. He took a considerable interest in the students, making himself available during coffee breaks and at the end of sessions; did his best to assuage anxieties about complications in the case studies; interacted without airs or graces; admitted candidly that he did not necessarily know all the answers; and acknowledged that his own view of an issue was only one of those possible.

To reinforce the idea that he was on the student's side, KW to some extent distanced himself from the Grapefruit system. He stated that he was against exams and hated marking papers, and implied that the assignment had been included only to assuage the administration. He also mildly mocked his colleagues' reputation for scholasticism, amiably remarking during one exposition: 'Grapefruit wants to have models, so here's a model.'

The students There were nearly fifty students registered on the course, three-quarters men, predominantly aged twenty-five to thirty-five, from a wide range of different national backgrounds, with the largest group (around fifteen) coming from the Indian subcontinent.

The sessions
(a) Approach KW stated that his twin objectives were to underline the importance of business models in organisations and to outline how they should be analysed, so that there could be improvement. His concern, in short, was both with 'how the world works' and with 'how to think about how the world works'.

As the sessions developed, KW put more and more emphasis on the analytical element, and the cases reflected this, as they dealt not just with problems in companies but also with consultants reflecting on how they had tried to put things right.

In discussing the process of analysis, KW placed great importance on taking a measured and rational approach, using a set of common questions to uncover systematically what was occurring. Building on this, he recommended a two-stage approach: the construction of a short narrative, describing the basic elements of the subject's business model, including its producer and customer economics; and then a more detailed focus on 'the numbers'.

Regarding the latter, KW noted that they were sometimes overlooked at Grapefruit, in favour of a softer approach, but he emphasised his belief that this was a mistake. At the end of session six, KW elaborated on this theme at some length, and indeed his final advice to the students was the admonition: 'Search for numbers – they tell great stories.'

Nevertheless, KW also cautioned the students against expecting easy results. He constantly warned against being seduced by preconceptions, and told the class: 'For every good point, I want the negative.' Moreover, he stressed that the search for solutions might well be indeterminate, baldly stating: 'There is no equation and formula by which the answers will pop up . . . If anybody says the answer will pop up, they're wrong.' Interestingly, he contrasted this need to accept complexity with his own experience of doing an MBA at Harvard many years previously, 'when we *did* think we had all the answers'.

The issue was raised particularly vividly in session four. The class had spent a good deal of time looking at Universal Consulting's interaction with Bank Seventeen, and KW was summing up. One student put her hand up and said she was very disappointed with what the consultants had recommended because it was too mundane – just common sense. This gave KW his opening. 'There is no magic wand,' he stated. 'They are human beings like us . . . They are people like you,' adding again, 'There is no magic wand.'

(b) The lecture segments Early in the week KW inserted brief lecture segments into the sessions, going through models – for example, McKinsey's '7 Ss'. Subsequently he concentrated on 'summing up the learning', going through the lessons that had emerged from the case study discussions.

Little reference was made to printed material. KW announced that there was no textbook for the course, and made only sporadic reference to either the very short reading list that was part of the course materials or the limited handouts that he provided.

(c) The case studies The main case studies analysed were Hard Group, Nippycar, Pharmacy-Mart, Bank Seventeen Corporation/Universal Consulting, Confidence Corporation/High Hat Consulting, Utah Telephones and Geriatric Care (the latter four involving written and video components). In addition, KW showed a well-known Harvard video dealing briefly with various international companies.

KW told the students that they had to read these case studies carefully, in particular paying attention to their various appendices.

His teaching style was to analyse the information provided in terms of the two-stage model that he had proposed and write extensive notes on the whiteboards as he went along. Some of the time he asked questions about the sequence of events, but more usually he threw out analytical challenges, and pushed the students to explore possible answers, sometimes getting them to debate between themselves.

In session five KW developed this technique further, by dividing the class into three groups, and giving them twenty minutes to come up with a list of the three most important issues in the Confidence story. The result was enlightening. The groups discussed animatedly and then proposed their answers. There was a significant degree of consensus. KW appeared to agree, but then began insinuating that some obvious and very important factors had been overlooked. A student picked up the prompt and soon attracted supporters. Within ten minutes the original list of suggestions had been modified. In conclusion, KW chided the class gently for not being braver in its initial thinking, but also observed that this was an important lesson, because the exercise had demonstrated to them some of the seductions and pitfalls that could so easily happen in real life. The key, he reiterated, was never to stray from rigour.

Throughout the sessions, KW remained receptive to questions or challenges. In session two, for example, he made extensive reference to a consultant's model (really just a checklist), but was then asked by a student why he had not used the scoring system or quantifier that went with it. At this KW laughed, and commented: 'I was hoping you wouldn't bring that up. How did you find it?' The student proudly announced that he had discovered it on the Web. KW took all this in his stride, and explained that he had ignored the system because he did not believe in it, though he also conceded that 'it might be useful for some sectors'.

There was only one occasion when the class nearly teetered out of control. The Nippycar case was accompanied by nine pages of exhibits and involved some complicated economics. KW proceeded with his standard analysis, but a student disputed one particular component, relating to the returns that would be earned under certain conditions. The information in the case turned out on closer inspection to be confusing, so there was no real way of establishing who was right or wrong. The argument raged and became heated. In the end, KW started to move on, though whispered disputation continued in the class for a further ten minutes or so afterwards. The next day the student at the centre of the altercation approached KW when he entered the auditorium and started the debate anew, having worked on the figures overnight. In the end, others in the class reacted jocularly, and the issue was finally put to bed.

Observations Measured in terms of its stated aims, this was a successful elective. KW explained his recommended mode of analysis clearly and used the case studies to demonstrate its efficacy in practice, drumming home the message by dint of repetition. The class was unusually responsive. A large majority had read the case studies beforehand; there was good participation in the sessions, with only one or two students not contributing at all; and debate tended to be lively, committed and even on occasion (as has been suggested) somewhat emotional. KW ended the week exhausted but satisfied, while the class showed its appreciation with an obviously heartfelt round of applause.

Assessed in a wider perspective, the balance sheet is perhaps more chequered. There were certainly positives. KW of course remained for the most part in charge of the discussion throughout the week, but there was also a degree of knowledge sharing. For example, in session one, when KW discussed Hard Group, he implied that it was successful, but a student pointed out that recent press coverage of the company had in fact been largely negative. Similarly, in session two, after KW had examined a series of companies that had broken the mould with startling innovations, a student brandished a journal article that apparently stated that such occurrences were statistically very rare, challenged KW about this and as a consequence provoked a short discussion about the difficulty of deliberately imitating such a strategy.

In addition, the course was also notable for the way it – more or less explicitly – questioned easy assumptions about knowledge and its interpretation. KW stressed that, when outsiders such as consultants interacted with firms, they rarely found all the data that they desired. Indeed, he observed, if some of the case studies were written in a fragmentary and unsatisfying way, it was precisely to illustrate this point ('The case did not come to you in a very neat package; this is real life.'). There was even the possibility, he added, that certain types of knowledge might not have been collated ('Organisations *think* they know their business well. It's amazing what organisations *don't* know about themselves.'). In addition, KW several times pointed out that understanding the significance of data was hazardous anyway because of the problem of bias. What a firm or manager stated, he advised, always needed to be carefully considered, perhaps sifted, certainly contextualised. Accordingly, when discussing the somewhat saccharine video about Geriatric Care, KW repeatedly asked: 'Do you believe what it's doing, or is there a lot of hot air?'

Nevertheless, in a wider perspective, there were some less satisfactory aspects of the module, too, which largely related to content issues, and they may be grouped as follows:

(a) Ethics Ethical issues were hardly raised at all. Indeed, KW embraced a model of capitalism in which making money was perceived as the sole concern. He underlined that a firm's mission was to create a need before consumers had even thought of it. And, in discussing business models, he repeated on several occasions that the point was not the elegance or coherence of what was being proposed but the simple test of whether it produced returns. As he put it: 'The model is not sacred, profit is sacred.' The message was reiterated, too, in several of the case studies, particularly the Harvard video, which featured a stentorian voice at the beginning and end asking: 'Who will transform the industry of today – you or your competitors?'

Significantly, KW's use of the Geriatric Care case reinforced rather than diminished the prevailing ethos. He pointed out that this was a rather different kind of organisation, dedicated above all to service, and then explained why he had included it: 'I said to you "make money!", "make money!", "make money!" all the time – but I want you to know I'm also human.' The impact of these words was certainly to underline that material values were not everything in life; but they also acted to reinforce the idea that there was a boundary, with 'normal business' on one side and a few, very different, 'ethically driven' organisations on the other.

(b) Diversity The course made few concessions to the non-developed world. This was true of the cases, as has been suggested, but equally so of the examples that KW drew on in his expositions – a predictable melange of Amazon, M&S, IBM, Hewlitt-Packard, GM, Dell, FedEx, and so on.

At the beginning of session six KW addressed the issue. He began by stating that '[s]ome of you have wondered why there are only American cases [in this course]', and then went on to claim: 'I guess it's just chance.' What he meant by this, it turned out, was that, since US schools had produced the best cases about consulting, it would have been perverse not to use them. If there was pain, he added, it was worth it for the gain: 'I appreciate the problems of understanding the language, etc., but it's where the quality is.'

Unsurprisingly, given this orientation, few of the class members from eastern Europe, Asia or Latin America made much reference to their national business systems. Indeed, it was noticeable that when students spoke, for example, they all did so largely in the idiom of Anglo-Saxon business.

(c) 'The view from the top' Most of the cases, predictably, privileged managerial voices, and in discussion the fundamental issue was normally what consultants or their clients should do next. Against this background, the class frequently lapsed into playing god, moving the various pieces round the board to see how they worked in different combinations. In this game the vocabulary could be brutal, with workforces 'downsized' or 'chopped', and incentives arranged to 'force' maximum output.

KW did little to discourage this trend, and in fact largely ignored the one or two students who wanted to challenge some of its premises. A good example of this occurred in the discussion of the Geriatric Care case. KW suggested, as has been noted, that this company's image was almost unnaturally wholesome, and in the light of this he asked class members what information they would seek to establish the truth. As suggestions were called out, he wrote them on the board. Much of what followed was predictable. A popular choice was to interrogate the customer. One student argued, however, that the real litmus test would be the way that the company treated its most junior employees – its trainee nurses, porters and cleaners. Interestingly, this option was not recorded.

(d) Context KW spent relatively little time examining contextual issues. At the end of session one, it is true, there was a ten-minute discussion as to why Hard Group appeared to be going awry, which was triggered by KW's observation that '[w]e have a problem with an individual', and then touched upon the CEO's character and background. For the most part, however, wider questions remained unexplored. At the end of session three KW underlined that middle management was often 'the treasure house' of the organisation, pre-serving important memories and truths, yet simply failed to respond when a student then pointed out that this stratum was nowadays precisely often the first to be 'downsized' in the search for 'flatness'.

Perhaps most surprisingly, given the nature of the course, this lacuna also extended to the treatment of consultancy itself. KW gave the impression that, provided the students followed his suggested rules of analysis, they would be able to untangle any problem that came their way. There was no reference to the literature on consult-ing; no consideration of why consulting frequently produces poor results; and only fleeting recognition of the fact that insiders may not necessarily exactly welcome enquiring outsiders. Thus, the activity of consulting was largely constructed as a technical exercise, devoid of questions of power and social interaction – further echoing the implicit assumption that the MBA bestowed a special kind of superi-ority.

The significant features of this example largely speak for them-selves. The tutor's general approach was in many ways admirable – informed, sceptical, committed and humane. His relationships with the class remained informal and friendly, which produced a good level of interaction. He continually encouraged critical thought. This was not someone who believed in the didactic monologue. On the other hand, the substance of what was being offered appeared to some extent locked in a very narrow frame of reference – for example, untouched by current concerns about cultural difference, fairness, sustainability and social responsibility. Nowhere was this more apparent than in relation to the question of how managers should treat their employees. The modern axiom, much repeated, might hold that a firm's greatest asset is its people, yet it was quite possible to walk away from this module and conclude that a workforce was essentially expendable – mere cannon fodder in the battle for higher profits. This was an instance, therefore, in which, in terms of content at least, essentially conventional perspectives both dominated and remained largely unquestioned. We have argued that case studies as printed on the page often present a rather partial and outmoded view of reality. Our observations suggest that, when they are actively taught in the classroom, there is no guarantee that such faults are necessarily rectified.

EXPLAINING INERTIA

What accounts for this inertia over the curriculum, the lacunae and evasions, the apparent unwillingness to sanction real change? During our discussions with faculty, various explanations were suggested. In the following paragraphs, we concentrate on three of the most frequently cited factors: the accreditation agencies, the alleged phenomenon of 'corporate capture' and the supposed proclivities of business school students.

It is not difficult to see why the three big accreditation agencies – AACSB International, AMBA and the EFMD – are sometimes viewed as the seat of the problem. These are leading players in the business school world, with long-standing connections to the elite institutions. They are often characterised as part of the establishment. Against this background, it is but a short step to imagining that, when all is said and done, accreditation itself must be merely an exercise in spreading and maintaining one particular vision of what business education should be about. Yet, in reality, the situation is a good deal less clear-cut. There is no doubt that accreditation as a whole does encourage a degree of mimicry. Schools seeking to be accredited will always be inclined to monitor their previously successful peers carefully. In addition, the fact that, partly for practical reasons, the agencies tend to use trusted partners on their evaluation panels inevitably tends to privilege the status quo.[53] Nevertheless, this is only part of the story. All three agencies (as has been suggested) are ambitious for growth, and instinctively recognise that overprescription may prove limiting. In any event, increasing sensitivity to cultural difference, here as elsewhere, has produced a general wariness about promoting common models. In these circumstances, what is actually most notable about the agencies today is not their insistence on uniformity but their relative tolerance of difference. AACSB International is a case in point. The basis of its accreditation procedures is a series of standards. Some contain direct guidance. For example, Standard 15, which deals with course content, includes the following:

> Normally, the curriculum management process will result in undergraduate and master's level general management programs that will include learning experiences in such management-specific knowledge and skill areas as:
> - Ethical and legal responsibilities in organizations and society.
> - Financial theories, analysis, reporting, and markets.
> - Creation of value through the integrated production and distribution of goods, services, and information.
> - Group and individual dynamics in organizations.
> - Statistical data analysis and management science as they support decision-making processes throughout an organization.
> - Information technologies as they influence the structure and processes of organizations and economies, and as they influence the roles and techniques of management.
> - Domestic and global economic environments of organizations.
> - Other management-specific knowledge and abilities as identified by the school.[54]

When AACSB International actually explains how these standards are to be interpreted in practice, however, it is clear that there is a good deal of leeway available for all concerned. The *Eligibility*

Procedures and Accreditation Standards for Business Accreditation handbook begins by declaring: 'Member schools reflect a diverse range of missions. That diversity is a positive characteristic to be fostered. One of accreditation's guiding principles is the acceptance, and even encouragement, of diverse paths to achieving high quality in management education. Thus, the accreditation process endorses and supports variety in missions in management education.'[55] Thereafter, the same point is repeated again and again. For example, a passage on the intricacies of assessing candidate schools advises: 'In the practice of accreditation evaluation, Peer Review Teams must exercise flexibility. Deviations from standards may be encountered that represent innovation or cultural differences that the standards have not anticipated. Evaluations must be based on the quality of the learning experience, not rigid interpretations of standards.'[56] When all the evidence is considered, therefore, it is difficult to conclude that the agencies' impact on curricula is anywhere near as potent as is sometimes claimed. They do make suggestions about course content, no doubt, and some schools may heed them, but there is little sense of either compulsion or the imposition of a monolithic view.

The second argument that has been put to us revolves around the notion of 'corporate capture'. The allegation is, in effect, that business and professional interests are now so powerful in the business school world that they can and do twist curricula to their own rather conservative ends.[57] This is a difficult matter to judge. It would be a strange situation indeed if business and the business schools did not interact at all; after all, there are large areas of legitimate common interest. The issue, therefore, is one of degree. How insistent is business pressure? Are alternative voices being drowned out? Is academic freedom being jeopardised? The evidence, such as it is, at first sight hardly seems reassuring. It is incontrovertible that a number of big companies very publicly set out to influence what business schools teach. Thus, Wal-Mart, operating through the Walton Family Foundation, finances retail centres in several American universities, and actively helps faculty interested in its operations with information, interviews and site visits.[58] In addition, there is palpably much activity behind the scenes. For example, some businesses energetically lobby for particular courses or specialisms, such as a focus on the local economy or the incorporation of a subject area that is key to their operations.

More generally, there is no doubt that the corporate sector continues with the active policing of the whole way that case studies are put together. Some idea of what is involved can be gleaned from the published handbooks that guide putative faculty researchers through the necessary conventions and possible pitfalls. In many instances, it seems, the case study is far from a neutral piece of academic enquiry. The process of research is said to depend upon sustained negotiation about what can or cannot be revealed, with the company always granted the final right of veto. Moreover, this is clearly a world in which the quid pro quo is the common currency. One experienced case study writer provides the following illuminating advice about how to get a project off the ground:

> I never approach a company asking for a favour. It is necessary
> to give the company reasons to accept. These are as follows:
> exposure in the best business schools and universities worldwide;
> diffusion of messages within as well as outside the company; a
> definitive ready reference account of the story; offering limited
> feedback to managers involved in the research . . . The company
> should find the relationship an interesting and rewarding
> exercise.[59]

This contrasts markedly, it hardly needs to be said, with the more independent way that research is usually ordered and conducted in many other parts of the academy.[60]

Sometimes the relationship between author and subject seems to have become almost too close for comfort. Some of the fallout from the corporate scandals of the early 2000s was indicative. It turned out that Harvard faculty had produced nearly a dozen cases on Enron in the period immediately before the company's spectacular collapse (including the indicatively named *Enron: Entrepreneurial Energy* and *Enron's Transformation: From Gas Pipeline to New Economy Powerhouse*), and that Enron had in turn cross-marketed a selection on its own website.[61] One Harvard luminary had reportedly written his case while earning $50,000 a year as a member of the company's board of advisers.[62] Academics at rival business schools were shown to have produced equally questionable material about some of the other disgraced companies. Looking back at these revelations in 2003, John Shank, a professor at Babson and Amos Tuck, commented drily: 'For the most part . . . you can't use those cases now, because you'd get laughed out of the classroom.'[63]

With all this accepted, however, it is still not easy to reach a watertight conclusion about the real extent of corporate sway. One underlying assumption in this discussion is that business has a common agenda. This is unrealistic. For example, there are certainly instances when corporate donations have been given to bolster or develop broadly progressive courses in schools.[64] To complicate matters further, accurately measuring influence is notoriously difficult. Observing that companies try to exert control over business school curricula is one thing; proving that they have actually done so is quite another. We have identified instances, perhaps even significant instances, in which some kind of 'capture' seems to be occurring, but a good deal else remains opaque. It is also worth remembering that however much business pushes its agenda, and in whatever form, there will always be countervailing forces present. For example, in regard to case studies, it is a fact that many universities and academic funding bodies have their own research protocols, and expect them to be observed. Indeed, the faculty who we have spoken to are generally as aware as anyone else of ethical issues in research matters. In this sense, talk of a 'corporate takeover' is an exaggeration. That said, however, there is certainly enough known about, for instance, the machinations over case studies to give considerable cause for concern.

A third argument that we have heard places the blame firmly on the customer – the business school student. The contention here is that those who enrol on courses such as the MBA have limited but very definite ambitions. What they want, above all, is a quick and uncomplicated grounding in those skills that will advantage them on graduation. What they do *not* want, by contrast, is anything that departs from this agenda. In this conception, therefore, curricula simply reflect the market. If innovation is absent, that is simply because there is no demand for it.

Such claims are, again, far from easy to evaluate. Some of the relevant data is unambiguous. Business school students certainly tend to be markedly instrumental in their orientations. For example, one UK survey of 2003 found that 96 per cent had embarked on an MBA to improve their career opportunities, whether in a general sense or specifically to help with a change of direction.[65] Second, there is substantial evidence that, amongst both undergraduates and postgraduates, many are uneasy about non-traditional teaching methods.[66] The latter's attitudes, in particular, are hardly surprising. Since Peter Cohen's *The Gospel According to the Harvard Business School* of 1973,[67] at least, the MBA has been popularly characterised as an ordeal, something that is much more arduous than other post-graduate programmes – 'the ultimate exercise in time management', as one journalist described it.[68] Symptomatically, there is an extensive literature on how to cope – for example, *The Business School Survival Guide*[69] – and a sophisticated underground apparatus that facilitates cheating.[70] Against this background, what many MBA graduates dwell on most is the difficulty of what they have to accomplish – the fevered study, the pressure, the constant deadlines, the long hours and the accompanying lack of sleep.[71] A British MBA succinctly encapsulated this view when he recalled: 'On day one, the director of the business school welcomed us to "Alcatraz", and he wasn't joking.'[72] In this climate, anything that appears to be a deviation or frill will obviously be judged harshly. The overwhelming desire is for teaching that is well delivered and straightforward.[73]

Nevertheless, whether this means that business school students are necessarily hostile to wider curriculum change remains more debatable. At one time, the fashion, especially amongst liberals, was to dismiss MBAs as both grasping and intellectually shallow. Harold Leavitt's jibe that they were 'critters with lopsided brains, icy hearts, and shrunken souls' was much repeated.[74] Various research findings apparently confirmed the picture. There was considerable amusement when American academics James Stearns and Shaheen Borna measured MBA students against 'felons imprisoned in minimum-security prisons' and found that the latter were in some ways more ethical.[75] Similar reaction greeted Robert Williams, Douglas Barrett and Mary Brabston's study of corporate crime in 184 US companies, since this suggested that the likelihood of criminal activity strengthened when members of the senior management team had either graduate business education or prior military service.[76]

From the early 2000s, however, a somewhat more positive picture of business school students began to emerge. Some studies, it is true, still repeated earlier themes. Fuqua School surveys of 2000 and 2003, which polled several hundred students in ten leading US institutions, discovered that, as the *Financial Times* reported, '[w]hen the going gets tough, ethics fly out of the window'. Across the Atlantic, Sweden's Universum Communications questioned 768 students in sixteen European business schools, and found that most were driven by money, prestige and power. For example, far more described their career goals in terms of 'working internationally' or 'influencing corporate strategies' than 'contributing to society' or 'achieving work/life balance'.[77] Yet elsewhere the findings were very different. In 2002 Aspen ISIB (associated with the Beyond Grey Pinstripes initiative) questioned 1,700 students at twelve leading international graduate schools and uncovered a previously unrecorded (and, in some quarters, unimagined) degree of introspection:

> Survey findings reveal that the events of the past two years
> have had a significant impact on MBA students' thoughts about

business, their careers and the content and structure of their MBA programs. Today's MBAs have a far more sober view of their own career prospects than MBA graduates in the spring of 2001. They are concerned about possible value conflicts and unsure that their business schools are adequately preparing them to deal with such conflicts. Their belief in the importance of the integration of issues of social responsibility into all business school disciplines also suggests that today's MBAs are thinking more broadly than past students about the role of business in society.[78]

Later the same year an online survey conducted by GradSchools.com discovered that 'more than 80 percent of prospective business graduates' felt that 'MBA programs today need to include a greater emphasis on ethics'.[79] Subsequent research continued to produce similar conclusions. For example, in 2004 the Chicago-based Committee of 200 commissioned a study that found that more than a half of MBA students and graduates believed that US businesses were 'unethical, care little about their employees and pay their top executives too much'.[80] The obvious lesson was that easy stereotypes were no longer viable. The student body, it appeared, was both less monolithic than had sometimes been imagined and a good deal more reflective.

In the light of this evidence, it is difficult to agree that business and management students represent as great an impediment to change as is sometimes alleged. The pervasive instrumentalism sets limits, of course. Most MBAs want to complete their courses as quickly and painlessly as possible, in order to enjoy the rewards that are available on graduation. To extrapolate further, however, and suggest that this cohort has always been somehow uniquely superficial or blinkered appears far more questionable, essentially a matter of prejudice rather than fact. The strong likelihood is that those studying at business school think in ways that largely mirror the evolving ideological currents in the world around them.

Our objective in the preceding paragraphs has been to understand why the current impasse over business school curricula is occurring. We have examined three frequently repeated hypotheses, and concluded that, though each contains some truth, all are in certain respects wanting. In our view, the real crux of the problem in fact lies in a rather different – and perhaps more prosaic – direction. The general presumption in the discussion so far has been that business schools place high importance on pedagogy and actively wish to keep their curricula up to date. It is clear, however, that, whatever deans and senior faculty avow, this is no longer necessarily always the case. Indeed, there is a sense in which, at least in some parts of the sector, teaching has been downgraded, to become in essence a second-class activity. And the reason for this is simply that many schools are now concentrating elsewhere – on consulting and other kinds of moneymaking, not unexpectedly, but also on research, which has become a kind of universally pursued Holy Grail. In the following chapter we examine aspects of this latter phenomenon more closely.

NOTES

1 Nigel Andrews and Laura D'Andrea Tyson, 'The upwardly global MBA', *Strategy + Business*, 36 (Fall 2004), 60; Della Bradshaw, 'Wider teaching as a matter of course', *Financial Times*, 15 November 2004; and Jeffrey Gangemi, 'Pushing MBAs beyond the books', *BusinessWeek Online*, 10 August 2005.

2 See, for example, Jean Evangelauf, 'Business schools are urged to rethink MBA curriculum', *Chronicle of Higher Education*, 23 May 1990, and Robert Jacobson, 'Transforming the MBA', *Chronicle of Higher Education*, 15 December 1993.

3 Jeffrey E. Garten, 'The need for wider horizons', *Financial Times*, 17 April 2005.

4 Mark Haskins, 'The GHP ("great homogenization process")', *BizEd* (January/February 2003), 54–5; anon., 'B-school blues', *Financial Times*, 29 April 2005.

5 www.businessweek.com/bschools/04/index.html#top30.

6 These figures have been calculated from the *BusinessWeek* profiles for

2004, listed at www.businessweek.com/bschools/04/index.html. They relate to a total of 280 schools – the number for which complete comparative data was available.

7 Tricia Bisoux, 'The extreme MBA makeover', *BizEd* (May/June, 2005), 26–33.

8 Constance Hays, 'The Wal-Mart way becomes topic A in business schools', *New York Times*, 27 July 2003; Christopher Stewart, 'Outsourcing joins the M.B.A. curriculum', *New York Times*, 28 March 2004.

9 AACSB International Management Education Task Force, *Management Education at Risk*, 9.

10 Anon., 'Is greed America's new creed?', *Business and Society Review*, 87(61) (1987), 6.

11 Porter and McKibbin, *Management Education and Development*, 86.

12 Julian Cummins, *The Teaching of Business Ethics* (London: Institute of Business Ethics, 1999), 8.

13 See anon., 'Business ethics?', *McGill Reporter*, 31(1) (1998), 5–7, and Frederic Greenman and Joseph Sherman, 'Business school ethics – an overlooked topic', *Business and Society Review*, 104(2) (1999), 174–5.

14 See, for example, www.beyondgreypinstripes.org/results/findings/top100.cfm; Della Bradshaw, 'How to make an idealist think again', *Financial Times*, 8 April 2002; Loredana Oliva, 'Ethics edges onto courses', *Financial Times*, 16 February 2004; and Sharon Shinn, 'Sustainability at the core', *BizEd* (July/August 2005), 30–8.

15 AACSB Ethics Education Task Force, *Ethics Education in Business Schools* (St Louis, MO: AACSB International, 2004).

16 See, for example, Philip Walzer, 'Virginia MBA programs split on question of ethics', *Virginian Pilot*, 25 August 2003.

17 Dirk Matten and Jeremy Moon, 'Corporate social responsibility education in Europe', *Journal of Business Ethics*, 54(4) (2004), 328; Dirk Matten and Jeremy Moon, *Survey of Teaching and Research in Europe on CSR: Overview and Highlights* (Brussels: European Academy of Business in Society, 2003), 2; and Christopher Stewart, 'A question of ethics: how to teach them?', *New York Times*, 21 March 2004.

18 Diane Swanson and William Frederick, 'Are business schools silent partners in corporate crime?', *Journal of Corporate Citizenship*, 9 (Spring 2003), 24–6; anon., 'Professor to speak on issues of business schools failing to require ethics courses', *Presswire*, 2 May 2005.

19 See, for example, Sheb True, Linda Ferrell and O. C. Ferrel (eds.), *Fulfilling*

Our Obligation: Perspectives on Teaching Business Ethics (Kennesaw, GA: Kennesaw University Press, 2005).

20 See, for example, John Pulley, 'More business schools are teaching social and environmental ethics, survey finds', *Chronicle of Higher Education*, 28 October 2005.

21 Fred Evans and Leah Marcal, 'Educating for ethics: business deans' perspectives', *Business and Society Review*, 110(3) (2005), 235–6.

22 Tricia Bisoux, 'Lights . . . cameras . . . learning', *BizEd* (November/December 2003), 46.

23 www.bath.ac.uk/management/courses/mba.

24 For further stimulating reflection on this point, see Pfeffer and Fong, 'The end of business schools?', 78–95, particularly 84.

25 It is worth noting that systematic content analysis of business school curricula is, in general, comparatively rare. For several recent examples, however – which, interestingly, broadly reach conclusions similar to our own – see Albert Mills and Jean Hatfield, 'From imperialism to globalization: internationalization and the management text', in Stuart Clegg, Eduardo Ibarra-Colado and Luis Bueno-Rodriguez (eds.), *Global Management: Universal Theories and Local Realities* (London: Sage, 1999), 37–67; John Ferguson, David Collison, David Power and Loma Stevenson, 'What are recommended accounting textbooks teaching students about corporate stakeholders?', *British Accounting Review*, 37(1) (2005), 23–46; and David D. Van Fleet and Daniel A. Wren, 'Teaching history in business schools: 1982–2003', *Academy of Management Learning and Education*, 4(10) (2005), 44–56.

26 Malcolm P. McNair, *The Case Method at the Harvard Business School* (New York: McGraw-Hill, 1954); Andrew Towl, 'The evolution of the case method', at www.ecch.cranfield.ac.uk.

27 This estimate has been calculated from the *BusinessWeek* profiles for 2004 (see above, note 5).

28 Bradshaw, 'Darden's dean finds inspiration in Socrates'.

29 For a parallel study of this kind, see Neng Liang and Jiaqian Wang, 'Implicit mental models in teaching cases: an empirical study of popular MBA cases in the United States and China', *Academy of Management Learning and Education*, 3(4) (2004), 397–413.

30 See, for example, John Heath, *Teaching and Writing Case Studies: A Practical Guide* (Wharley End, Beds.: European Case Clearing House, 2002), 61–9.

31 Brian Rogers and Nirmalya Kumar, *easyJet: The Web's Favorite Airline* (Lausanne: IMD, 2000), 1.

32 Don Sull, 'easyJet's $500 million gamble', *European Management Journal*, 17 (1999), 20–38.

33 Rogers and Kumar, *easyJet*, 1.

34 Rogers and Kumar, *easyJet*, 4, 6–7, and Exhibit 6.

35 Sumantra Ghoshal, Annette Gardner, Rebecca Hansen, Louise Marchant, Hanno Ronte and Indira Thambiah, *Lufthansa: The Challenge of Globalisation* (London: London Business School, 1996).

36 Ghoshal et al., *Lufthansa*, 2–3.

37 K. Labich, 'Europe's sky wars', *Fortune*, 11 February 1992.

38 Deutsche Lufthansa AG, *Annual Report* (Frankfurt: Deutsche Lufthansa AG, 1995), 12; N. Moss, 'Lufthansa needs to sell its shares at home (privatization continues)', *European*, 10 February 1997.

39 Anon., 'Optimistic Lufthansa "poised for takeoff at reduced weight"', *Interavia Business and Technology*, 1 June 1994.

40 Christopher H. Lovelock, *Federal Express Quality Improvement Programme* (Lausanne: IMD, 1990).

41 Lovelock, *Federal Express Quality Improvement Programme*, 3, 9–11.

42 Lovelock, *Federal Express Quality Improvement Programme*, 10.

43 Lovelock, *Federal Express Quality Improvement Programme*, 13.

44 Martin Everett, 'Court of last resort', *Across the Board*, 28(11) (1991), 53.

45 Everett, 'Court of last resort', 51.

46 There appear to be few studies of teaching notes as such, though see Craig Lundberg and Joan Winn, 'The great case-teaching-notes debate', *Journal of Management Education*, 29(2) (2005), 268–83.

47 Thus, in their easyJet teaching note, Rogers and Kumar provide a brief synopsis; advise on 'use' (with sections on 'audience', 'sequencing', 'time' and 'issues'); identify some specimen 'assignment questions', and explain in detail how these should be answered; cite references, together with 'supplemental reading and background information'; and append five pages of useful 'exhibits': see Rogers and Kumar, *easyJet*, 'Teaching note'.

48 See, for example, Louis B. Barnes, C. Roland Christensen and Abby J. Hansen, *Teaching and the Case Method* (Boston: Harvard Business School Press, 1994), esp. 47–50, and Heath, *Teaching and Writing Case Studies*, 103.

49 K. R. S. Murthy, 'Future of the case method', in S. K. Srinivasan, M. R. Dixit, S. Manikutty, S. S. Rao, M. M. Monippally, R. Bijapurkar, G. Raghuram, T. K. Rishikesha, S. Mirra, K. R. S. Murthy, J. Joseph and

A. K. Jain, 'What is the future of the case method in management education in India?', *Vikalpa*, 30(4) (2005), 119.

50 J. Paul Mark, *The Empire Builders: Inside the Harvard Business School* (London: Harrap, 1987), 22.

51 See, for example, David A. Garvin, 'Making the case', *HBS Working Knowledge*, 15 September 2003, and, more generally, Graeme Currie, Sue Tempest and Alison Seymour, 'The development of "critters": a critical appraisal of the teaching case method within the MBA', forthcoming.

52 On this point, see also Mary Margaret Weber and Delaney J. Kirk, 'Teaching teachers to teach cases: it's not what you know, it's what you ask', *Marketing Education Review*, 10(20) (2000), 59–67.

53 Swanson and Frederick, 'Are business schools silent partners?', 25.

54 AACSB International, *Eligibility Procedures and Accreditation Standards for Business Accreditation* (Tampa, FL: AACSB International, 2005), 15–16.

55 AACSB International, *Eligibility Procedures* (2005), 1.

56 AACSB International, *Eligibility Procedures* (2005), 2.

57 This argument has, of course, been made more generally in relation to the academy as a whole. For one highly perceptive example, see Washburn, *University Inc.*

58 Hays, 'The Wal-Mart way'.

59 C. Pinson, 'How to write a winning case', *ECCHO*, 2 (1992), 2. See also Heath, *Teaching and Writing Case Studies*.

60 For further illuminating discussion of the corporate influence on case writing, see Mark, *The Empire Builders*, and Roy Harris, 'The case against cases', *CFO.com*, 1 April 2003.

61 HarvardWatch, *Trading Truth: A Report on Harvard's Enron Entanglements* (January 2002), at www.harvardwatch.org.

62 Katherine S. Mangan, 'The ethics of business schools', *Chronicle of Higher Education*, 20 September 2002.

63 Harris, 'The case against cases'.

64 See, for example, Francis Beckett, 'Conflict of interests', *EducationGuardian.co.uk*, 9 July 2003.

65 Association of MBAs, *The Official MBA Handbook 2003/2004* (London: Pearson Education, 2003), 13. See also, for example, Deone Zell, 'The market-driven business school: has the pendulum swung too far?', *Journal of Management Inquiry*, 10(4) (2001), 331–2.

66 See, for example, Charles Booth, Stuart Bowie, Judith Jordan and Ann

Rippin, *The Use of the Case Method in Large and Diverse Undergraduate Business Programmes: Problems and Issues* (Bristol: Bristol Business School, n.d.), and Graeme Currie and David Knights, 'Reflecting on a critical pedagogy in MBA education', *Management Learning*, 34(1) (2003), 27–49.

67 Peter Cohen, *The Gospel According to the Harvard Business School* (New York: Doubleday, 1973).

68 D. Hinds, 'Managing the workload (without getting divorced)', *Independent*, 23 October 1997.

69 Jon Housman, *The Business School Survival Guide* (London: Random House, 2001).

70 Anon., 'The pressure to cheat', *Financial Post*, 15 December 2003; Tim Elliot, 'Top in enterprise, bottom in integrity', *Financial Times*, 2 June 2003. See also Pfeffer and Fong, 'The business school "business"', 1504–5, and Donald L. McCabe, Kenneth D. Butterfield and Linda Klebe Trevino, 'Academic dishonesty in graduate business programs: prevalence, causes, and proposed action', *Academy of Management Learning and Education*, 5(3) (2006), 294–305.

71 See, for one example amongst many, Peter Robinson, *Snapshots from Hell: The Making of an MBA* (London: Nicholas Brealey, 1994).

72 Anon.,'Welcome to Alcatraz', *Daily Telegraph*, 26 January 2002.

73 It is fair to point out that some would make this point in rather bleaker terms: see, for example, Pfeffer and Fong, 'The business school "business"', 1509; and Deone Zell, 'Pressure for relevancy at top-tier business schools', *Journal of Management Inquiry*, 14(3) (2005), 272–3.

74 Harold Leavitt, 'Educating our MBAs: on teaching what we haven't taught', *California Management Review*, 31(3) (1989), 39.

75 J. M. Stearns and S. Borna, 'A comparison of the ethics of convicted felons and graduate business students: implications for business practice and business ethics education', *Teaching Business Ethics*, 2(10) (1998), 175–95, and anon., 'Jail the MBA's?', *Multinational Monitor*, 20(1/2) (1999), 4.

76 R. D. Williams, J. D. Barrett and M. Brabston, 'Managers' business school education and military service: possible links to corporate criminal activity', *Human Relations*, 53(5) (2000), 691–712.

77 Della Bradshaw, 'Pragmatism wins the day', *Financial Times*, 5 May 2003, and Ian Wylie, 'Passport to riches', *Guardian*, 24 May 2003. See also Mintzberg, *Managers not MBAs*, 71–5.

78 Aspen ISIB, 'Where will they lead? MBA student attitudes about business and society' (2003), 2, at www.aspenbsp.org.

79 Anon., 'Students focus on ethics in education', *BizEd* (November/ December 2002), 10.

80 S. Jones, 'MBA students distrust biz', 8 October 2004, at www. chicagobusiness.com. See also Archie B. Carroll, 'An ethical education', *BizEd* (January/February 2005), 36–40.

5   Business school research

A quick tour of business school websites today encourages the belief that schools are primarily focused on teaching. There is copious material on courses, virtual tours round state-of-the-art teaching and learning facilities, and panegyrics about the alleged benefits of this or that qualification. By contrast, an informal conversation with business school faculty often produces rather different impressions. For many, teaching seems to be a bit of a chore. There are grumbles about increasing class sizes or changing student expectations. If the subject of research is mentioned, however, the response will in all probability become animated. Sometimes this is fuelled by an enthusiasm for the subject at hand. More often than not it is because faculty recognise that what they produce in terms of reports, articles and books now largely determines their academic, and perhaps personal, fates – for example, whether or not they will gain promotion or be able to engineer a lucrative move to a better institution. The basic fact is that, regardless of the public facade, it is research and not teaching that has become the real fulcrum of much business school life. In this chapter we begin by examining how such a situation has come about, and then discuss its overall significance, focusing on two issues that are currently causing particular controversy: the quality of what is produced, and its relevance (in other words, usefulness to potential end users).

THE RISE OF RESEARCH

For most of the twentieth century only a few elite business schools really concentrated to any great degree on research. From the1970s onwards, however, there was accelerating change. The United States, inevitably, led the way. Thus, Porter and McKibbin reported in 1988 that the 'research genie' had recently been well and truly 'let out of the bottle', and was unlikely to be returned. Indeed, they noted, as many as 40 per cent of provosts in their sample wanted to see their schools place significantly more emphasis precisely on this aspect of their mission.[1] Across the Atlantic similar developments soon followed. In 1994, it is true, a commission of enquiry chaired by George Bain (dean of London Business School) reported that British schools still had 'a weak commitment to research and inadequate policies and resources to support it'.[2] Nevertheless, within a few short years the position in the United Kingdom, as in many other countries in Europe and elsewhere, had essentially been transformed.

The drivers behind this shift were similar, though not identical, worldwide. Growing competition between schools provided the basic stimulus. Deans increasingly recognised that research performance could impact on reputation, and hence influence important stakeholders (from government departments, through grant-giving organisations and private donors, to students, current and future), thus making or breaking the bottom line. Accordingly, the improvement of research quality came to be seen as yet another integral weapon in the battle for long-term survival. One area in which this new priority surfaced most publicly was that of hiring and firing. 'Research stars' found themselves in great demand. By contrast, those classified as 'research inactive' frequently struggled. There were some spectacular redundancies. When David Begg was appointed to revive the flagging business school of Imperial College in London during 2003, he immediately announced that one of his top priorities was to develop 'a stronger culture of research'; within twelve months seventeen out of fifty staff had been 'persuaded' to leave. Across London, at Cass, the approach taken was rather similar. In a restructuring exercise, the dean 'moved on' 20 per cent of the faculty, and candidly told the *Financial Times*: 'Are the people coming in through the door better? [. . .] Yes, in every case.'[3] What gave this new emphasis on research an added twist was the fact that, simultaneously, written outputs were being more and more closely monitored. Several specialist league tables appeared. The University of Texas School of Management was a pioneer, ranking schools' research contribution on the basis of their publications record in twenty-two leading academic journals.[4] Subsequently, some of the better-known general rankings incorporated 'intellectual capital' elements into their overall assessment criteria. Before long, accreditation agencies, too, had begun to take an interest, demanding that applicants either had goals such as 'a clearly defined research and publications policy' (the EFMD's EQUIS arm) or the means to produce 'intellectual contributions that advance the knowledge and practice of business and management' (AACSB International).[5] The inevitable outcome was that both schools and individual faculty found it harder and harder to remain aloof.

In the United Kingdom there was an added ingredient: the government. The British university sector had traditionally been liberal and non-directive. Scholars could effectively choose whether to research and publish or not. From 1988 onwards, however, the major official funding body instituted an increasingly rigorous Research Assessment Exercise (RAE) – basically a periodic audit of output, department by department, that rated each on a scale – and tied quite large slices of grant allocation to the outcome. Before long, university managers were responding with vigour; newspapers and periodicals were highlighting the results and discussing the winners and losers; and many staff across the board were gripped, endlessly discussing their individual and collective prospects. Business schools found themselves swept up just like everyone else.[6] There were dummy runs, internal reviews, benchmarking exercises and detailed analyses of previous leading players' performances. Some schools offered big cash bonuses for publication in the most prestigious journals – in one case, allegedly as much as £3,000 per article, an unheard-of sum in UK academic life. Recalcitrant staff courted remedial or perhaps even disciplinary action. By 2005 Australia, New Zealand and other European countries had begun to take notice, and were beginning to think about instituting similar systems. Again, the overall result was to ingrain further the American dictum 'Publish or perish'.

Against this background, it is unsurprising to find that over the last two decades or so the amount of management and business research, both published and unpublished, has increased at an ever faster rate. There is no easy way to measure the magnitudes involved, but a simple, if very crude, counting exercise gives some indication. *Ulrich's International Periodicals Directory*, the standard reference work, listed 931 journals under the heading 'management' in 1990, but 1,800 in 2005 – a doubling in only fifteen years.[7] Indicatively, the output of research has become so large that even specialists struggle to keep up with it. There was a revealing insight into these problems in 2001, when the RAE panel adjudicating on UK research in management and business reported that it had been 'all but overwhelmed' by the explosion of journals that was revealed in the different submissions. It added:

> As an illustration of this point, at least two colleagues found it necessary to call for papers from more than 200 separate journals, and it often became apparent that their author(s) were not aware of established work in the field in which they were publishing. More worryingly, it is reasonable to assume that the papers had been reviewed by colleagues who also were not very familiar with research in the field in which they were acting as referees.[8]

What all of this means in practical terms is that, in most business schools today, a substantive concern with research and getting published will be apparent at every level. Junior faculty will be busy writing their first journal articles, hopeful of gaining tenure or promotion. Their more senior peers will be aiming at the most prestigious journals. Groups will be meeting to discuss grant applications to support new projects. There will be a constant flow of refereeing, reviewing and editorial work. Some staff will be measuring their colleagues' performance and chasing the laggards. Others will be advising commercial, professional or government bodies on this or that aspect of research policy. And keeping the closest watch of all on developments will be the deans and the school management, cognisant of the fact that performance in research and publishing is currently more crucial than ever in determining their institutions' future.

CALCULATING THE BENEFITS: (I) QUALITY

We now look at how the growth of research should be evaluated, and start with the issue of quality. It is immediately obvious that there are competing views here. Deans and university managers are predictably upbeat. They argue, in essence, that the spur of competition, together with the associated introduction of various carrots and sticks, has worked its magic. Researchers nowadays can call on greater resources; have expanded ambitions; enjoy extensive cross-fertilisation with other social sciences; and utilise a growing array of sophisticated methodologies and techniques. Accordingly, so the story goes, what they actually produce is more proficient and estimable than ever before. Nonetheless, for many others who observe the business school sector, this is simply anathema. What has really happened, they argue, is that developments such as the RAE and the research league tables have turned business schools into academic treadmills, with the volume of output prioritised regardless of almost any other consideration. In this scenario, scholarly values have steadily been jettisoned, to be replaced by an unattractive mixture of expediency and cynicism. The consequence has been a torrent of verbiage that for the most part is quite inconsequential.

Untangling the precise truth about this issue is far from easy, partly, of course, because 'quality' is a rather nebulous concept that remains difficult to measure. In very general terms, the overall thrust of the optimists' case seems uncontentious. For much of the twentieth century management and business research was unarguably limited – small-scale, over-functional and rarely enriched by the insights of other disciplines.[9] Today the situation is, in almost all respects, quite obviously much improved. That said, however, it is also necessary to enter one or two significant caveats. First, there is the question of the actual magnitude of change. It is sometimes claimed – though more often simply assumed – that the amelioration of research has been substantial, but this is in fact debatable. The British experience is particularly significant here, because the RAE apparently lends itself so well to comparisons over time. Certainly, at first glance, the evidence from this source appears conclusive. The 2001 RAE Business and Management Studies panel observed:

> The last five years have seen a steady improvement in the quality of research in the discipline. In the 1996 exercise, 26 per cent of the submissions were rated 4 or above [on a seven-point scale] but by 2001, the comparable figure was 40 per cent. This is due primarily to the continuous improvement in the quality of the research in a wide range of the sub-areas.

Its conclusion was that 'the management sciences are healthy, and developing an international dimension not seen in the 1980s'.[10]

On closer examination, however, these judgements are rather less robust than they appear. The key point is that the RAE's effectiveness as a measuring rod of change remains open to question. It is noteworthy that the 2001 panel itself admitted 'some slight grade inflation' since the preceding exercise.[11] But a bigger problem is the fact that, as this was the fourth RAE in little more than a decade, many of those who submitted departmental returns had learnt to play the game – that is, by hook or by crook optimise their chances of gaining a better rating than they probably actually deserved. Interestingly, when we talked with an academic who had been very closely involved in the actual minutiae of assessment, he quite openly admitted that such manipulation had occurred, and indeed added: 'I can point to tons of criticisms if I had to.'[12] Thus, while the 2001 return may have illuminated the hierarchy that existed at that particular moment, its usefulness as a tool to quantify developments since RAE 1996, let alone RAE 1992, cannot be assured.[13]

Adding a relative perspective does little to remove the doubts. Unsurprisingly, given its history, business and management research was long considered a poor relation of many more established academic disciplines.[14] How far this has changed remains unclear. The evidence is fragmentary but hardly encouraging. Those in the surrounding university community still seem to be distinctly unenthusiastic about what business schools produce. A detailed assessment of citation patterns in a range of social science journals indicates that scholars in such subjects as economics, psychology and sociology are markedly less likely to have digested their management peers' work than vice versa.[15] Occasionally there is more forthright disdain. For example, in reviewing the publications of three highly rated UK business schools in 2003 a group of public health specialists with considerable academic and practical experience concluded that they were sloppily conceived and executed, and ended up wondering whether the 'emperor had got any clothes'.[16] It would appear, then, that business and management research still has some way to go before it is considered genuinely first-class in any meaningfully comparative sense.

Finally, the critics' allegations about the way that audit and ranking are proving corrosive in a wider sense cannot simply be dismissed. Long-established norms and conventions regulating scholarship do seem to be becoming increasingly beleaguered. The retiring dean of the Oxford's Said School, Anthony Hopwood, himself a distinguished editor, recently remarked upon a growing obsession with journal 'hits', and regretted that this was leading to the spread of what he termed '[c]areerist and institutionally orientated research'.[17] Others bemoan the spread of a more general kind of cautiousness – in essence, a preference for pursuing bland and inoffensive projects, perhaps dressed up in fashionable jargon, at the expense of anything truly challenging or experimental – as well as a questionable willingness to recycle material whenever possible so as to conjure the illusion of fecundity.[18] Reflecting on these various trends in 2005, the *Financial Times* columnist Lucy Kellaway satirised 'the senseless dumbing up of management theory', and produced a telling illustration:

> The story was a little one, down towards the bottom of a page in the current *Harvard Business Review*. Trust, it said, isn't the

great thing we have all been led to believe. In fact, within teams, you can have rather too much of it.

According to research carried out at Washington University in St Louis, teams that trust each other a lot don't perform very well because they never check up on what each other is up to, and therefore can't communicate properly.

To arrive at this conclusion, Professor Claus Langfed spent four months solemnly studying 71 self-managing teams of MBA students. The *Harvard Business Review* then solemnly reported his findings, including the banal recommendation that 'managers may want to require a modicum of oversight rather than let a team decide for itself'.

And now I am reporting the research too – not so much solemnly as despairingly.[19]

Beyond all this, there are more fundamental concerns about what the appetite for audit and ranking is doing to the notion of excellence itself. One persistent allegation is that the new paradigm has further cemented US domination of relevant definitions and meanings.[20] Because American schools have greater organisational coherence and bigger resource bases, it is argued, they are able to monopolise judgements about what is good and what is not, and thus, in effect, simultaneously perpetuate their own superiority and force the rest of the world to follow them. Whether any of this is true remains a matter of dispute. American academics certainly cast a long shadow. For example, US business and management journals continue to top almost all hierarchies – they are simply more cited,[21] and more widely accepted as prestigious.[22] In addition, there is persuasive evidence that many American scholars to some extent share their own idiosyncratic assumptions about what constitutes, and does not constitute, valid enquiry.[23] What this means in practice for the rest of the world, however, is less easy to ascertain. There are intellectual currents in Europe – for example, critical management studies in the United Kingdom – that are vigorous enough to have carved out their own space and reputation. On the other hand, it is certainly true that many here, as in other continents, strive to publish in American journals but struggle with the barriers to entry – language, of course, but also norms of custom and practice. It is a sobering fact, which goes some way to substantiating the critics' case, that Americans apparently continue to find it far easier to publish abroad than their overseas peers do in the United States.[24]

CALCULATING THE BENEFITS: (II) RELEVANCE

We now turn to the question of relevance, and try to assess the extent to which the recent upsurge of business school research has interested, and been helpful to, potential end users (whether individual managers, corporates or others). It is worth underlining that this matter, too, remains highly controversial. Most agree that, until the mid-1980s, business schools were sometimes rather lax about responding to the intellectual and practical needs of the outside world. Where opinions differ is about what has happened subsequently. The establishment view is that business schools have learnt their lesson, and are now much better at producing ideas and techniques that can actually be implemented. In 2005 AACSB International went so far as to claim that '[m]anagement education and research contribute directly to – and even drive – business productivity and strengthens [sic] organizations at virtually every level'.[25] Dissenting voices are unconvinced, however. There might have been some toying around the edges, they maintain, but the reality is that the schools remain largely isolated. The same criticisms have echoed down through the years. In his 1993 presidential address to the Academy of Management, Donald Hambrick memorably described what he saw as his profession's penchant for navelgazing: 'Each August, we come to talk with each other; during the rest of the year we read each other's papers in our journals and write our own papers so that we may, in turn, have an audience the following August: an incestuous, closed loop.'[26] A decade later the *Financial*

Times columnist Michael Skapinker was struck by how little had changed:

> This year's Academy of Management conference in Seattle was crawling with management teachers. They came from the University of Oregon, the Stockholm School of Economics, the Auckland University of Technology and hundreds of schools in between. They presented papers on everything from the role of compensation committees to the influence of gender on career success. But what was striking about this international festival of management was the almost complete absence of managers.[27]

Writing to the paper subsequently, a correspondent added the piquant detail that the academics in question could be distinguished from business leaders 'not only by their lack of practical experience but also by their predilection for facial hair'.[28] Quite clearly, the whole subject of engagement and relevancy easily raises hackles, and is informed by a host of wider debates and prejudices.

How should these different viewpoints be assessed? First, it is important to stress that much of the comment about business schools in this context – whether pro or contra – tends to be overstated, perhaps more fashioned by self-interest or the desire for notoriety than respect for the facts. A detailed look at one example is revealing. In 2003 Thomas Davenport and Laurence Prusak published a book that (amongst other things) investigated where efficacious business ideas came from. They focused in particular on business gurus, and asked how many had been produced by business schools and how many by consultancies.[29] Their methodology was to construct a ranking of the top 200 gurus, using Google hits, entries in the Social Sciences Citations Index and media mentions in the LexisNexis online database, and then exploring each individual's background. The conclusions drawn were not flattering to business schools. Davenport and Prusak admitted that there were some gurus who came from academia, but argued that they were 'exceptions'. Their overall assessment was harsh: 'We believe that most business schools – and most academics who inhabit them – have not been very effective in the creation of *useful* business ideas. Sure, a lot of business ideas are explored in business school research, but for the most part, they are created elsewhere and are seldom even discussed in an accessible fashion by academics' (emphasis in original). Significantly, Davenport and Prusak's judgement that 'the realm of business academia' was largely 'a wasteland for the practicing manager' contrasted with their characterisation of management consultants as 'some of the most prolific idea creators in the 1980s and 1990s'.[30]

This book seemed to be an important piece of work, which as a result received considerable favourable publicity. Reviewing the study today, however, reveals that it is in fact somewhat less convincing than might be imagined. To begin with, it is not clear that Davenport and Prusak's condemnation of the business schools is actually justified by their data. The authors list the top 200 gurus in rank order, but add significant biographical data only for the top ten. Of this latter grouping, three (Porter, Senge and Valarian) have full-time jobs at management schools, while one (Hamel) is a consultant but also a visiting professor at no less than London Business School. This compares well with the totals for what might be termed 'other academics' (Drucker and Becker), professional pundits and consultants (Peters, Toffler and Goleman) and 'others' (Reich). Looked at in terms of these figures alone, therefore, the business school seems far from 'a wasteland'.[31]

Moving beyond the numbers, there are, of course, horrendous problems anyway in classifying exactly who is what. Academics such as Porter also do consultancy work. Polymaths such as Hamel – to repeat – play multiple roles. Some consultants turn out to have had academic careers, perhaps prestigious ones (something that is true, for example, in Goleman's case). Indeed, it may be a feature of gurus as a whole, perhaps, that they are exactly the people who are most likely to have feet in several camps. As Davenport and Prusak remark in a parallel commentary on their listing, 'nothing boosts a guru's ranking like the combination of brand and academic credentials'.[32] In addition, it is by no means clear that Davenport and Prusak's method of measuring 'gurudom' is in fact generally robust. To take but one of the issues, it is apparently by no means unknown for consultants to buy large numbers of their own books, hoping to get them on the best-sellers lists and thus secure precious publicity,[33] which raises questions about whether any of the chosen indicators can really be considered an objective measure. Finally, there is also the thorny problem of how an idea arises in the first place, and who therefore should take credit for its origin. Little here is clear-cut. 'Borrowing' or 'building on' others' work is common in many different walks of life. Davenport and Prusak themselves notice the similarities between Gary Hamel and C. K. Prahalad's very influential 1990 *Harvard Business Review* article on 'The core competencies of the corporation' and previous work by academics, stretching back to a seminal study by Edith Penrose in 1956.[34] To complicate matters further, the origins of some other big ideas are fairly obscure. Peters and Waterman's enormous 1982 best-seller *In Search of Excellence* is built around the proposition that firms require eight key attributes. Sometime after the book was published, one of the researchers on the project revealed that these 'came not from thoughtful analysis but straight from [the author's] head when he had less than one day to prepare a talk'.[35] Finally, it is also worth noting that, in any event, the word 'author' tends to be used in somewhat elastic fashion in the world of business books. This is simply because there is sometimes such a significant input from ghostwriters, or specialist ghostwriting companies, that the boundaries of who contributed exactly what are completely blurred.[36]

The lesson, therefore, is that this whole area of enquiry comes with significant health warnings. That accepted, however, it is still possible to make some informed observations on the issues, and these can be summarised as follows. First, it is incontrovertible that many business school academics are not only engaged with outside individuals and organisations but also clearly valued for their specific knowledge and advice. One example will suffice. As part of the 2001

RAE, the University of Leeds Business School (like its peers) produced a report headed 'Research dissemination: appointment as policy advisers and consultants'. Amongst other things, this showed that school staff had involvement with international bodies ('Lead consultant, UNCTAD investment policy review of Egypt'), the UK government ('Joint author of manual on the use of multi-criteria analysis commissioned by the Department of the Environment'), various businesses ('Adviser to the Greater Manchester Pension Fund'; 'Member, boards of Yorkshire Enterprises, NLC, Lynx plc, advisory panel of the Northern stock exchange; adviser for incubator project of Chase Manhattan Bank'), professional societies ('Input to the Institute of Credit Management on consumer credit issues') and even the trade unions ('Consultancy and research on partnership for Manufacturing, Science, and Finance Union').[37] Leeds was clearly not an institution that was either isolated or unloved. A glance at school websites and faculty profiles in most other countries of the world suggests that such engagement remains, by and large, the norm.

If we then turn to look beyond this, however, at the difference that business school research per se has made, a rather different picture emerges. There are, it is true, a handful of great success stories, such as finance, where academic researchers have historically supplied practitioners with much of their stock-in-trade – most obviously, the capital asset pricing model.[38] Yet, if anything, these are the exceptions that prove the rule, for in recent years, at least, business school research often seems to have disappeared into the ether, and thus dissipated without any measurable effect at all. Some business practitioners have registered their awareness of this phenomenon, and expressed their puzzlement or irritation at it. One group of corporates recently told a semi-official enquiry in the United Kingdom that business school research had 'no relevance to practice' and was 'published in academic journals in inaccessible language'.[39] Elsewhere, there is straightforward indifference. The British authors Paul Ankers and Ross Brennan interviewed a group of experienced marketers, and discovered that none referred to, or even seemed to be aware of, academic research. Their colleagues Nigel Slack, Michael Lewis and Hilary Bates compared articles in the academic *Journal of Operations Management* and the *International Journal of Operations and Production Management* to survey data provided by practitioners, and reached the striking conclusion that there were simply 'two worlds' in existence that did not match.[40]

Studies that have taken a more oblique approach invariably reach similar conclusions. In 2002 Pfeffer and Fong pointed out that academics featured comparatively rarely in either *BusinessWeek*'s list of best business books (the adjudication of expert judges) or its list of business best-sellers (the adjudication of the market).[41] Moreover, they also produced a highly significant analysis of the origins of 'business tools' – the 'ideas and techniques used in management consulting, things that businesses actually pay money to implement'. Their starting point was a well-known annual list prepared by Darrell Rigby of Bain and Company that charted the most popular tools in circulation.[42] What Pfeffer and Fong did was take the list for one year (2001) and (in collaboration with Rigby) meticulously investigate who had put that particular set of tools together. Their findings are worth repeating at length:

> Seven out of the 25 management tools came out of academia, and 18 came out of either corporations, consulting firms or some combination. The [Bain] survey asks about satisfaction with the tools, their utilization, and gives estimates of a defection rate, or the proportion of companies that stopped using a tool. The tools that came out of consulting firms and companies had a higher utilization rate than the tools from academia . . . had a higher level of satisfaction . . . and a lower defection rate. Rigby's data suggest that less than one third of the tools and ideas that companies are paying money to implement came out of academia and those that originated in universities were used less often and were abandoned more often.[43]

In a wider perspective, too, it is notable that the business and management oeuvre seems to have been equally marginal.

Significantly, informal listings of public intellectuals in the United States and United Kingdom rarely if ever mention the business school professorate.[44] Moreover, business schools as a whole have had surprisingly little impact on public policy debates. Some deans are frank about their sector's impotence. On his retirement from Yale, Jeffrey Garten told the *Financial Times* that he was hard-pressed to identify any schools, including his own, that had made 'significant contributions to the biggest policy challenges that senior executives face in conjunction with other parts of society'.[45] Clearly, if all this evidence is to be believed, it is right to conclude, with Pfeffer and Fong, that the influence of business school research across the board has been only modest.

EXPLAINING THE LIMITED IMPACT

At first sight, the business schools' failure to make more of an impression is puzzling. The schools themselves frequently underline the fact that they aim to be in tune with the outside world. Moreover, the accreditation agencies all now emphasise that this is not just desirable but necessary. A recent AACSB International task force observed: 'The goal is for business schools to adjust dynamically to the shifting agendas of the global marketplace with strong scholarship that both informs what is taught and connects with current and emerging business issues and practices.' EQUIS takes a similar line, stating that it prioritises 'a balance between high academic quality and professional relevance provided by close interaction with the corporate world'.[46] What is preventing the schools from delivering?

It is important to keep a sense of perspective here. Business school research simply cannot always be immediately relevant. There has to be room – as in similar endeavours – for 'blue skies' thinking, whilst the evolution of a potentially useful idea or technique can be convoluted, and thus involve significant time lags. In addition, relevance itself may be difficult to pin down anyway – conceptually elusive, varying between quite brief time periods, sectors and countries, and perhaps even contested. Thus, for example, while business leaders and business school academics no doubt both cherish higher productivity in general, they may well disagree fundamentally as to how it can be best achieved. Finally, and more practically, it is important to remember that some of the business schools' difficulties over relevance are directly related to the rise of the global consulting industry. Many business school professors, as we have seen, have involvement of some sort in the corporate sector, but only a minority have actually run a company (see table 5.1). Consultants not only make their living from solving day-to-day management problems but are often somewhat better connected and resourced. In this sense, it is hardly surprising that business schools are to some extent finding it less and less easy to make a mark.

Nevertheless, these points accepted, we believe that the business schools are themselves also culpable. In our view, the problem in the end is not really that the schools have been trying to generate relevant research and then failing, for whatever reason, when it comes to implementation but, rather, that – contrary to their own rhetoric, and perhaps intuition – they have been insufficiently concerned about relevance in the first place. To substantiate this hypothesis, we need to look in more detail at how the whole field of business and management studies has developed over time.

For much of the twentieth century, as has already been noted, business and management studies occupied a subordinate position in the academic pantheon, and was much looked down upon by older and more established subject areas. As the business schools expanded and prospered, however, so those who taught in them began to feel that they deserved to be accorded higher status, and especially a greater degree of recognition from their peers. When refugees from declining disciplines such as sociology joined business schools in the 1980s and 1990s, the demand for respect became even stronger. The key underlying desire was to demonstrate that business and management were 'proper subjects' in their own right, with relevant 'theory' and rigorous methodologies. The upshot was an increasing willingness to mimic the natural sciences – in other words, to copy the approach of

Table 5.1 *Business experience of tenured professors at selected top business schools, 2004*

School	Number of tenured professors	Members of company boards/ directors of boards of advisers (%)	Have owned a business (%)
BusinessWeek top thirty US MBA schools (where information available)			
Stanford	61	25	8
Dartmouth	31	4	0
Virginia	41	37	39
UCLA	66	60	25
UNC Chapel-Hill	61	23	18
Texas–Austin	83	16	n.a.
Yale	30	66	20
Washington	26	4	n.a.
Notre Dame	65	8	5
Georgetown	41	12	13
Babson	93	13	9
Southern California	79	16	26
Rochester	18	22	5
Vanderbilt	27	18	3
BusinessWeek top ten international MBA schools (where information available)			
Queens	60	15	35
IMD	46	20	13
ESADE	70	60	37
LBS	42	45	n.a.
IESE	37	54	40
HEC Paris	103	n.a.	10
Toronto	53	35	7

Source: BusinessWeek Online.

those who were considered most unimpeachable in terms of their seriousness about creating 'real knowledge'. There was growing interest in designing appropriate 'experiments', and much greater emphasis on quantification. Business school faculty now wrote what they termed 'papers', which, like those in natural science journals, featured specialist language and a rigidly prescribed format: first a literature survey, then summaries of methods and findings, and finally a discussion. Before long the new approach, with its promise of academic respectability, was sweeping the board. Meanwhile, older traditions, such as qualitative investigations of messy but real human situations, were increasingly viewed as inferior – subjective meanderings that belonged to a bygone and best forgotten 'pre-scientific' era.[47]

From our point of view, the most interesting feature of this evolution is that, as it matured, so the issue of relevance became ever more marginal. Dabbling in theory building or conducting laboratory-like experiments, it was believed, constituted real scholarship. Worrying about practical problems, on the other hand, was for lesser minds. By the turn of the century such attitudes had nearly become all-pervasive. The hierarchy of priorities could be detected at every turn. For example, it was quite apparent that, in their basic thinking about research, academics now barely acknowledged the concerns of practitioners. Indeed, an exhaustive American study went so far as to suggest that there were two 'incompatible' models at play, each with its own coherent set of assumptions, techniques and objectives:

> Under the 'academic model' for producing management knowledge, researchers ought to begin with [an] interesting research question and end with adds [additions] to theoretical knowledge. Along the way, first, they should establish sound premises from which they can develop hypotheses that can be tested. In order to do so, they need an appropriate sample to collect the necessary data. After rigorous analysis of data, they need to make some logical inferences making sure that their findings are internally consistent. Whatever conclusions they draw must be defensible

generalizations, and their findings must be able to be replicable by others. And, 'of course', the results should add to theoretical knowledge . . .

According to the 'executive model', exemplary research ought to start with explain(ing) managerial reality. It should have a short and crisp write up with direct implication for actions. Such implications should have explicit recommendations that lead to solving real management problems. Thus, as a result, business school research should improve corporate performance, and for the executives be helpful in running a business.[48]

The content of the field's major journals was equally indicative. More and more articles involved the micro-analysis of obscure aspects of firm or management performance, while the study of broader controversies and pressing issues languished.[49] Outsiders, who had little comprehension of the required mindset and jargon, felt baffled. An *Economist* correspondent spoke for many when he regretted that too much of the management literature had come to be dominated by 'academic clones who produce papers on minute subjects in unreadable prose'.[50]

The growth of audit and league tables (described at the beginning of this chapter) only reinforced further the existing trends. Those who constructed the new measurement criteria inevitably picked up on and then formalised how the profession itself had come to think about relevance. Thus, for example, in assessments, articles in scholarly journals virtually always counted for more than articles in practitioner journals. When we talked to deans about this they tended to be rather sheepish, realising that many people outside the business school world would find it inexplicable. Invariably, they also, however, pointed out that their hands were tied. In conversation, the head of a top-rated UK school explained both the pressures and their consequences:

> *The implication of what you're saying all through this is that the RAE is a very important overhanging objective of all of this.*

Yes it is.

Shaping what you're doing.

Yes it is, both for external profile and reputation but equally for internal political reasons as well.

Within the university?

Yes. If we weren't a Five [the second to top rating] now we'd have a lot less power, and be told to do a lot more, but because we are a Five and we aim to become a stronger Five I think they listen to us a lot more, they ask us what we need a lot more, and they involve us much more, so it's vitally important that we hold on to that . . .

A criticism of that . . . would be that it's ignoring . . . having . . . communication to users?

Well, I don't know . . . I think it's almost undoubtedly going to be the case that the gold standard will still be the sorts of academic journals that we know and that we are familiar with . . .

But pinning you down to a specific journal . . . Management Today *is . . . the popular user journal in Britain. Would that be thought to be a worthwhile thing to put something in?*

Generally, I don't suppose it would, no.[51]

Needless to say, the situation across the Atlantic was almost identical. For example, when American deans were asked to rank 'top items used to evaluate scholarship performance' on a scale of one to five, with one being highest, they scored 'article in refereed journal' at 1.15, but 'business/professional presentation' at 2.55, and 'article in non-refereed publication' at 2.66.[52]

In some ways, therefore, business schools today display what one perceptive insider called 'a type of organizational schizophrenia'.[53] In their everyday lives, faculty regularly interact with a range of businesses and other stakeholders, often providing valued assistance. When it comes to research, however, they are confronted by a culture and an incentive system that hardly seem to recognise the practitioner at all. Some are oblivious of the tension, and enthusiastically play the publications game, hoping for preferment. Many feel to a greater or lesser extent disgruntled. When we talked to rank and file staff members they frequently complained that the system was out of control and dysfunctional. Perhaps our most interesting discussion in this context was with a lecturer who had recently launched an entrepreneurship module in a UK business school. At the time, this was a hot topic. The British government had decided that universities needed to be more enterprising, and was beginning to put some extra funds into new courses and centres. Our informant recounted that he had been much feted by the university administration because of this initiative. But he also told us that, within the school, he was basically treated as a second-class citizen, not really 'a true academic' at all. His explanation for this said much about the wider developments that we have been discussing:

> I spent about 18 months flogging away, developing this degree programme and now it's an embarrassment to the Business School . . . And you just think, well, I wish I hadn't bothered . . . The people at the top of the university and at the top of the Business School will say: 'Wonderful, you know, this is exactly the sort of thing that . . . [we] should be doing.' But the individuals concerned, who are actually having to run it, think: 'Well, why am I doing this, why are none of the readers or professors involved?' They haven't a clue what's going on. So what's in it? [. . .] It comes down . . ., I think, [to] the RAE, [which] has developed an extremely selfish culture: you know, why should I do anything that isn't focused on the RAE? Because if I do, there's no rewards in it . . . [Y]ou just finish up feeling . . . resentful of the time that you're spending on it . . . You know, people who are ruthless and selfish and are never here, and are just writing; they're the ones who are climbing up the greasy pole.[54]

NOTES

1 Porter and McKibbin, *Management Education and Development*, 173–4.
2 Commission on Management Research, *Building Partnerships*.
3 Bradshaw, 'Deans vie for the world stage'.
4 See http://citm.utdallas.edu/utdrankings.
5 European Foundation for Management Development, *EQUIS: The EQUIS Quality Standards* (Brussels: European Foundation for Management Development, n.d.), 1; AACSB International, *Eligibility Procedures and Accreditation Standards* (2005), 13.
6 For a detailed analysis of British business schools' performance in the 2001 Research Assessment Exercise, see J. Bessant, S. Birley, C. Cooper, S. Dawson, M. Gardiner, J. Gennard, A. Gray, P. Jones, C. Mayer, J. McGee, M. Pidd, G. Rowley, J. A. Saunders and A. W. Stark, 'The state of the field in UK management research: reflections of the Research Assessment Exercise (RAE) panel', *British Journal of Management*, 14(1) (2003), 51–68, and Janet Geary, Liz Marriot and Michael Rowlinson, 'Journal rankings in business and management and the 2001 Research Assessment Exercise in the UK', *British Journal of Management*, 15(2) (2004), 95–141.
7 *Ulrich's International Periodicals Directory 1989–90* (New York: Bowker, 1989), 822–47, and *Ulrich's International Periodicals Directory 2005* (New Providence, NJ: Bowker, 2004), 1715–79. We are grateful to Sarah Ashton for suggesting this source.
8 Bessant et al., 'The state of the field', 65.
9 See, for example, Porter and McKibbin, *Management Education and Development*, 183.
10 Anon., 'Overview report from UoA43: Business and Management Studies', 1–2, at www.hero.ac.uk/rae/overview/docs/UoA43.pdf.
11 Anon., 'Overview report from UoA43', 2.
12 Interview, 27 April 2004.
13 It should be noted that these problems are by no means confined to business and management, and to some extent dog the RAE as a whole: see, for example, anon., 'Top scorers play dirty in RAE game', *Times Higher Education Supplement*, 20 May 2005.
14 See, for example, Porter and McKibbin, *Management Education and Development*, 183.
15 Andy Lockett and Abagail McWilliams, 'The balance of trade between disciplines: do we effectively manage knowledge?', *Journal of Management Inquiry*, 14(2) (2005), 139–50. See also, for a rather different view,

Arthur G. Bedeian, 'Crossing disciplinary boundaries: an epilegomenon for Lockett and McWilliams', *Journal of Management Inquiry*, 14(2) (2005), 151–5.

16 R. J. Lilford, F. Dobbie, R. Warren, D. Braunholtz and R. Boaden, 'Top-rated British business research: has the emperor got any clothes?', *Health Services Management Research*, 16 (2003), 147–54.

17 Quoted in Donald MacLeod, 'The hit parade', *Guardian*, 14 June 2005. See also Nigel Piercy, 'Why it is fundamentally stupid for a business school to try to improve its research assessment exercise score', *European Journal of Marketing*, 34(1/2) (2000), 27–35.

18 See, for various examples, Mark de Rond and Alan N. Miller, 'Publish or perish: bane or boon of academic life', *Journal of Management Inquiry*, 14(4) (2005), 321–9.

19 Lucy Kellaway, 'Beware the senseless dumbing up of management thinking', *Financial Times*, 23 May 2005.

20 Stewart R. Clegg and Anne Ross-Smith, 'Revising the boundaries: management education and learning in a postpositivist world', *Academy of Management Learning and Education*, 2(1) (2003), esp. 88–90.

21 See, for example, Lars Engwall, CEMP Report no. 7, *The Carriers of European Management Ideas* (Uppsala Sweden: Uppsala University, 1999), esp. 35–42.

22 See, for example, telling remarks in A. M. Pettigrew, 'Management research after modernism', *British Journal of Management*, 12 (2001), S65.

23 For some interesting reflections on this issue, see B. Üskiden and Y. Pasadeos, 'Organizational analysis in North America and Europe: a comparison of co-citation networks', *Organizational Studies*, 16(3) (1995), 503–26; Lars Engwall and Cecilia Pahlberg, CEMP Report no. 11, *The Content of European Management Ideas* (Uppsala, Sweden: Uppsala University, 2001); and Naomi Olson, Stephen Perkins, Saku Mantere, Behlul Üskiden and Mark Wexler, 'The Oxford Handbook of Organizational Theory: meta-theoretical perspectives/the Blackwell Companion to Organizations', *Organizational Studies*, 25(4) (2004), 669–80.

24 See Engwall, *The Carriers of European Management Ideas*; Silviya Svejenova and Jose Luis Alvarez, CEMP Report no. 9, *Contents and Influence of Management Academic Outlets* (Barcelona: IESE, 1999), esp. 44–7; and Yehuda Baruch, 'Global or North American? A geographical based comparative analysis of publications in top management journals', *International Journal of Cross Cultural Management*, 1(1) (2001), 109–26.

25 AACSB International, *Why Management Education Matters* (Tampa, FL: AACSB International, 2005), 8. See also Susan M. Philips, 'How B-schools drive productivity', *BizEd* (November/December 2003), 54–5.

26 Donald Hambrick, 'What if the Academy actually mattered?', *Academy of Management Review*, 19(1) (1994), 13.

27 Michael Skapinker, 'Hotshots from business school leave managers cold', *Financial Times*, 5 November 2003.

28 Letter, *Financial Times*, 10 November 2003.

29 Thomas H. Davenport and Laurence Prusak, with H. James Wilson, *What's the Big Idea? Creating and Capitalizing on the Best Management Thinking* (Boston: Harvard Business School Press, 2003).

30 Davenport and Prusak, with Wilson, *What's the Big Idea?*, 81, 85.

31 Davenport and Prusak, with Wilson, *What's the Big Idea?*, 219–22, 79.

32 Thomas H. Davenport and Laurence Prusak, with H. James Wilson, 'The 50 top business gurus', *Outlook*, 1 (2003), 13.

33 Crainer and Dearlove, *Gravy Training*, 74.

34 Davenport and Prusak, with Wilson, *What's the Big Idea?*, 71.

35 Robert Birnbaum, *Management Fads in Higher Education* (San Francisco: Jossey-Bass, 2001), 7.

36 Crainer and Dearlove, *Gravy Training*, 83–90.

37 University of Leeds, RAE return for Business and Management Studies, form RA6a, at www.hero.ac.uk.

38 Peter L. Bernstein, *Capital Ideas: The Improbable Origins of Modern Wall Street* (Hoboken, NJ: John Wiley, 1992).

39 Council for Excellence in Management and Leadership Business Schools Advisory Group, *The Contribution of the UK Business Schools*, 26.

40 Paul Ankers and Ross Brennan, 'Managerial relevance in academic research: an exploratory study', *Marketing Intelligence and Planning*, 20(1) (2002), 15–21; Nigel Slack, Michael Lewis and Hilary Bates, 'The two worlds of operations management research and practice', *International Journal of Operations and Production Management*, 24(4) (2003), 372–87. See also Stephen Rutner and Stanley Fawcett, 'The state of supply chain education', *Supply Chain Management Review*, 9(6) (2005), 55–60.

41 Pfeffer and Fong, 'The end of business schools?', 87.

42 Darrell Rigby, 'Management tools and techniques: a survey', *California Management Review*, 43(2) (2001), 139–60.

43 Pfeffer and Fong, 'The end of business schools?', 88.

44 See, for example, Richard A. Posner, *Public Intellectuals: A Study of Decline* (Cambridge, MA: Harvard University Press, 2003), and anon., 'Top 100 British public intellectuals', *Prospect*, 100 (July 2004), 23.

45 Jeffrey E. Garten, 'The need for wider horizons', *Financial Times*, 18 April 2005.

46 AACSB International Task Force, *Management Education at Risk*, 19, European Foundation for Management Development, *EQUIS: The European Quality Improvement System*, 2.

47 See Warren Bennis and James O'Toole, 'How business schools lost their way', *Harvard Business Review* (May 2005), 96–104.

48 Nasswan Dossabhoy and Paul Berger, 'Business school research: bridging the gap between producers and consumers', *Omega*, 30(4) (2002), 309.

49 James P. Walsh, Klaus Weber and Joshua D. Margolis, 'Social issues and management: our lost cause found', *Journal of Management*, 29(6) (2003), 859–81.

50 Anon., 'Trusting the teacher in the grey-flannel suit', *Economist*, 19 November 2005.

51 Interview, 11 February 2004.

52 Anon., 'Ranking the research', *BizEd* (March/April 2003), 11.

53 Zell, 'Pressure for relevancy at top-tier business schools', 274. See also Zell, 'The market-driven business school: has the pendulum swung too far?', 324–38.

54 Interview, 13 January 2005.

6   Experiments and innovations

In the previous chapters we have looked at the business school scene today in some detail, and underlined our belief that there is much to be uneasy about. We do not wish to suggest that the situation is wholly gloomy, however. As will have become clear by now, many are equally critical of what is currently taking place in business education, and, against this background, some – at least – have taken the bull by the horns and have aspired to introduce genuine changes. The most common move is to experiment with courses and research programmes that seek to close the gap between 'theory' and 'practice', and thus bring the academy into better balance with its stakeholders. In the following pages we explore some examples of constructive innovation, and attempt to evaluate their quality and effectiveness.

REFASHIONING THE MBA: 'CAN A NEW BUSINESS
SCHOOL TEACH TECHIES TO LEAD?'[1]

One trend that is occurring on both sides of the Atlantic is a reassessment of the MBA so as to make it more suited to the way that business is currently evolving. In a knowledge society, so the argument runs, boundaries between different specialisms are dissolving rapidly. What companies need are polymaths – in a nutshell, managers who are as at home discussing the latest technologies as the intricacies of business strategy. In this scenario, training and education need to adapt accordingly. One outcome of this line of reasoning has been a series of initiatives aimed at moving the MBA away from its traditional roots, towards entrepreneurship and the natural sciences. In 2004 Queen Mary College, part of the University of London, introduced an MBA in technology management and innovation. The course director explained: 'We thought there was a need for graduates to marry technology skills and management theory, for the benefit of business.' The course included modules on, amongst other things, 'international business and the economics of high-technology industries', 'technological entrepreneurship', 'business law and international property', 'managing research and development' and 'strategic management of technology'.[2] A year later the United Kingdom's Open University announced MBA programmes 'designed for the Life Sciences and Health universe', and an MBA (Technology Management) aimed at 'managers, engineers, technologists and scientists whose job includes managing technology'. Perhaps the most interesting example of this reorientation was occurring in San Diego at what in 2004 was christened the Rady School of Management.

The roots of Rady lay in the 1990s. San Diego had nurtured a formidable high-tech sector. One of the key institutions feeding growth was the University of California, San Diego (UCSD), world-renowned for scientific research. There was a perception, however, that the full potential of the relationship between the university and local business was not being achieved. UCSD programmes and projects prompted many start-ups, but a significant minority failed, often allegedly because of insufficient business acumen. While this was occurring, however, San Diego was also experiencing something of a brain drain. Simply put, too many of those MBAs who studied in the city (whether at UCSD or the other local players, San Diego State and the University of San Diego) were tending to leave the area in order to advance their careers.[3] The challenge, therefore, was to find a way of coaxing the cream of local business graduates into the burgeoning start-up economy on their doorstep. By the turn of the century the consensus view was that this could best be achieved by launching a wholly new business school for the city – one that upheld the highest academic standards and would therefore be considered prestigious, but also one that was fundamentally attuned to local needs. The upshot was that, in October 2002, Robert Sullivan, a highly experienced dean who had previously worked at Kenan-Flager Business

School, amongst others, was appointed to carry this mission through.[4]

Right from the word go, Sullivan lost little time in articulating his vision. In his view, this was a 'once-in-a-lifetime opportunity'. He explained:

> That's [what's] . . . being presented to me. If you had a clean slate,
> no legacy effect, what would you do in an ideal world if you had
> the magic to do it? A good way to view this is to call it the 'new'
> graduate school of management. It should be redefining, just like
> CMU in the late 1940s. The goal and the aspiration in the charter
> of this B-school is to redefine the discipline for the 21st century.[5]

Given this chance, what he wanted to do was make sure that the new school was as well connected to the practicalities of day-to-day business as it possibly could be. In everything that was done, he emphasised, 'real-world application' would be 'key'. Asked candidly by *Business 2.0* whether the world really needed yet another business school, he insisted: 'It needs a different kind of school. Most spend too much time on general management – leadership, organizational behaviour, marketing. Growth industries today are technology industries, and they need individuals who not only speak the language of business but also have credibility among scientists and engineers . . . Industry focus is a top priority for us.'[6] When dealing with more prosaic issues of pedagogy and recruitment, Sullivan was equally bold. He repeatedly underlined that he aimed to 'toss' the traditional curriculum, and replace it with an approach that blended science skills and management know-how. His 'grand experiment', he stated in one interview, would be 'to thread the business program together with UCSD's medical and engineering schools and other affiliated institutions'. He also emphasised that he intended to angle for students with a very particular set of aptitudes. What he wanted was those who were 'bilingual and bicultural' – 'folks who are credible with the scientists . . . [and] also understand business models and what's needed in terms of raising capital'.[7]

During 2003 and 2004 Sullivan and his team began the process of implementation. The new school, they announced, would cost $117.5 million, and be based in a state-of-the-art 80,000 sq. ft. building, boasting four tiered classrooms, four conventional classrooms, four seminar classrooms, twelve breakout rooms and a computer laboratory. When complete, it would employ sixty-five full-time faculty and thirty-five adjuncts, and teach 1,200 MBAs, a half of them full-time, together with fifty PhDs.[8] Nevertheless, as time passed, it became increasingly obvious that realising such an ambitious endeavour was going to be even more challenging than it had appeared at first sight. Sullivan faced problems on a number of different fronts. The school had been initially conceived during the dot.com boom. Now business conditions were much harsher. Accordingly, fund-raising tended to be considerably more difficult than originally envisaged. Sullivan spent many hours talking to the local corporate community, and set up a number of schemes for donors. A gift of $15 million from Irwin Jacobs, former UCSD engineering professor and founder of local wireless telecom giant Qualcomm, helped greatly, but by late 2003 80 per cent of the school's total projected cost remained to be found.[9] At the same time, institutional problems also proved vexing. University of California regulations meant that Sullivan had to consult with the other business schools in the system about proposed curriculum developments and faculty appointments. Worse, state policy pegged fees for local full-time MBAs at about $11,000 per year (about one-third of the average at good private schools), and thus constrained earnings from this potentially vital source.[10] Finally, and not unexpectedly, there were also some neighbourly anxieties and jealousies. For example, it was quite evident that not everyone on the UCSD campus was exactly delighted at the thought of a big new constituent department suddenly arriving out of the blue. Interviewed by the *Chronicle of Higher Education*, Maria Loftuss, the school's chief of staff, cited a familiar complex of prejudices: 'The campus reaction was always that it didn't feel right. We were a science-and-engineering university focused on the pursuit of knowledge, and people worried that the pursuit of money or publicity could taint that.'[11]

On the other hand, the situation was by no means all gloomy. In January 2004 Ernest Rady, a local financial services magnate, announced a donation of $30 million (half for the building and half to be used at the discretion of the dean), with the school being named in his honour – a development that considerably eased the fund-raising pressures.[12] Behind the scenes, too, Sullivan was achieving significant gains. For example, he greatly improved his ability to hire top-quality faculty when he persuaded some San Diego corporates to provide such appointments with consulting and board positions.[13] His incessant networking and public relations work also seemed to be gradually changing UCSD campus opinion. At any rate, by early 2005 he felt confident enough to tell a reporter: 'Everyone wants to be a piece of us . . . I even had the head of the history department come in saying that we need a joint M.B.A./history degree.'[14]

While these developments were playing out, the new school began its teaching programmes, using temporary facilities. Initially, Sullivan sensibly concentrated on executive training, particularly for companies such as Qualcomm that were, in effect, fairly close partners. In September 2004 the school's first real class began work, studying for a two-year flexitime MBA. There were sixty-four students, 80 per cent with science or technology backgrounds, each paying $36,000 per year. One year later Rady enrolled its founding group of full-time MBAs, a cohort of sixty from a pool of 238 applicants. Again, the profile of the students clearly matched the vision that Sullivan had enunciated earlier.[15] The press saluted an extraordinary achievement: the creation of an ambitious new institution in less than three years. Nevertheless, there were still one or two clouds on the horizon, predictably centring on finance. In the autumn of 2005 Rady announced, in quick succession, that its fund-raising had reached $70 million, and that work on its new building had begun. Within a few weeks, however, stories began to appear in the local press about cost overruns and delays. The root of the problem, it appeared, was overheating in the construction sector in the San Diego area, which meant, first, that raw material costs were increasing quickly and, second, that fewer contractors than had been anticipated were prepared to bid for the planned work.[16] In the end, Sullivan opted to apply to the University of California regents for extra funds. Informed journalists speculated that the Rady campus would not now be completed until sometime in the spring or summer of 2007, nearly a year later than originally intended.[17]

How should this story be evaluated? At the time of writing, in early 2006, the Rady School remained a work in progress, but much had been achieved. Sullivan constantly trumpeted 'the Rady revolution', and, thanks partly to the employment of marketing consultants Townsend Inc., the school had gradually established a brand image along these lines.[18] Press comment was voluminous and generally positive. The scale of student applications proved that the new school had appeal. The critics who wondered whether science graduates would enrol at a management school with a technology bent appeared to have been proved wrong.[19] Faculty strength was gradually increasing. What remained less clear was how far Rady had actually departed from the pedagogic concerns of its competitors. The problems of technology-driven firms were woven into many of the new modules, but the curriculum as a whole seemed surprisingly traditional in shape and approach. Sullivan's ambition to 'thread' his programmes through UCSD's science faculties was, as yet, largely unrealised. Much would clearly depend on how Rady developed when it finally took possession of its new home.

A FRESH APPROACH TO RESEARCH: FROM 'THE SUBJECT
UNDER THE MICROSCOPE' TO COLLABORATION

We now examine innovations in business school research, and in particular those involving matters of conceptualisation and strategy. Some background is illuminating. In the past such research was usually a relatively straightforward matter, which rarely attracted any great degree of controversy or questioning. The researcher, fortified by his or her academic qualifications, followed the classical mode of scientific enquiry, venturing out to study 'subjects' (usually practitioners in one or other branch of business) and then writing up a set of 'findings' for peer-reviewed journals. There was no doubting exactly who was in control of the process. The 'subjects' in question might have spent a lifetime juggling with the practical problems of their calling, but it was the academic who allegedly had the skills to contextualise, and therefore fully understand, what was really going on. When we interviewed a leading researcher at one of the United Kingdom's top schools, he put the matter to us as follows:

> You see, the problem with working with practitioners . . . there's two ways really of working with practitioners. If you go to a practitioner and say, 'Tell us what your problems are,' well, then you could get anything. So, we have a fairly focused idea . . . you see, practitioners don't know what hasn't been researched, and academics know that. So, you know, we have an idea. Now, of course, when we go to them, if they say: 'This is a stupid thing to be studying,' then we might . . . [but] we haven't had that reaction so far; everyone's said, 'This is a really interesting idea that few people have studied.' So we are really getting the help on 'the how' rather than 'the what', and it is quite dangerous, to some extent, to ask practitioners 'the what', because they don't know what academic research is and they can often ask you for insoluble things and things that academics can't solve.[20]

More recently, however, some have begun to criticise this model, and explore alternatives in its place. One increasingly popular methodology is to seek collaboration: the active participation of the 'subjects' in the research, and not just intermittently, but from the outset of the project right through to its culmination. The objective is to co-produce knowledge – in other words, hopefully blend theoretical and practical perspective into a more insightful synthesis. The typical vehicle that has been used for this kind of project is a forum, a semi-permanent institution, focused on one theme or set of themes, that brings academics and practitioners together on a regular basis to discuss pertinent issues.

A recent estimate is that as many as seventeen UK business schools have such institutions, and it is possible that a proportionate number of their US equivalents are similarly involved.[21] In what follows, we focus in detail on a single example – the Financial Services Research Forum (FSRF) at Nottingham University – in order to try to understand how the new paradigm is different, and what it ultimately promises.

THE FINANCIAL SERVICES RESEARCH FORUM: 'SCRATCHING WHERE WE'RE ITCHING'?

The Financial Services Research Forum brings together business school academics, industry practitioners and other interested parties in order to 'stimulate collaboration between management in financial services and business/management academics . . . promote, facilitate and disseminate leading edge academic research of relevance to management; [and] . . . raise the profile of such collaboration through networking and publishing'.[22] In the following paragraphs, we look in turn at how this body has developed, what it actually does and the extent of its various achievements.[23]

The FSRF's roots stretch back over twenty years. In the mid-1980s the Trustee Savings Bank decided to set aside significant charitable funds to support academe. The school of management at the University of Manchester Institute of Science and Technology (UMIST) bid for some of this money, and in 1987 received £500,000 to launch what it christened the Financial Services Research Centre (FSRC). This quickly became quite a success story, promoting multi-disciplinary research, supporting a variety of publications and drawing in substantial additional funding from a range of public and private bodies, including the Association of British Insurers, the Chartered Institute of Banking and the Economic and Social Research Council.[24] Indeed, by the early 1990s the FSRC had a considerable institutional presence. The director at the time, David Knights, later recalled:

> There were seventeen people involved. Now, they weren't all working full-time in the financial services area, a lot of them

were PhD students or research assistants working on projects that had got funded from the public sector, so ESRC. I had a secretary, I had a deputy director, obviously, and I had a few bits of consultancy projects that I'd bring people into, to run. So . . . it had got pretty big.[25]

Buoyed up by this success, the FSRC then decided to branch out. Knights was the catalyst. He had worked in the financial services sector before embarking on a very successful university career, and was convinced that business and the academy should interact to a much greater extent than they had in the past. Accordingly, in 1993 he created the Financial Services Forum, which aimed to encourage the two sides 'to establish a regular dialogue and debate on issues of common concern'.[26] The model here was an interesting one. Companies were canvassed to pay an annual subscription, and offered the opportunity to participate in fashioning a research agenda that was much more long-term, original and strategic than was normal from such collaborations. And, significantly, this was something that touched a nerve. In 1995 Knights reported: 'Although our forum has only been in existence for 18 months, we now have an annual research income of £120,000 generated through 24 participants who all describe the experience so far as a win-win situation.'[27]

Shortly afterwards, however, the situation imploded. In May 1997 Knights and his team launched a further associated body, the Consumer Finance Education Centre (CFEC), 'to inform the public about financial matters by producing independent educational literature on matters such as banking, pensions and insurance'.[28] Some fifteen business sponsors, including the Halifax and the Co-operative Bank, agreed to give support. Both the UMIST hierarchy and the financial press were enthusiastic. After only a few months, however, the mood changed drastically. The CFEC seemed becalmed, and some of the corporates involved began to worry about their reputations. At the same time, there was growing unease within UMIST itself, fuelled by claims that the new body had in fact been launched without the formal blessing of the management school's policy committee. Behind this, it appeared, lay a tangled web of suspicion and perhaps envy. *The Times Higher Education Supplement* reported that '[t]he root of the problem' was 'opposition from a group of academics in the school of management who feared that links with commerce could threaten their academic credibility'.[29] When we interviewed Knights he concurred by and large, and reflected:

> I think they were partly probably threatened by it a little bit, in the sense that you're in a business management department, all the noises coming out of government, all the noises coming out of . . . generally out of university vice chancellors, that, you know, business should be bringing money in, working with industry, that kind of thing. And very few people in the department were doing that, in the school of management were doing that. My own colleagues . . . constantly were always fairly critical of it. I remember, you know, they'd be critical to the deputy . . . never to me directly, it was always indirectly to my deputy; but on the basis that, you know, 'Oh, I don't think that's really research, that's not genuine research, that's selling out to the industry.'[30]

Whatever the exact truth here, the fallout was spectacular. Knights left UMIST after twenty-six years, and took up a senior post at the Nottingham University Business School (NUBS), while the deputy director of the CFEC negotiated a £50,000 severance payment.[31]

After settling into his new job, Knights had to decide what he wanted to do with the Financial Services Forum. The position was complicated. One or two of the senior corporate members met with the vice chancellor at Nottingham, and came away with the impression that he was keen for the forum to continue. Knights himself had by now developed a sense of ownership, and was very reluctant to see his efforts wasted. But NUBS was going through a period of change, particularly at leadership level, while UMIST was predictably reluctant simply to hand over the money that remained in the forum's account. In these circumstances, Knights struggled to keep things ticking over: there were one or two meetings in the ensuing year, but the membership dropped from twenty-six to eleven. When Knights then decided to move on again, this time to Keele, it appeared that the forum's days were numbered.

In the end, a fresh appointment saved the day. Nigel Waite had enjoyed a successful career at Glaxo, Mars, Lloyds TSB and Barclays Bank, but was now looking to set up on his own as a consultant. Unusually, he had always maintained strong academic interests, having gained a PhD in marketing at Cranfield, and was in fact teaching a module on the NUBS MBA at exactly this time. A colleague introduced him to Knights, and it was agreed that they would try together to rescue the forum. The remaining corporates were called together and persuaded to contribute £7,000 per annum each in membership fees. In addition, Waite negotiated with UMIST over the funds that were in dispute, and secured £50,000 in final settlement. The challenge now was to decide exactly what the forum should do to build a long-term future.

The context was not wholly propitious. The financial services industry's public reputation had suffered greatly because of a series of mis-selling scandals. Morale amongst practitioners was low. Moreover, in the general economic downturn of the time, businesses were becoming increasingly unwilling to carry extraneous costs. Big players appeared relatively unconcerned about the forum's fees, but others demonstrated a much greater degree of price sensitivity. In addition to everything else, there was the enduring problem that those representing the corporates sometimes changed jobs and had to be replaced, which at best undermined continuity, and at worst threatened their companies' involvement altogether. On the academic side, there were also problems. Both the outgoing and the incoming deans of NUBS were supportive, as was a small group of leading professors, but, amongst the staff in general, doubts remained. The school had ambitions to win a five-star rating in the forthcoming Research Assessment Exercise, and this inevitably meant that many were interested only in activities that would lead to publication in top-ranked journals. At the same time, lurking suspicions about the wider morality of the endeavour continued to eddy, with some believing that the academics involved were self-interested and perhaps 'on the make'. Finally, there were some taxing practical problems as well. For example, Waite quickly discovered that the forum's established financial year and accounting procedures were at odds with those used by the university administration, a situation that in turn made presentation of timely and accurate annual statements difficult to compile.

Against this background, the forum embarked upon a rebuilding strategy that, essentially, had two major interlocking facets. First, there was a sustained attempt to make the forum more professional. Initiatives occurred at several different levels. Much was done to tighten up organisation. The forum's name was tweaked so as to include the word 'Research'. Waite was appointed executive director and placed on a contract whereby he worked for a fixed number of days per year. The accounts were harmonised with those of the university. The existing steering committee was strengthened, so that it could take on a wider array of work. Improved communication with members became a priority, with developments including the launch of a dedicated FSRF website and the institution of an annual dinner. Similar steps were taken to improve the organisation's events and research. Waite believed that the forum's meetings could be improved, and he determined to ensure that, in future, more care would be taken over the selection of invited speakers and the format of individual sessions. Branding and a new logo were introduced to reinforce the FSRF's image. An attempt was made to systematise the commissioning of research, and ensure that results were written up in common form. The overall objective was to present the forum as a proficient and well-oiled machine, and then ensure that it lived up to this image.

At the same time, considerable effort was made to improve the FSRF's focus. At first, it was agreed to organise around core themes: initially 'education and regulation', 'consumer behaviour and distribution' and 'strategy and decision-making' and, later, 'risk and financial behaviour', 'markets and consumption', 'financial education and regulation' and 'strategic management and organisational learning'. By late 2002, however, it was becoming clear that such an approach had drawbacks. Waite's epiphany occurred when a company that was resigning from the forum told him: 'The thing is, you're not scratching where we're itching.'[32] Provoked by this comment, he then started investigating what other members felt. His findings were sobering. It was an unwelcome fact, Waite believed, that, for all its burgeoning activity, the forum had yet to punch its potential weight. It was pursuing a schematic conception of the industry's problems, but avoiding any real engagement with the most pressing issues. The result was something of a disconnect. The academics at NUBS were producing work of high intrinsic value, no doubt, but this was only occasionally stimulating the membership, which indeed remained somewhat indifferent.

In these circumstances, the FSRF began an urgent reorientation. The key driver was a bold reconceptualisation. Previously, the forum had operated largely as if the financial services sector consisted only of providers. What Waite and his colleagues on the steering committee now proposed was that they should start thinking in terms of a financial services *domain* – consisting of the providers, certainly, but also consumers and regulators. From this, much else followed. A decision was taken to broaden the membership base, and this quickly led to the recruitment of organisations such as the Financial Services Authority, the Consumers' Association and Pfeg (an educational charity) as non-fee-paying associates. Concurrently, there was a reformulation of the priorities for discussion and research. In future the forum would concentrate on studying how the main players interacted, so as to help them achieve closer and better alignment.

In 2004/5 much was done to put this new approach into practice. Forum meetings were increasingly themed, organised in terms of a regular thrice-yearly cycle and held at high-profile locations, including the Hongkong and Shanghai Banking Corporation headquarters and the Treasury. Attendances were buoyant, with good representation from a wide array of stakeholders. The issue of trust became increasingly salient in FSRF deliberations, and much effort was spent on producing a 'trust index', measuring what consumers thought of providers. The change of policy engineered by Waite and his colleagues appeared to have produced considerable dividends.

How should the FSRF be assessed? One approach is to examine it simply as an organisation, and, from this perspective, there is much to admire. The basic facts are as follows. The forum has managed to keep operating, in one guise or another, since 1993. A core membership has remained loyal, stabilising in recent years at about seventeen full members and ten or so associates. The finances have been healthy: in 2004, for example, the accounts showed that £127,734 was carried forward. The level of outputs, too, has been impressive. The forum's website currently provides links to fifty-eight comprehensive research reports on a wide range of issues, dealing with both ordinary people's behaviour ('Can consumers be educated to save for retirement?') and providers' conundrums ('Outsourcing in the UK financial services industry: the Asian offshore market'). The quality of meetings is now usually first-class, with well-crafted presentations and lively discussion. Less tangibly, the FSRF has also managed to build a considerable reputation. Government ministers have recently demonstrated that they believe the forum to be a credible voice, which deserves to be taken seriously. Perhaps even more indicatively, consumer organisations, too, are now in most cases highly favourable. One new associate member from the charity sector commented to us:

> I think the organisation is very good, I think the way they communicate is very good. I think you get proper information, you know – I mean, it sounds simplistic but you wouldn't believe how often people don't bother to tell you what time things are starting. You know, all of that kind . . . what I see as being like the bedrock of administration, which enables things to happen, I think is very good. I think that . . . [they] have a nice way of doing

things, which is very inclusive and friendly and it has a nice tone
to it . . . So I have nothing but warm feelings towards the forum,
I think it is a good thing.[33]

This is not to suggest, however, that every problem has been
overcome. On the corporate side, personal and organisational churn
continue to cause difficulties. Moreover, commitment remains questionable. An internal review of 2004 concluded: 'Some notable
progress has been made in broadening participation in the work of the
Forum among member companies but we remain far too dependent
upon the key representatives.'[34] The situation with the academics is
something of a mirror image. The number of NUBS staff involved has
gradually increased but it is also true that long-standing prejudices
persist. In these conditions, frustrations on both sides wax and wane.
The practitioners tend to remain puzzled that commissioned research
takes so long to complete, and wonder what academics actually do
with their time. Some also criticise the way that results have been
presented. When interviewed, the representative of one of the big corporates elaborated:

> No, I don't enjoy their presentations, I've got to be frank. I think
> they're too slow and cumbersome in many cases and there's too
> much data transferred. I mean, I always like to . . . imagine what
> would happen if I put one of those presentations in front of my
> chief executive, and I'd last about three minutes, you know. The
> fact is, in industry, it needs to be more concise.[35]

One of his colleagues made essentially the same point, though
more laconically: 'I think there is a tendency to [say] . . . "I've got this
bunch of findings, and they're numbers one to twenty, and so, therefore, I'm going to run through one to twenty, whether you're all still
sat there at the end of it or not."'[36] Not unexpectedly, broad political
or cultural differences sometimes surface as well, and can prove
irksome. One practitioner, who believes that the private sector gen-
erates the wealth 'for all the public sectors [sic] to sort of enjoy and

spend', expressed himself mildly irritated that not all academics shared his views:

> There's one in particular who . . . [makes] lots of little sighs and comments . . . you know . . . it's just little things, like the way the word 'profit' is pronounced, you know, like it's a dirty thing. I mean, you can just tell . . . 'Oh, the profit', you know. And it just strikes me, if I was managing this individual . . . I would be saying 'Now look, these people on the supply side are actually our customers, they're the only ones that are paying £7,000 a year, all the others are coming in free, you know, I mean this whole thing will collapse if we don't have that . . .' – you know, and it just needs a little bit of counselling. But I don't get the impression that that's done in academic circles.[37]

The academics have their own complaints. From their perspective, the business members too often remain inexplicably inert – unresponsive, for example, even when asked to suggest new and relevant research projects, or provide practical help. Not untypically, one of the senior professors recounted to us that, when he asked forum members for contacts to help with a project that they were formally backing, 'only one guy came back'.

Nor has the addition of new members from charities, quangos and the civil service necessarily proceeded smoothly. The fact that prejudices of one kind or another are still quickly rehearsed is significant. Our interviews were replete with examples. A practitioner member commented of a government department: 'There's a small part at the top of very bright intellectuals. And then there's a large rump of pretty average-intelligence bigots.' A representative of a charity believed that FSRF academics too often speak as if they work at 'the university of the bleeding obvious'. And a highly qualified statistician who worked for one of the regulators described some forum discussions as 'no better than the *Daily Mail* . . . on a Wednesday'.[38] Of course, while some of this is harmless, and has no impact on collaborative working, in other cases it may be more debilitating.

Nevertheless, with this litany accepted, there is no doubt that, from a purely organisational angle, the forum must still be judged positively. Bringing people together from different walks of life will always be difficult. Stresses and strains are to be expected. If the important facets are weighed against each other, however, the successes well outweigh the failures. What about the perhaps more interesting and important question of influence? Has the forum achieved its aim of creating and disseminating the kind of knowledge that will make a difference in the real world?

The record as regards the research output – strictly defined – is probably at best mixed. As already noted, the FSRF has, over the years, involved itself in a whole series of projects, and thus built up a formidable array of reports. There is no doubt that some of this material has proved of interest to policy-makers and journalists. Thus, for example, forum papers have been cited by commentators as diverse as the UK Treasury's Myners Review on the Governance of Life Mutuals, the Financial Services Authority, the Organisation for Economic Co-operation and Development and the BBC's *Money Box* programme. It seems to be the case, however, that the impact amongst the FSRF's own industry members has been rather less marked. When interviewed, one or two practitioners claimed that they read the circulated material if it was germane, and added that they sometimes judged it beneficial. For instance, a medium-sized player estimated that he has found 'about 25 per cent' of the reports to be valuable, and quoted the following example:

> The very first one that I remember which impressed me was one which looked at whether or not there was a market for advice or whether stakeholder products would largely do away with that . . . I'm a marketer and as a marketer you are like a jack of all trades – you know, probably master of none . . . But I did a lot of market research, I spent about eighteen months actually in a market research department, doing nothing but market research. So I've got some idea of how to do market research and, you

know, I've got a feel for whether the approach looks rigorous enough or whether the questionnaires are right and all the rest of it. And I know having looked through it . . . this was a good piece of research, and what came out was that a lot of people didn't really understand the stakeholder products, and certainly, when it came to things such as fund choices and so on, they did need investment advice. And when you looked at the detail of that and what came back, I thought, 'Yeah, this is a credible piece of work; I believe the results, you know.'[39]

On the other hand, there is no doubt that such a response is quite unusual. An FSRF document of 2004 concluded rather drily that '[a]ll too often' the reports had 'failed to make their mark among relevant constituencies'.[40] When we asked if this was still true, many members concurred, and indeed were disarmingly forthright about how little of the material they read. One simply commented: 'I've got a cupboard behind me at work and it's full of research papers that fall into the category of "interesting, must get round to reading some time".'[41] Another made much the same point, and placed the issue in context:

It's just one of those typical things in today's working environment, that people don't have much time. And there's a whole load of information being flung at us from every direction and, you know, basically what's going to make them turn round and say 'Well, as a priority, I'll read the latest paper from the Research Forum'? It's a battle. And the fact that you've got such good participation at meetings means that that's really the prime opportunity.[42]

After long experience in the field, Waite was unsurprised. He expanded: 'With very few exceptions, I might say to somebody at that company, "Hand on your heart, now tell me honestly: when you get a research report from the forum, what happens to it?" "Honest, Nigel, it goes on the shelf." '[43]

Interestingly, because the FSRF's steering committee has been aware of this problem for some time, there has been sporadic discussion about solutions. One idea was that practitioners should sponsor individual research projects from their inception, certainly advising, and perhaps even cooperating in data collection and evaluation, thus gaining firmer ownership of the final report. Nonetheless, although this arrangement apparently worked – at least to some extent – on one or two occasions, there has been no large-scale uptake. The problem is simply that only a tiny proportion of the corporates have ever had adequate time for such an endeavour. Thus, Knights recollected of the policy: 'It fizzled out because I think . . . it's very difficult to take their time, you know. It would mean them coming to extra meetings. It's hard enough to get them to the meetings that there are.'[44] In this situation, fundamental issues about what research is, and how it should be conducted and reported, remain to be fully resolved. A senior member from the business side explained as follows:

> Yeah, I think . . . the practitioners . . . do take a very different view. They want to do research and they want to see X, Y and Z result. They don't want to see, you know, a bunch of hypotheses that may or may not be true, with a whole bunch of, you know, correlation factors. I remember one particular report that I was interested in, and I thought it was a good report, but I found it very hard going as a practitioner, to go through it and drag out the relevant bits. In effect, the relevant bits you could have sort of condensed into half a page. So I think, once you start writing for the practitioners, you know, you say: 'We found this, here's the data and these are our conclusions.' It becomes a really rather short report. Whereas the academic side wants rigour, it wants its proof, it wants its correlation and all this, that and the other. And I think the two reports are very different . . .[45]

If a broader perspective on the question of knowledge activity is adopted, however, one that encompasses the forum's signature events, with their manifold discussions and networking opportunities, then a rather different – and arguably more positive – picture emerges. To substantiate this point, it is necessary to look in some detail at the different ways in which the FSRF members describe actually interacting. One key feature of forum meetings is that they are held under 'Chatham House rules' – that is, comments are not repeated later to outsiders. The consequence is that debate tends to be fairly unbridled. It might be thought that such frankness could cause division and perhaps resentment, but in fact it is almost universally welcomed. Joining from the consumer politics sphere, one senior participant recalled being pleasantly surprised by his new colleagues' acceptance of the need for give and take:

> I thought, 'Well, OK . . . let's go and see if these industry guys want to come along and tell you the truth' – you know, they want to have a frank and open discussion. And so I thought, 'Well . . . I see it when I believe it . . .' But it's actually turned out that way – you know, it has been a fairly open forum . . . and most of the industry have left their sort of guns at the door when they've come in, you know, and . . . they've been open.[46]

On the practitioner side, too, forthrightness is a big attraction. The point is that the corporates to some extent recognise their own introversion, their entrapment within idiosyncratic interpretations and jargon, and understand that these characteristics represent a weakness. Hearing other opinions, therefore, can be like a breath of fresh air. This is particularly so because, in the context of the FSRF, all comment is likely to be accepted as credible; it might be 'left-field', as one interviewee described it, but it also comes from people whose good faith and expertise is largely guaranteed. A representative from one of the large financial institutions told us:

> I think . . . we all have a – what's the word in marketing? – a self-referencing criteria [sic], don't we, where we see . . . the world through our eyes and our experiences. And I think . . . [critics are] useful, whether you agree with them or not. I mean, I remember

having the [FSRF] dinner recently with [XXX, the guest speaker], where he was . . . very controversial and scathing about different things, and, you know, whether you agree with it or not, it's good to be challenged. And I think that, you know, it's back to 'perception is reality': if people are saying that about our industry, then we've got a perception problem. And so I think, from that point of view, it does challenge you and it does make you think. And you might not agree with them, whether that's a political or personal stance, but you've got to be open to these things.[47]

In this situation, knowledge diffusion is frequently both tangible and widespread. Practitioners learn about the surrounding landscape, the way that their peers think and in particular how they should evaluate new products and trends. One remembered how a particular discussion at a forum meeting developed his thinking:

We were talking to them about stakeholder products, for instance that we're thinking of doing post-April of this year, and so on. And these people [doing the presentation] are actually quite candid about, you know, what their plans are, what their views are, and the fact that in that particular case it's by no means certain that there's going to be a tremendous explosion in demand for stakeholder products, and therefore . . . [their institution] will take a very softly-softly way to the approach. You canvass round some of the others . . . exactly the same. You're talking to people who are at the heart of this, you know, sort of equivalent positions to me in their respective companies, either from marketing or whatever . . . So that when I'm talking to our board, and part of my job is to keep abreast of what's going on in the market, I have that much more confidence about saying: 'Look, I don't think we need to be scared to get those stakeholder products and go rushing in, you know what I mean, I think there is definitely going . . .' And, yes, . . . it's the sort of thing that you pick up bits of in the press, but to hear it from the people is really helpful.[48]

For those from the non-commercial sector, the benefits may be less about specifics and more about gaining broad experience and understanding, even confidence to argue their corner. The leader of a charitable organisation described how she attended her first FSRF meeting with trepidation but was soon reassured by just how 'clueless' some of the other participants appeared to be. She elaborated: 'You always think everybody else knows so much more than you do but actually it's [not true] . . . so I sometimes think, "Oh, I'll be really out of my depth in this one and I won't have anything to say." And then actually I listen to what the people are saying and I'm thinking – well, you know.' What she valued about the forum was that it constantly expanded her horizons, and thus helped in other interactions. She commented:

> I mean, a lot of the stuff is a bit peripheral for us but . . . what I get out of the forum, which other things don't do, is it gives me a knowledge base about things which it would be impractical for me to find out about otherwise . . . So, although I technically don't need to know some of the stuff there, it really helps my credibility if I can drop things into conversations in other contexts, you know.[49]

Turning to look at the networking activity that goes on in and around the FSRF, the situation is at first sight rather different. To begin with, it is worth underlining that members take networking very seriously indeed, and in fact rate it as the prime benefit that is available to them.[50] Moreover, there can be no doubt that much of this activity is straightforwardly instrumental – a matter of lobbying, building alliances, perhaps even gaining commercial advantage. Thus, for example, one of those interviewed was quite open about the fact that his company only joined the forum because it represented 'an opportunity to make contacts in other areas'. He elucidated:

> Maybe five years ago, we really had to go out and . . . persuade our clients that they really needed us. Then the game changed, a

lot of things happened in the market and . . . our clients suddenly found that they needed us more than we needed them . . . And that was the happy situation we were in up until about a year ago. And that's really the sort of period when our membership of the Research Forum was something that we were actually looking for. The reason for that was that we kind of foresaw the time when the world would change again, and that's happened. We didn't know why it would change but we just thought it would change . . . So we're sort of saying to ourselves, 'Well, where in the future is our bread and butter business going to come from?' And the answer is that it's not going to come from our traditional sources, it's going to come from elsewhere . . . So our objective really was to make contacts outside of our own immediate sort of circle of clients, if you like – that was what we were trying to do. And when you look at the Financial Services Research Forum, the membership of that is very wide across financial services organisations. So it was primarily a sort of networking, contact-making opportunity that we saw. And that was it.[51]

Nevertheless, the boundary between such networking and the apparently more esoteric world of knowledge sharing is rather less fixed than might be imagined. A member with a sophisticated notion of lobbying – and, indeed, long experience of doing just that for a living – also underlined his commitment to discussion, to reach beyond the easy stereotypes.

I think everyone has something to offer – you know, when you go there . . . for example . . . sometimes if I'm sitting there having a pint with somebody after the forum meetings, you know, and they say to me, 'Well, how come you're so anti this because we read what you said in the paper?' And that gives me a chance to say: 'Well, actually, you know, you didn't see the other 95 per cent of me saying it was actually positive' – you know, the media picks up the 5 per cent that's controversial or confrontational, you know. So it gives you the chance to explain, it gives you the chance to explain where you're coming from, you know.[52]

Thus, while the primary motive for networking is almost always to gain influence, the content of the subsequent exchanges can prove educational – and, moreover, for both the participants.

In summary, it is clear that, when FSRF members interact, knowledge is offered and accepted in multiple different ways. But, it then needs to be asked, does any of this actually make a difference? It is clear, to begin with, that the diffusion of knowledge has certainly altered personal opinions. Talking to Waite in 2002, one member reflected: '[The forum] helps create white space which I rarely get . . . [and] enables you to challenge your thinking.'[53] When interviewed by us, his colleagues made similar observations. Moreover, there is evidence that such change can then ripple – with the individuals involved in turn influencing departmental colleagues and those managers or board members who they report to. Significantly, several members described themselves as 'gatekeepers', who analysed knowledge gained through forum activities, and then circulated it as they saw fit.

Whether any of this in the end actually modifies corporate behaviour remains far harder to determine. When Waite questioned the membership in 2002, his findings were decidedly downbeat. He reported: 'Respondents felt that the Forum, in general, has made no impact upon the conduct of strategy within their respective organisations, some nine answered "none at all".'[54] On the other hand, the position seems to have improved subsequently. Some members on the industry side readily acknowledged in our interviews that their immersion in particular forum events had reinforced existing hunches, and so helped fashion hard and fast judgements. Beyond this, identifying what impact there has been becomes messy, and difficult to pin down. Other influences are, of course, always at play. Nevertheless, it is still possible to discern linkages. Not untypically, a senior figure with considerable internal responsibilities credited the forum with improving his everyday decision-making, albeit rarely in a straightforward way: 'You might take that and a bunch of other things, and you might extract a few, you know, key points out of it, and then that might go towards a formulation of a strategy.'[55] Another very active member agreed, analysing the benefits that the forum had brought him as follows:

> It's not necessarily going to be something . . . where I'd say: 'Oh, actually yeah, that's going to really make a difference strategically in the next two or three years, directly.' It may be . . . an insight which makes you want to go off and look at something else we haven't thought about or something . . . [Y]ou're saying have a look at something or my colleagues look at something or this is what we need to do, it's sometimes interesting getting a different interpretation on that. And sometimes you get into quite interesting insights.[56]

Against this background, it is perhaps reasonable to conclude that the forum's recent reorientation has to some extent achieved what the organisation envisaged.

In 2003 the United Kingdom's Lambert Review of Business–University Collaboration argued that 'the best forms of knowledge transfer involve human interaction', and added pointedly: 'Forums that bring academics and business people together are likely to increase the chance that people with common interests and goals will find innovative ways to develop partnerships.'[57] The FSRF has done much to prove the point. Participants no doubt aim to enjoy a variety of advantages through their involvement in forum affairs, but all are committed to the exchange of ideas, and the benefits of partnership in problem-solving. Whether this represents a qualitative advance in research methodology is perhaps still a moot point, however. The FSRF certainly aids the circulation of existing knowledge, and has also produced its own stock of research and ideas. What remains more difficult to assess is how far any of this involves real co-production. The academics have certainly dominated much of the activity, if only by default. On the other hand, it is evident that some of their opinions have evolved because of contact with practitioners. An interview with one of the senior professors included the following indicative exchange:

> *So what . . . about co-production, then?*
>
> Oh God! That's difficult, extremely difficult. I mean . . . they [the practitioners] are too busy to really spend a massive amount of time on this . . .
>
> *Has co-production ever happened in your view?*
>
> Not really, no, I don't think so.
>
> *In a sense, you produce research, it's been discussed . . . but has it ever changed your view of things particularly?*
>
> Oh, I think, yeah, I think my view can change through the discussion that we have, yeah . . . I mean, more in detail than in a generic sense.[58]

It will be interesting to see if this kind of 'reverse influence' deepens as the FSRF matures in the future.

THE POSSIBILITY OF CHANGE

The stories rehearsed in the preceding pages provoke contrasting reflections. First, they confirm that the business school firmament is not fixed, and that constructive initiatives are possible. Rady and the FSRF have to some extent broken the mould. They are departures from the norm; they show what can be done if the will is there. This is an optimistic message.

Nonetheless, that acknowledged, there are also grounds for caution. Our subjects both enjoyed substantial advantages of various kinds. Sullivan, Knights and Waite all provided unusually clear and perceptive leadership. The Rady donation was, obviously, an exceptional windfall. In the FSRF's case, the wider environment, too, was favourable; after all, if the financial services industry had not been continually buffeted over the past twenty years, first by the impact of 'Big Bang' and later by mis-selling scandals and tighter regulation, would its constituents have been likely to sit down and talk in the first place? It is quite reasonable to argue, therefore, that both cases are essentially *sui generis*.

In the forthcoming chapters we look at the issue of business schools and change more broadly, first following a fictitious MBA class, in order to highlight some of the central dilemmas that need to be resolved, and then examining a handful of possible future scenarios.

NOTES

1 This quotation is taken from an article in *The Economist* on the Rady School of Management: see anon., 'MBAs for anoraks', *Economist*, 24 January 2004.

2 Stephen McCormack, 'Meet the material girls and boys', *Independent*, 6 May 2004.

3 Brian Hindo, 'A new blueprint for B-schools?', *BusinessWeek Online*, 25 November 2002; Rachael Laing, 'Breaking new ground', *SignOnSanDiego. com*, 17 August 2003.

4 Sullivan is well profiled in Katherine S. Mangan, 'The business school as a start-up', *Chronicle of Higher Education*, 9 September 2005.

5 Mangan, 'The business school as a start-up'; Brian Hindo, 'Building a B-school from scratch', *BusinessWeek Online*, 3 October 2002.

6 Mathew Maier, 'Reengineering the MBA', *Business 2.0* (April 2004).

7 Laing, 'Breaking new ground'; Andrea Siedsma, 'Reform school: UCSD on course to train next-gen tech leaders', *UCSD Connect*, 24 September 2004.

8 Hindo, 'A new blueprint for B-schools'; Laing, 'Breaking new ground'; Mangan, 'The business school as a start-up'; and Bruce V. Bigelow, 'As construction costs spike, so does price of UCSD school', *SignOnSanDiego.com*, 8 October 2005.

9 Laing, 'Breaking new ground'.

10 Hindo, 'A new blueprint for B-schools'.

11 Mangan, 'The business school as a start-up'.

12 The donation was in the name of Ernest Rady and the Rady Family Foundation: for the background, see anon., 'UCSD names school of

management in recognition of $30 million gift from Ernest Rady and Rady Family Foundation', *Business Wire*, 22 January 2004.

13 Sullivan himself became a director of Cubic Corporation (a defence contractor): see Laing, 'Breaking new ground', and Siedsma, 'Reform school'.

14 Mangan, 'The business school as a start-up'.

15 Siedsma, 'Reform school'; Bruce Bigelow, 'Weekend MBA program begins', *SignOnSanDiego.com*, 11 September 2004; and Eleanor Yang, 'UCSD opens its new business school', *SignOnSanDiego.com*, 22 September 2005.

16 Bigelow, 'As construction costs spike'.

17 Bigelow, 'As construction costs spike'; Charles Nguyen, 'UC-San Diego business school budget to include campus funding', *University Wire*, 29 September 2005; and University of California, Office of the President, memorandum 103, 20 September 2005.

18 See www.townsendinc.com/casestudies/radyschool.php.

19 Mangan, 'The business school as a start-up'.

20 Interview, 27 March 2004.

21 See Catrina Alferoff and David Knights, 'Making and mending your nets: the management of uncertainty in academic/practitioner knowledge networks' (forthcoming), 6.

22 Financial Services Research Forum mission statement, at www.nottingham.ac.uk/business/forum/.

23 This case study is based upon, amongst other things, extended interviews with FSRF members, FSRF internal minutes and papers, and participant observation at FSRF events. We are grateful to all those who have given us the benefit of their opinions, particularly David Knights, and to Nigel Waite, who also provided documentation.

24 David Knights and Chris Green, 'A winning ticket', *Times Higher Education Supplement*, 3 November 1995; interview, 25 January 2005.

25 Interview, 25 January 2005.

26 Knights and Green, 'A winning ticket'.

27 Knights and Green, 'A winning ticket'.

28 Alison Utley, 'Two quit in sponsor row', *Times Higher Education Supplement*, 19 December 1997.

29 Utley, 'Two quit in sponsor row'.

30 Interview, 25 January 2005.

31 Utley, 'Two quit in sponsor row'.

32 Interview, 11 January 2005.

33 Interview, 13 April 2005.

34 Financial Services Research Forum, 'Item 2 re Forum situation review', 13 January 2004, 1.

35 Interview, 31 March 2005.

36 Interview, 14 February 2005.

37 Interview, 25 February 2005.

38 Interviews, 25 February 2005, 13 April 2005, 26 April 2005.

39 Interview, 25 February 2005.

40 Financial Services Research Forum, 'Item 2 re Forum situation review', 1.

41 Interview, 14 February 2005.

42 Interview, 12 April 2005.

43 Interview, 11 January 2005.

44 Interview, 25 January 2005.

45 Interview, 29 March 2005.

46 Interview, 22 February 2005.

47 Interview, 31 March 2005.

48 Interview, 25 February 2005.

49 Interview, 13 April 2005.

50 Financial Services Research Forum, 'Feedback on member research exercise, September/October 2002', para. 10.1; interview, 7 April 2005.

51 Interview, 29 March 2005.

52 Interview, 22 February 2005.

53 Financial Services Research Forum, 'Feedback on member research exercise', para. 10.2.

54 Financial Services Research Forum, 'Feedback on member research exercise', para. 9.1.

55 Interview, 31 March 2005.

56 Interview, 7 April 2005.

57 R. Lambert, *Lambert Review of Business–University Collaboration: Final Report* (London: HM Treasury, 2003), 31.

58 Interview, 25 February 2005.

7   Imaginary MBAs

Our focus now shifts to an imaginary MBA class. The class revolves around a screening of Oliver Stone's film *Wall Street*.[1] The professor intends to use the discussion of the film to explore different perspectives on contemporary capitalism. His touchstone is the great sociologist Max Weber's pessimistic vision of the inexorable rise of capitalism. He is also concerned to encourage the students to reflect critically on their MBA experience. For the sake of dramatic purpose, rather than verisimilitude, the characters are presented as somewhat one-dimensional 'ideal types'. Any similarity with real MBA students is totally fortuitous.[2]

PROLOGUE

The scene is set in an MBA lecture theatre. A professor enters, checks his technology, wipes his glasses and looks at the class. He clears his throat and speaks.

Professor: Good afternoon, ladies and gentlemen. I'd like to start this afternoon's session with a quote from the eminent social scientist Max Weber's most famous work, *The Protestant Ethic and the Spirit of Capitalism*. Weber was European and one of the founding fathers of social science, that strange hybrid that thinks that we can study society scientifically and come up with laws that describe its functioning. Weber is summarising how the spirit of capitalism has reached its climax in the United States, thus picking up on a theme we have discussed previously: the different variants of capitalism and whether globalisation is leading us all in the same direction. In the context Weber is describing, the pursuit of wealth for its own sake has become a kind of sport. In the process a mode of living and of society has become established that he compares to a cage. We are all, willingly or unwillingly, trapped in this cage.

Weber ends his great book with the following words: 'No one knows who will live in this cage in the future, or whether at the end of this tremendous development entirely new prophets will arise, or there will be a great rebirth of old ideas and ideals, or, if neither, mechanised petrifaction, embellished with a sort of convulsive self-importance. For of the last stage of this cultural development, it might well be truly said: "Specialists without spirit, sensualists without heart; this nullity imagines that it has attained a level of civilisation never before achieved." '[3]

Today we will be looking at a film – Oliver Stone's *Wall Street* – that sets out to tell a story but also to capture, like Weber, the spirit of its time, the spirit of capitalism in the 1980s, when MBAs were well on their way to becoming masters, and mistresses, of the universe. Some would argue that things have got worse since the film was made. We barely survived the roaring nineties and the dot.com boom. We have had Enron and the rest, Sarbanes–Oxley, the Chicago gangster theory of life elected to the White House. We have had the first MBA elected president of the United States.

Wall Street, the film we are going to analyse, offers the viewer a flawed hero, Bud Fox, pursuing a career in investment banking, who lives the spirit of his time. He embarks on a roller coaster ride to success that takes him over the line of ethical and legal practice into the murky world of insider trading, riding on the shoulders of his employer and mentor Gordon Gekko, who, as events unfold, becomes his nemesis. Success gives way to criminal charges as Fox finally sees the error of his ways. By the time he is arrested he has become disillusioned with his lifestyle and has gained some hard-won insight into his own character, into the reasons for his fall from grace and into a way of life and a world that he comes to see as intrinsically corrupt. The film is, in its way, a modern morality tale.

A film, a fictional film at that, provides a different and, I would argue, an alternative perspective on and an alternative way of understanding business. A film, this film, does not pretend to hold a mirror up to life. It does not claim to be a case study with easily understandable lessons, once you have done the hard work of decoding what the case stands for. Works of fiction – novels, plays, films – provide us with myths and metaphors, the kinds of things that, whether we are aware of it or not, are indispensable for living the lives we choose to live. Some of us – a small number admittedly, but we are growing in number – think that such fictions have a potentially powerful role to play in the business school curriculum, that they challenge the metaphors and myths by which business schools live their lives. The knowledge they contain is at least as important as that contained in other vessels of so-called knowledge. At the very least they provide an antidote to the shortcomings of other, more scientific ways of picturing the world – survey-based studies of occupations and organisations, for example.

Let me quote from an excellent study of work as an arena of struggle, confrontation and the search for meaning, entitled *Living with Capitalism*: 'So much of what passes for "theory" . . . fails to connect with the lives that people lead, whereas most descriptive social surveys too often fail to grasp the structure of social relations and the sense which people make of them. It is almost as if another way of writing has to be developed; something which "tells it like it is" even though in any simple sense this is not possible; something which is theoretically informed yet free from theoretical pretentiousness, and which destroys the gap between the abstract and the concrete.'[4]

Films such as the one we are about to watch can fill that gap. And fiction can, at least, be fun, something which cannot always be said for other methods. *[There is a small wave of rueful laughter in the room.]*

There is, I would argue, a correlation between enjoyment and learning, and between laughter and longevity! Fiction can also provide a counterbalance to the overwhelmingly favourable views of managerial work that we find in the non-fiction management literatures you spend most of your time on, and in the case studies you pore over as part of your MBA. Name me the last case study you read that was critical of its target company. I too have read some of the Enron cases. We now know what kind of revolution Enron was leading when the lights went out in California. *[Pause.]* Well, art is better at teaching us how to cope with a precarious and often terrifying world where the lights are going out.

As students and teachers we need to look for data that will allow us to understand and improve the living meaning of the collective situation that is work. We also have to broaden our horizons, extend our mental models, realise that the best choices for the future will not be deduced from economic data or from abstract quantitative measures that purport to capture, wriggling on a pin, the essence of organisational behaviour. We need to probe more deeply, empathically, to wrestle with the messy reality of daily life at work. See Zuboff's *In the Age of the Smart Machine* for an elaboration of this argument.[5]

Art, novels, films provide us with an unparalleled opportunity for doing this probing, both into ourselves and into others, into society, because the role of art is to penetrate to the heart of our existential dilemmas, in part by examining 'the ethical trials and temptations that a competitive industrial order always puts in the way of those who want to become its forceful protagonists'. The power of art is to stimulate our 'moral imagination' and, in the process, 'to unnerve people – get them worried about what they might be doing or not doing . . . [and to] suggest various moral, social and psychological possibilities'.[6]

DeMott, in a *Harvard Business Review* article, argues that fiction has played a key role in contributing to cultural change, not least in its contributions to public perceptions of the business world.[7] Sometimes it has presented business in a positive light but this doesn't usually make great literature and it fails to convince. On the whole, art has been critical of business, either overtly or implicitly. Look at Joseph Heller, for example, and lots of others. The leading literary critic Lionel Trilling wrote in 1961 about literature's contribution to an 'adversary culture'.[8] Some think this is due to lack of experience or the very limited experience of writers of the business world. The English novelist David Lodge's book *Nice Work* is one of the few to offer a balanced view of business and society, and to poke fun at the literary distaste for the dirty business world. But the converse is that the students of business have usually ignored broader cultural issues. It is intellectually myopic to isolate business and the study of business from these issues. The study of fiction can provide a way of breaking down barriers between the two. It might also be that work is more like fiction than we think.

Lodge, in the novel I have just referred to, captures very well a major cultural shift in the nature of work. He argues that the new technology of financial transaction has radically altered the nature of work to make it more like fiction than productive labour. Financial dealings are no longer business in the sense of buying and selling real commodities. As Lodge describes it, 'It's all on paper, or computer screens. It's abstract. It has its own rather seductive jargon – arbitrageur, deferred futures, floating rate. It's like literary theory.'[9] Brokers and traders are semi-automatons managing and being managed by information flows. Information is the new currency. Real commodities have lost their importance faced with this new immaterialism. Money isn't really real. As Gordon Gekko says in the film we are about to watch, 'Money isn't lost or made, it's simply transferred from one perception to another. Like magic. I create nothing. I own.'

Literature has long been justified by its proponents, such as Lionel Trilling, as a means of developing critical intelligence, that form of intelligence that can pull out from multifarious and apparently disconnected parts a sense of an overarching whole. In the words of E. M. Forster, 'Only connect.' Ironically, perhaps – tragically, even, for those who try to distance culture from the world of business and, indeed, justify it as business's antithesis: art for art's sake, not mammon's – it is increasingly being recognised that the development of such critical intelligence could be an important managerial skill, a core competence, even.

The notion of management as the negotiation of meaning, as the management of systems of symbols, is becoming increasingly significant. Management is, in Jeffrey Pfeffer's phrase, 'symbolic action'. Environments have become so interconnected, regulated, legislated, complexified that effective managerial action increasingly depends upon the manipulation of various sorts of symbols to make sense of and for the members of an organisation and to motivate its members. This key management skill has been neglected for too long. In Pfeffer's words: 'If management involves the taking of symbolic action, then the skills required are political, dramaturgical, and language skills more than analytical or strictly quantitative skills . . . Language, symbols, settings, stories, ceremonies, and informational social influence to produce socially constructed realities are as much the tools of managers as are economic analysis, finite mathematics, and theories of leadership and organisation design that stress the rational, objective results of managerial action.'[10]

To approach the study of management and organisations in this way is also to take an important step, perhaps a first step, in attempting to locate a theory of managerial action in the context of the changes, the crises, the wars – for example, the culture wars – that have disrupted the cosy structure the human sciences used to enjoy. These transformations reflect a widespread reaction against the assumption that natural science is the correct model for social science methodology. This has led to a rejection of positivist empiricist methodology in some quarters and has led to

the suggestion that the explanation of human behaviour and the explanation of natural events are logically indistinct undertakings, and thus that the positivist contention that all successful explanations must conform to the same deductive model must be fundamentally misconceived. From many different directions the cry has instead gone up for the development of a hermeneutic

approach to the human sciences, an approach that will do justice
to the claim that the explanation of human action must always
include – and perhaps take the form of – an attempt to recover
and interpret the meanings of social actions from the point of
view of the agents performing them.[11]

Let us try and bear some of these issues in mind while looking
at the film. In particular, let us reflect upon the meaning the actors in
the film attribute to their actions and the broader social significance
of their interpretations of self.

[He fiddles with the control panel and the lights of the auditorium dim.]

THE FILM
The film traces the formation of Bud Fox's character, a form of combat
training in the less ethical ways of Wall Street. Bud embodies the
spirit of one form of capitalism, a fervent dedication to his chosen
career, the self-discipline of the worldly monk in pursuit of this
calling, and grand aspirations. In his working environment, the harsh
competitive market of investment, mergers and acquisitions, lever-
aged buyouts, the manipulation of information, knowledge and loyalties, it is the law of the jungle, with everyone out for his or her own
survival. Bud has given himself up to the morals, or lack of them, of
the herd mentality that dominates this world, inhabited as it is by
individuals who are both barbarians in some of their working practices but also the most educated, talented and well-paid professionals
of their generation, the best and the brightest, veritable masters and
mistresses of the universe.

Bud is warned early in the film that 'good things take time', but he
has a different definition of what is 'good' and he is in a hurry, marching,
sprinting to a different drumbeat. He is sick of spending his days cold-
calling clients to try to explain to them the extraordinary opportunities
in the world debt market. He realises the importance of being connected
and courts the most talented dealer of them all, Gordon Gekko, the 'big

game'. Bud wants to be a player in the big game, he wants to get into the 'kill zone', make a killing. His father wanted him to be a doctor or a lawyer but Bud argues that 'there is no nobility in poverty', strangely equating membership of a profession with low rewards, unaware, perhaps, of how much plastic surgeons or top lawyers earn. Anyway, he would have been too impatient to go through the years of training.

Gordon Gekko, Bud's role model and, at first, his hero, had 'an ethical bypass at birth', so what he has to do comes easy to him. He does have a sense of values, however. He is a man with a mission. He justifies his insider dealing as a form of populism. He is, he argues, on the side of the people and the shareholder, battling the corporate dinosaurs and their stifling, self-indulgent and vastly over-expensive managements, who have only their own interests at heart. He justifies his activities in terms of wealth creation and wealth liberation. For Gekko, greed is indeed profoundly good. His counter-argument to the charges of speculation, venality and obscene profits is that he is restoring accountability to badly managed companies and sloughing off the inertia of years of bad management that has cost America dear.

Gekko attacks the time-servers, the bureaucrats with their steak lunches, hunting and fishing trips, corporate jets and golden parachutes. He represents the forces of evolutionary progress, a necessary counter-force to 'the survival of the un-fittest'. He says that he wants to eradicate the conglomerate and to liberate the efficient company lurking within. He casts himself not as a destroyer but as a liberator. His call to arms echoes the real-life words of Ivan Boesky: 'Greed is good.' For Gekko, greed is right, greed works: 'Greed clarifies, cuts through, and captures the essence of the evolutionary spirit . . . Greed will save the malfunctioning corporation of the USA.'

Before he even meets Gekko, Bud has sold his soul to him, seduced by his success and power. Gekko is drawn to Bud by his youth and persistence. In Bud he recognises a similar ambition to that of his own youth and the gnawing fear of failure. Bud makes a pact with Gekko's Mephistopheles. Also, Bud and Gekko develop a sort of father–son relationship, an ideal type almost, 'the best of youth combined with the wisdom of age'. And, as the myths tell us (for the film is replete with mythic echoes), in the end the son betrays the father, saving himself in the process.

Gekko is well versed in the language of modern management and its practices. He woos Bud with words from Sun Tzu's *The Art of War*: 'Every battle is won before it is ever fought.' He also makes it abundantly clear what he wants and what he has recognised in Bud's greed. 'I got twenty other brokers out there analysing charts. I don't need another one. If you're not inside, you're *outside*.' He wants intelligent, driven, smart and hungry individuals with no feelings to do his dirty work. He warns Bud, tempts him, again with images of war: 'It's trench warfare out there . . . Sheep get slaughtered . . . Money never sleeps.' And Bud is ready – prepared, even – when the moment comes and he has to trade on inside information gleaned from his biological father, to let overweening ambition overtake honour. Gekko liberates ambition bereft of moral purpose. Unlike Luke Skywalker, Bud is unable to resist the temptation 'to explore his darker side'.

Bud becomes a pro, he learns quickly, and soon he is adept at searching out the forbidden fruit of knowledge by any possible means. He finds that he is good at it and satisfies Gekko's demands. Fame, fortune, his first yuppie apartment, the girl all inexorably follow. Bud, too, studies Sun Tzu, to impress his master. He embodies the insight that 'all warfare is based on deception'. He liberates friends from their 'golden handcuffs' by making them accomplices in the deals he sets up, convincing them that this is the way to become masters of their own destiny. He becomes 'a yuppie Frankenstein'.

Then he makes a mistake that makes his illegal dealings visible to those who are charged with safeguarding 'the purity of the marketplace', the Securities and Exchange Commission (SEC). He makes a second mistake, trusting Gekko to allow him to manage one of their targeted acquisitions, the company his own father works for. For Bud is not satisfied with the nature of his work, despite its rewards. He aspires not to be a power broker but to be a power player, an entrepreneur, to run a company, to become a Lee Iacocca or a Jack Welch. Now

Gekko betrays him. Like Dr Faustus, Bud discovers that he hasn't even left hell when he finds out about Gekko's restructuring/dismemberment plans for the company he coveted. He realises the tragedy of it all, that he has betrayed friends, violated taboos, even committed a form of patricide – at the very least in contributing to his father's heart attack and perhaps even literally 'breaking' his heart.

He confronts Gekko, asking him 'How much is enough?', arguing that he has given his word to the employees of the airline company of which he is now president. Gekko's reply cuts to his essence: 'It's all about bucks. The rest is conversation . . . It's not a question of enough . . . Money is simply transferred from one perception to another. Like magic. The more real the illusion is the more they want it . . . I create nothing. I own. We make the news. It's the free market . . . You're part of it. You've got the killer instinct.' He could have added that it is also about the thrill of the chase, the excitement of the hunt and the climax of the kill.

But Bud has changed, or has rediscovered thoughts and values he had lost touch with. He conspires again, but this time in the right cause, to entrap Gekko and prove his wrongdoing. Gekko, he now realises, was only a projection of his own dark desires. Suffering and the lessons he has learnt from his real father combine to give Bud the beginnings of wisdom and maturity. He sabotages Gekko's deal, even though it proves his own guilt and leads to his own arrest. Bud is wearing a wiretap so that Gekko too is implicated and arrested. He and Gekko fight. Betrayed, Gekko accuses him: 'I showed you how the system works. I gave you everything. You could have been one of the great ones. I look at you and see myself.' Bud replies: 'I guess I realise I'm just Bud Fox as much as I wanted to be Gordon Gekko.'

A colleague has counselled Bud just before his arrest: 'Man looks in the abyss. There is nothing staring back at him. At that moment man finds his character. And that is what keeps him out of the abyss.' Bud has found himself on the edge. If he had accepted the golden parachute that Gordon offered him to go through with the last deal there would have been no way back. His father congratulates him: 'You did the right thing. You told the truth and gave the money back. You helped save the airline.' A happy ending of sorts! Bud has negotiated his dark rite of passage. He returns to the bosom of his family, who support him in his court case. It is his father's wisdom that triumphs. Punishment is the price of atonement. The price of going to jail is worth it. About to enter the cage – prison (the film ends on the steps of the courthouse) – he is liberated from the cage of his slavery to Gekko and all he stands for.

His father's words sum up the business moral: 'It's going to be rough on you, but maybe, in some screwed-up way, that's the best thing that can happen to you. Stop going for the easy buck and go *produce* something with your life, *create* rather than living off the buying and selling of others.'

INTERPRETATION

Professor *[as the lights go up]*: Well, what is the film saying? Is it correct? Does the film capture the essentials of contemporary capitalism? Does it confront the key issues? Does *Wall Street* present an image of work and organisations that we need to think about, worry about? *[Pause.]* Are these the right questions? *[Pause.]* Let's assume that they are. We can raise other issues later. Let's address the question of 'essentials'.

Let me quote Weber again, one of the leading theorists of capitalism, who identifies the principal features of the spirit of capitalism as follows: 'The earning of more and more money, combined with the strict avoidance of all spontaneous enjoyment . . ., is thought of so purely as an end in itself that vis-à-vis the happiness of, or utility to, the particular individual it appears as quite transcendental and wholly irrational. Man is dominated by acquisition as the purpose of his life; acquisition is no longer a means to the end of satisfying his material needs. This reversal of what we might call the "natural" situation, completely senseless from an unprejudiced standpoint, is evidently as definitely a leading principle of capitalism as it is foreign to all peoples not under capitalistic influence.'[12]

[Long pause.] Do these conditions still apply and does *Wall Street* reflect them? What kind of cage have we trapped ourselves in? *[Pause.]* Obviously, the asceticism has gone out of the window and it is also about conspicuous consumption and hedonism, the yuppie lifestyle.

Moralist: I think, at one level, it's pretty accurate. And pretty critical, obviously a radical critique of the system. A bit one-dimensional, perhaps, too black and white. And the ending is too optimistic, isn't it, too simplistic?

Professor: Justifiably so?

Beancounter: Well, let me start the ball rolling. You know what I'm going to say. *[Laughter.]* Okay, obviously that kind of thing goes on, but it's a very partial picture of a system that has been phenomenally successful. Look at the quality of life that capitalism has made possible. The financial system is just one part of that system. Obviously it's the most important part, it keeps lean and fit *[Laughter.]*, but to see Bud and Gekko as representative is way out of line. Most people don't act that way. Finance people are mostly men, and women, of honour.

Sociologist: Like the Mafia. *[Laughter.]*

Beancounter: Well, I'm from Chicago, and while we may be most famous for our gangsters *[Laughter.]* there's a lot more to us than that . . . Like Chicago economics, the business of business is business, the business of business is to look after the interests of those who own the business, property rights, the rule of law and all that stuff. Anyway, I just make sure the figures add up.

Moralist: Isn't the film trying to suggest that Bud and Gekko – or, more accurately, Gekko perhaps – might not be truly representative, in the sense that everybody doesn't act like they do, but it is representative in that they represent the system in an ideal-type sort of way. The underlying dynamics of the system do foster, or at least facilitate, this kind of extreme behaviour. Its seed lies in the everyday dynamics of this kind of work and organisation. That's what I meant when I said it was radical.

Sociologist: The film is not radical enough. It isn't really a radical critique of the system. I agree with the criticism that it is, essentially, a conservative apologia. Its resolution is facile. It suggests that everything will be okay if you repent and your family forgives you. The film does not seriously examine the systemic roots of the corrupt behaviour it depicts. It explains this in terms of individual psychological problems, Freudian Oedipal tensions concerning fathers, sons and father figures, and individual ambition. It harks back to the old American myths. It fails to seriously interrogate the inner market structures that produce unethical commodity trading and which fuel the desire for money and fame. It doesn't examine the ethical contradictions that lie at the heart of late market capitalism, the real destructive forces of a world economy gone wild and out of control. The film does not try to get to the real heart of the matter, how the broader social-historical moment itself created the conditions for Bud's fall.

Beancounter: But are gangsters the product of the system or aberrations, exceptions who justify the rules?

Sociologist: Which the lawyers help them get around.

Biologist: The biologists argue that it's all about our genes. After all this time the survival of the fittest means that the most selfish gene survives. Should we be surprised at how people act? I'm not. This is just another example, in a particular context, of social Darwinism.

Sociologist: Yes, but it is context-, so socially, specific. Remember the gangster, as we see in another film, *The Godfather*, was socially respected? In a harsh environment he created the rules for his clan and was, despite the violence, also a source of order and justice, of a sort. The gangster was also, and remains, a fantasy figure in deprived communities where crime often looks like the only possible source of rapid social mobility. And if you didn't want to be a gangster, in some ways you might have needed them. 'The clannish loyalties that held sway in gangland represented guarantees of community protection against the rapacious business elite.'[13] Gangster protectionism was a medium of parallel government in the absence or the corrupt semi-presence of official institutions.

Professor: Perhaps we should look for other forms of benign collective activity – Chicago jazz or blues musicians? Interesting that the market can be so naturally compared with gangster behaviour or the law of the jungle, red in tooth and claw. Of course, some biologists have a more positive view, more altruistic. Perhaps we need better, or, at least, different, metaphors. My own view is that we need to cultivate a view of the world, and of business, which is more than a permanent battle for survival, and war, competition and violence are the norm. We need to think more about system interactions and mutual dependencies. In the end Gekko goes down. The SEC catches up with him.

Beancounter: Eventually. And he was too greedy. He went too far. That's why I'm doing the MBA, to learn how the system works, to see how far you can stretch it, to make sure I don't get caught. *[Some laughter.]*

Historian: But we can be optimistic, can't we? There are enough examples of altruism. Okay, there's corruption, but the worse excesses are being dealt with. The system has the will and the power to police itself, clean up its act and heal itself. I think the film is starting to look dated. It's very mid-eighties, Ronald-Reaganish. It's history, no longer contemporary, a trip back into the dark ages of Reaganomics.

Moralist: And then you had the roaring nineties, Enron, WorldCom, etc., etc.

Historian: Yes, but we are getting better. We learn from the excesses. Now, when companies return supernormal profits, the question is not how to imitate them but: what are they doing wrong? At least, it is sometimes.

Moralist: But the norm is still to aspire to the supernormal, whatever 'normal' is. We do top MBAs because we want to join the business elite, we want to be players, we want to be masters, and mistresses, of the universe.

Sociologist: We say that people are our most important resource while in the same breath we do deals to offshore their jobs on cost grounds. We say that the customer is king but we're judged by the market in terms of how we outcompete others on profit grounds. We build companies, thinking about initial public offerings, and acquire companies to liberate value for senior management. We're all involved in a war against everyone. What I also like about the film is that it captures a historical moment. It's a film about a country where manufacture, making things, is a thing of the past, dominated by a service economy, an economy in the service of intangible figures. The money men dominate, not the manufacturers; the financial engineers, not the real engineers. It's a film about the recent past and the present and the future, unless we change course.

Historian: Some argue that history is dead, in terms of the clash of competing systems, and that there is, for better or worse, only the capitalist system. Look at the fate of the centrally planned economies – chaos, anarchy. It's the end of history.

Moralist: If there's no history can there be any progress? Have people become more ethical? Or just more scared?

Sociologist: Let's get real, people. We all know what happens in business. We're not all saints. George W. Bush is the first American president with an MBA from Harvard. This is what a former Harvard tutor wrote in an article 'Hail to the robber baron': 'Bush belonged to a minority of MBA students who were seriously disconnected from taking moral and social responsibility for their actions. Today, he would fit in comfortably with an overwhelming majority of business students and teachers whose role models are celebrated captains of piracy. Since the 1980s . . . business education has . . . increasingly become contaminated by the robber baron culture of the pre-Great Depression era . . . American economics study has increasingly become a pseudoscience of mathematical formula manipulation that is devoid of humanity. This economics has conquered America's business education and become fused with the robber baron culture of greed supremacy. American MBAs are taught to treat ordinary employees as disposable costs and to swallow uncritically the gospel that corporations exist only to reward abstract stockholders.'[14] Heavy stuff!

Beancounter: Look at the proliferation of courses in business ethics. They're big business now.

Historian: And, even if people remain the same, the system is far more sophisticated in terms of self-regulation. The system cannot function if there are too many Gekkos.

Immoralist: But Gekko serves a function too. He was essentially right in his core premise. Conglomeration is wrong in the sense that it does not work to make the system more efficient. Look at the evidence on unrelated diversification. Look at Michael Porter's arguments. Look at the case studies we have looked at. Think General Mills, CBS. Many companies need the kick in the pants that a takeover brings. They need new structure and management to survive in such a hostile competitive environment. You've got to adjust to survive.

Historian: Yes, but to go back to the point about capturing the zeitgeist, the values underpinning the story are essentially outmoded, they no longer work. They hark back to a golden age which probably never existed anyway, when people created instead of living off the buying and selling of others. It's pure outdated ideology. It harks back to a time when things were real, had real value, and when real things reflected the real values of hard-working individuals. It's the old American dream. That time is gone, if it ever existed in the first place. The Buds of today wouldn't go back.

Professor: So it's farewell the Prodigal Son? *[Pause.]*

Moralist: In the film everything is illusory. Money is information rather than commodity. All is illusory except the old-fashioned values. I don't think they're irrelevant. Even today we have the reactions against the big corporates and their power. Look at the open source software movement. Linux provides an alternative to Microsoft. Members of the community have a totally different motivation. They volunteer their knowledge for the good of creating through voluntary collaborations. We should think hacker, not gangster. Hackers built the internet. You create a bazaar of equal exchange to build a cathedral that is constantly evolving, just like when all those people coalesced on the plains of France and built Chartres. Now they come together in cyberspace. At least, the internet makes travel easier and you can sleep in your own bed. And it's not pure altruism, because the developers are doing something they enjoy more than almost everything. They volunteer their labour and understanding.

Professor: So, Linux and open source possibly provide us with a different model of organisation: organic, voluntaristic, disciplined not by management control but by excitement, a community of intrinsic interest. Richard Stallman and Linus Torvalds, the driving forces behind the movement, gave away what they owned, their knowledge, their code, for free. They built a new form of competition to the incumbent giants, Microsoft and the rest, an entity that can't be bought, can't be controlled or coerced or manipulated because it has a different value system. It stands outside the ecology of the traditional roots of corporate power. And, heresy of heresies, it's a free good, available to all. *[Pause.]* This is the real da Vinci code, perhaps?

Historian: This is a bit one-sided. *[Making an expansive gesture to include the rest of the class, the majority, who have not, so far, spoken.]* I want to speak for the silent majority here. Capitalist values have always been contradictory. Indeed, unless you're a fanatic and go for a quick value fix that you cling to come what may, there's always going to be at least some ambivalence about value choices. That's normal. Look at the consumer revolution. It brought amazing opportunities and previously unimaginable choice, but it also brought guilt. We feel guilt about our craving for more consumer goods. We feel anxious when we compare ourselves with others, anxious if we've got more, anxious and envious if they've got more. And we feel resentful because we take it all so seriously, realise it isn't but can't stop ourselves anyway. We continue to judge our success in life through the objects we do consume and aspire to consume. We all should go into marketing. That's where the real power lies.

Psychologist: But not everybody falls in the way Bud does. The majority – the moral majority – do their work according to the law. It is down to individual psychology, not the system. The film is surely essentially right in its optimistic ending: that the system is essentially sound, it is not in deep trouble – these are teething pains as we come to terms with new forms of work, new forms of technology, amazing new opportunities. There are people out there like Carl Fox, his father, like the SEC, who will police the system and bring wayward yuppies into line. The system is not in itself corrupt. Gekko is essentially an outsider. It is precisely his profound sense of being an outsider – of being beyond the social pale – that drives him to his excesses. He couldn't make it by legitimate means. At least, not to the level that he is driven to try to achieve.

Ecologist: Adaptation or apocalypse, isn't that the choice? The glass is half empty or it's half full. Unfortunately, I think, I believe that those who think it's half full are deluded. They don't want to change anything. I'm from southern California. Business has driven out any sense of a responsible land ethic. We fill our wildfire corridors up with expensive real estate, we turn our wetlands into marinas and the flood plains into industrial and urban districts. We construct high-density housing on earthquake fault lines.

Historian: Just what I said. You're optimists. Optimism leaves casualties in its wake, but what's the alternative?

Ecologist: It also leads to inaction and then it's too late. We're at the leading edge of apocalypse, all the horsemen have been released – floods, fire, earthquake, all avoidable with a little foresight and self-restraint, a little less greed. If they don't get us then it will be a volcano or the nukes or the jogger-eating mountain lions out in the canyons, swarms of killer bees or alien death machines.

Moralist: But don't money and power always corrupt? You can't be just a bit pregnant.

Realist: Are you arguing that having *any* money or *any* power makes one corrupt? One becomes more pregnant, relatively, as the pregnancy progresses.

Professor: I think it was someone called Bishop Wilson who argued, according to Matthew Arnold in *Culture and Anarchy*, that 'riches are almost always abused without a very extraordinary grace'. Arnold, who wanted to be on the side of the angels, agreed in his critique of the philistine rich.

Ecologist: Where does grace come from? We need new myths that demonstrate our need for connectedness with nature. We need new narratives to give us a sense of meaning, green narratives.

Materialist: Next you'll be telling us we need angels and asking us to fall to our knees and pray.

Immaterialist: We need to realise that science and the spirit are not two separate domains. We need a sense of the sacred. We need to cultivate a sense of the possibility of personal wholeness and social cohesion. From where else can we draw hope? It goes deeper than economics or aesthetics or enjoying consumption. We need to find things and activities that we can really celebrate.

Moralist: Bud's father thinks that 'money's one giant pain in the ass'.

Philosopher: But, as Gekko says (wasn't it in connection with his art collection but it applies to the whole thing?): 'The illusion has become real, and the more real it becomes the more desperately they want it.'

Immaterialist: He wants to own the art for ownership's sake, not for its intrinsic value as art.

Psychologist: You've got to be charitable. Gekko too is a victim, trapped, joyless, in a life devoid of intimacies, existing only, feeling only for his work, his greed. He sees survival only in terms of manipulation of everyone around him as short-term responses to need and greed. He has become a cerebral gymnast in some sort of virtual reality, oblivious to his surroundings, aware only of the endless flow of financial facts and figures on the computer screen and the endless possibilities of creative financing. Everybody is a victim. The unrelenting representative of good, Bud's real father, has a heart attack. Gekko does have his good side, though he might see it as a blind spot. He does feel for Bud. He's not just a lizard.

Philosopher: Yes, but it is only to manipulate him, to corrupt him. Nothing is real to him. Everything is only a simulacrum. Even Bud. Bud is important to him only as a simulacrum of his lost youth whom he has to corrupt to prove again that the path he took was inevitable. He feels for Bud when Bud feels for him, supports his corruption. When Bud rebels we realise how shallow his feelings are, and how conditional. Bud's family stand by him even though he violates all the virtues that they stand for – hard work, honesty, a concern for the working man. Gekko has allowed himself to be swallowed by the system. He has become, in the phrase you quoted from Weber, 'dominated by acquisition'. He has no real material needs. He exists for an illusion, an empty sign. In that sense he embodies a leading principle of the capitalist system. Of course, he's a victim too, in his own way, although he's a willing victim who benefits from his sins.

Sociologist: The signs are important. They are crucial, for example, in situating yourself, in gaining status, in a system where they do constitute the ultimate reality. *[Pause.]*

Professor: It used to be said, incidentally, that the film industry was the one area where art and commerce went hand in hand. Then, in the 1980s, MBAs gained control and art walked out. *[Nervous laughter.]* I think it was Reg Revans, the pioneer of action learning, who said that MBA stood for 'moral bankruptcy assured'.

Beancounter: But the bottom line is important. Surely art only serves to embroider the essentials. It is not in itself essential. It fulfils a higher need. Survival is basic.

Moralist: The philistine speaks. The bottom line isn't the ultimate reality – is it? There's a choice between culture and anarchy. Surely the film invites you to make a crucial value judgement? Was Bud right or wrong? Does the way his dreams were punctured justify his actions? Is his only mistake to have been careless and to get caught? Or is there a better, more ethical way of life? *[Pause.]* 'Where is the life we have lost in living?' Who said that? Art and its values highlight the emptiness of materialism.

Aspiring novelist: It's important to situate this in a broader cultural perspective. Novels help us do this. I've just been reading Scott Fitzgerald's novel *The Great Gatsby*. Gekko is a Gatsby for the 1980s. He even uses Gatsby's term of address, 'sport'. Both Gatsby and Gekko are corrupted by the world they aspire to, the world of the rich. Gekko is more corrupted by a more corrupt world. It is the careless rich who destroy Gatsby and it is the careless rich who make Gekko what he is. He needs to be what he is to climb the social ladder, to rise to the level of the rich and beyond, to gain control of his destiny. Both Gatsby and Gekko are moral innocents. Fitzgerald sees Gatsby as quintessential innocent America, not yet disillusioned, with a dream greater than himself. He carries this dream to his grave. Indeed, it is the dream that kills him – or, rather, the foul dust that 'floated in the wake of his dreams'.

Gatsby was the 1920s. In the 1980s the illusion is shattered, unreality is real, B-movie actors become presidents, dreams have become material. Gekko uses his energy, his will, to pursue power. He takes the rich on at their own game, the only game in town. It is a kind of sport to him, the term used by Weber in your opening quote, a gladiatorial contest. *[Pause.]* The analogy with *Gatsby* doesn't stop with the parallel between Gatsby himself and Gekko. Bud is like Nick Carraway, the narrator of Gatsby. Like Nick, he comes out of his experience of the world of the rich chastened. Having learnt about the nature of the system, like Nick he retreats into a form of moral vigilance. Both of them retreat from the centre of power. There is no way Bud wants to return to Wall Street. Carraway goes back to the Midwest, Fitzgerald's 'real' America. They're both damaged. They both leave the centre of power to find a separate peace. They give up on the spirit of capitalism – or its ghost. They don't finally challenge the core values of the system head-on. Neither the novel nor the film suggests a viable alternative, except for disengagement. *[Pause.]* There are also interesting parallels with Huckleberry Finn and his rejection of civilisation. His father even calls Bud 'Huckleberry'.

Moralist: Are you saying that these comparisons actually demonstrate a general decline in moral standards between the 1920s and the 1980s? Has it all been downhill? Surely not. Surely there is a moral progression, moral development, on Bud's part. At the beginning of his relationship with Gekko – the scene in the restaurant – he starts out scared not of doing something unethical but of losing his trading licence for doing something illegal. By the end he learns what is 'right'. His father congratulates him for doing right. He learns that the system is 'wrong' in at least one of its trends. It seems likely that when he gets out of prison he will work to produce things and not live off the buying and selling of others. Hopefully, we are more convinced of the immorality of insider trading after the excesses of the 1980s, we're not just scared of being caught.

Immoralist: But there's a heavy irony in Bud's supposed awakening. Just how profound is it? Bud behaves unethically in his manipulation of the airline's stock price using insider information to get Gekko. Is that ethical? Gekko, to his credit, is neither moral or immoral. He's amoral. He exemplifies a life, in Weber's phrase, stripped of religious and ethical meaning. But isn't what he does 'good' in making corporations more efficient, even if this does mean dismantling them? If we want an efficient system that uses scarce resources most effectively, surely we need Gekkos? His shortcomings are a small price to pay. *[Pause.]*

Professor: Karl Marx claimed that Robinson Crusoe is the representative capitalist myth. Do we need a new myth for our times, one closer to *Wall Street*? *[Pause.]* Let's go over some of the issues raised. Let's think about them as questions for further exploration. Essentialism and representativeness – what is a representative image of work for today? What is the film saying about Wall Street? Is it a radical critique or is it more problematic than that? Is it ironic, perhaps? Is Carl Fox, the father, the value centre for the director, Oliver Stone, or is Bud's retreat back to his origins only a sign of weakness, a failure to confront the real sources of power? Do we only live in a world of signs? Are signs the true reality not things? Have we lost the world of labour and honest exchange for ever? Are we all, at heart, Bud Foxes, to a greater or lesser degree?

How do we educate people to be good, to be critical of the system, to work to change it rather than uncritically accepting that there is no alternative? What is the role of those people who have the power – senior managers, for example? Is the system responsible for its excesses, does it programme people to act irresponsibly at the expense of others, or is it the fault of guilty individuals? Is there an alternative? Are we all, more or less, willing conspirators in a system dominated by acquisition? Is it too early to draw any firm conclusions? Is the jury still out? Does the film only reinforce the system? Is this what it really wanted to do?

[Long pause.]

Professor: We live in a world of marketisation. Shakespeare and Einstein are just products, like everything else. Education is, or should be, or used to be, about 'culture', the opposite of which is 'anarchy'. Look at Matthew Arnold on this and Trilling on the liberal imagination and conscience. Arnold argued that we needed education, a liberal arts education, to alert us to the possibilities of culture and civilisation and also to alert us to the dangers of anarchy. Without education we just *live* anarchy. Materialism triumphs. The philistines and the barbarians, ever present at the gate, take over.

Arnold defines culture as the great help out of our present difficulties, 'a pursuit of our total perfection by means of getting to know, on all the matters which most concern us, the best which has been thought and said in the world; and, through this knowledge, turning a stream of fresh and free thought upon our stock notions and habits, which we now follow staunchly but mechanically, vainly imagining that there is a virtue in following them staunchly which makes up for the mischief of following them mechanically . . . Culture, which is the study of perfection, leads us . . . to conceive of true human perfection as *harmonious* perfection, developing all sides of our humanity; and as a *general* perfection, developing all parts of our society'[15] – and the emphasis is in the original.

Bud shifts his position, from following mechanically to willing himself to move in another direction. And he is not alone *[Pause.]* nor is he uneducated. The predators of the 1980s included the best of their classes, the best educated, the most promising. But in what sense can you say they were educated at all, in the sense that Arnold or others talk about, if they never connect to a deeper culture? And to what extent is their shallowness, their philistinism (though Gekko collects works of art), their barbarism a result of deficiencies in their education? To what extent is it the educators' fault? *[Pause.]* Arnold criticises Puritans, champions of the original Protestant ethic, for having developed only one part of their humanity at the expense of all others. As a result, he argues, they become 'incomplete and mutilated' men. *[Pause.]*

The great Irish poet W. B. Yeats wrote that 'the best lack all conviction, the worst are filled with passionate intensity'. Can we conclude that the worst, perhaps, are most intense about the pursuit of wealth? Arnold judged that 90 per cent of Englishmen in his day believed that greatness and welfare are proved by being very rich. In the United States today he would no doubt conclude that the percentage is even greater. De Tocqueville argued that Americans are afraid of culture, afraid to exercise intellect. *[Pause.]*

But one does need to qualify Arnold. Wealth is not just an end sufficient unto itself. It is a means to an end. It provides an alternative to the precarious and often terrifying world that I mentioned earlier. By focusing on the pursuit of wealth to the exclusion of almost everything else, people avoid coming to terms with – by avoiding, by substitution, by transference – the precariousness and the terror of life. They remain uncivilised. Or, more fairly, they find nothing else in society – social relationships, family, education, work – to provide them with anything powerful enough, big enough, to fill the void, to socialise and civilise them. They latch onto the pursuit of wealth to fill this void. Only money constructs a reality for them. They are educated in the price of everything and the value of nothing.

Perhaps that is as good a place as any to finish. Thank you. See you next week.

[The class starts to disperse. The professor and the students collect their papers and head for the door. As they leave, three international students, two Chinese, one Indian, compare notes.]

Student 1: They are strange, these Westerners.

Student 2: Yes, very strange. What are they – how do they say it? – angst-ing about?

Student 3: Your English is getting very good.

Student 2: Yes, I'm learning.

Student 1: We will clearly win and they will lose.

Student 2: Yes, all this is just flotsam and jetsam. We take what we need, Black and Scholes, Michael Porter; we understand how they think, how they compete, what are their weaknesses, their vulnerabilities.

Student 1: Their lack of sense of purpose.

Student 2: We know what we are doing, helping to build a more assured, more powerful and wealthier society, more in control of its destiny.

Student 1: Yes, the investment has been very much worth it.

Student 2: They have greed but no hope.

Student 1: Yes, we will win and they will lose.

Student 3: We had better hurry or we will miss the next lesson.

NOTES

1 *Wall Street* was written by Stanley Weiser and Oliver Stone, directed by Oliver Stone and released by Twentieth Century Fox in 1987. The book of the film is Kenneth Lipper, *Wall Street* (New York: Berkley, 1987).

2 This chapter is a development of Ken Starkey, 'Eleven characters in search of an ethic, or the spirit of capitalism revisited', *Cultures, Organizations and Societies*, 5(1) (1999), 179–94.

3 Max Weber, *The Protestant Ethic and the Spirit of Capitalism* (London: Unwin University Books, 1930), 182.

4 Theo Nichols and Huw Beynon, *Living with Capitalism* (London: Routledge, Kegan and Paul, 1977), viii.

5 Shoshana Zuboff, *In the Age of the Smart Machine* (Oxford: Heinemann, 1988).

6 Robert Coles, 'Teaching ethics at Harvard Business School', *Dialogue*, 2 (1988), 59, 63.

7 Benjamin DeMott, 'Reading fiction to the bottom line', *Harvard Business Review* (May/June 1989), 128–34.

8 Lionel Trilling, *The Liberal Imagination* (London: Mercury Books, 1961).

9 David Lodge, *Nice Work* (London: Secker and Warburg, 1988), 153.

10 Jeffrey Pfeffer, 'Management as symbolic action: the creation and maintenance of organizational paradigms', *Research in Organizational Behavior*, 3 (1981), 44–6.

11 Quentin Skinner, 'Introduction: the return of Grand Theory', in Quentin Skinner (ed.), *The Return of Grand Theory in the Human Sciences* (Cambridge: Cambridge University Press, 1985), 6.

12 Weber, *The Protestant Ethic*, 53.

13 Andrew Ross, *The Chicago Gangster Theory of Life* (London: Verso, 1996), 255.

14 Yoshi Tsurumi, 'Hail to the robber baron', *Harvard Crimson*, 6 April 2005.

15 Matthew Arnold, *Culture and Anarchy* (Cambridge: Cambridge University Press, 1966), 6–7.

8   Business school futures: mission impossible?

In 1907 Charles W. Eliot, president of Harvard University, addressed the institution's general education board in an attempt to obtain funds for establishing a business school, arguing that such a school 'would soon demonstrate a great capacity for public usefulness'.[1] Others warmed to this theme, and justified the case for the new initiative in terms of 'public service and business'.[2] The rest is history. Today, Harvard Business School is a very prestigious part of what most consider the world's leading university, and regularly tops the league tables. It espouses a trifold mission: to train able men and women to become competent and responsible general managers; to prepare doctoral students for careers in teaching and research or in academic administration; and to contribute to the body of knowledge about management and business through leading-edge research.

Eliot is credited with the modernisation of Harvard during his four decades in office,[3] and the creation of the business school was an important component of this process. Whether the Harvard school or, indeed, any other has fulfilled Eliot's ambition concerning 'public usefulness' is still very much open to question, however. Our previous chapters have demonstrated that – as the critics suggest – the business school business is by no means all sweetness and light. In particular, we have shown that

- business schools are currently experiencing extreme institutional pressures (with hyper-competition an unwelcome and unforgiving fact);
- business school teaching is, to some extent, flawed, ossified around a limited and somewhat partisan model of capitalism;

- business school research is, in the main, of doubtful quality and relevance; and
- though a few business schools are experimenting with different models of teaching and research, it is unclear either whether genuine and lasting innovations are taking shape or, in any event, how far the system as a whole is equipped for change.

In short, strong doubts remain about the schools' viability, their intellectual standing, the qualities of their students and their contribution to society.

In this context we now consider the future, and examine in detail how business schools might traverse the next few decades. We outline some likely scenarios, and then go on to begin to explore our favoured alternative: a set of arrangements that we feel will regenerate the schools and give them an enhanced sense of purpose, to everyone's benefit. Before we embark on this discussion, however, we need to look at some context, and especially two unfolding developments that we feel inevitably shape the possibilities.[4]

THE CHANGING UNIVERSITY

To begin with, it is important to say something about the way that higher education as a whole is changing. This inevitably means starting with some history. The modern idea of the university emerged at the turn of the eighteenth century and owed much to the Prussian statesman and philosopher Wilhelm von Humboldt. He believed that the university should concentrate on knowledge production, and made the grand claim that it held primary responsibility for the cultural, and even spiritual, leadership of society, together with the provision of professional elites for the nation state. In Humboldt's thinking, the university had to be granted the status of an autonomous actor, robustly cushioned from outside interference. It was to engage solely in philosophical reflection, using research and teaching to achieve its broader goals. The key point was that the university's knowledge work should remain absolutely free from subservience to practical utility.[5]

Humboldt's ideas set the tone for much subsequent Western thinking about the university and its character. In the twentieth century Clark Kerr's classic study coined the term 'multiversity'[6] to reflect the increasing demands that were being made of many institutions, but, even as the range of its activities grew, the modern university's underlying rationale remained rooted in its sense of its own importance and authority as a unique knowledge site. As long as the university performed its 'fiduciary' functions – *inter alia*, professional training, general education and cultural development – then its mandate to define the bases for claims to knowledge, and, therefore, the legitimacy of its research practice, was largely unchallenged.[7] Its identity continued to be distinctively tied up with the validation of enquiry and learning as precious for their own sake, rather than for merely technocratic or instrumental reasons.

Even as the university sought to entrench itself as a privileged knowledge site, however, fault lines began to open up, primarily in the tension between the ideals of research and the professional training increasingly desired by students and society. In time, the pressure began to tell. Leading university administrators and academics might repeat their traditional mantras about the life of the spirit, the life of the mind, and knowledge as some form of transcendence, vital to the health of humanity and society, but they found themselves increasingly outflanked as competing discourses grew in volume. Policymakers and consumers had their own agendas, based upon more worldly considerations. The focus became ever more concerned with pay-offs. Governments demanded solutions to pressing social and economic problems. Students wanted credentials that would enhance their subsequent careers, and thus ultimately boost their living standards. In this sense, then, the university gradually became enmeshed in the rationalisation of modern life, subject to critical analysis and increasingly viewed through the lenses of measured performance and accountability. Today, therefore, the university often has to justify itself in terms of what it does for society as a whole, effectively bowing to the market's estimation of knowledge.

The French philosopher Jean-François Lyotard argued that the essence of this historic shift can be understood in the following terms:

> The relationship of the suppliers and users of knowledge to the knowledge they supply and use is now tending, and will increasingly tend, to assume the form already taken by the relationship of commodity producers and consumers to the commodities they produce and consume – that is, the form of value. Knowledge is and will be produced in order to be sold, it is and will be consumed in order to be valorized in new production: in both cases, the goal is exchange. Knowledge ceases to be an end in itself.[8]

Under the new regime, the key indicator tends to be the ratio of inputs to outputs, the goal to maximise return. Research teams, for example, routinely have to justify themselves according to how they will contribute to economic growth, and if they cannot do this they risk tapered funding, isolation and eventual 'termination'. The calculation of impact defines relevance and vice versa. The mission of higher education is less and less to do with the philosophical question 'Is it true?', and more and more to do with the practical market-led questions 'What use is it?' and 'Is it saleable?'. The life of the spirit or the emancipation of humanity might be indirectly boosted by such an approach but nowadays few academics articulate their claims for support and funding solely in these terms.

Of course, assessments as to quite how far these trends have developed inevitably tend to differ. In 1996 Bill Readings, an associate professor of comparative literature in Canada, described the university as a '*ruined* institution, one that has lost its historical *raison d'être*' (emphasis in original). Henceforth, he suggested, 'the question of the University is only the question of relative value-for-money, the question posed to a student who is situated entirely as a *consumer*, rather than as someone who wants to think' (emphasis in original).[9] Lyotard, too, believed that the university has been severely compromised. Perhaps such views are over-pessimistic, exaggerations to warn or gain effect. But there is no doubt which way the wind is blowing. Earlier we cited Kirp's assessment of the situation in the United States. We also note a recent study by academics at Bristol University, based upon interviews with more than 150 senior academics and administrators at sixteen institutions, which found that a 'new managerialism' imported from the private sector was emerging as 'the dominant force in British higher education', and that, in the process, traditional approaches to research and teaching were being steadily superseded.[10]

THE NEW PRODUCTION OF KNOWLEDGE

The second change that we need to take account of is in the mechanics of knowledge production in society as a whole.[11] In the past, those who assumed the mantle of 'experts' tended to rule the roost. When they spoke, people listened. Quite clearly, the university generally had a position of pre-eminence here. It gathered together great thinkers and pioneering scientists, whose authority was rarely questioned. More recently, however, this situation has begun to mutate. With the rise of the 'knowledge economy', all sorts of business players have become progressively more restless, not least with long-standing disciplinary boundaries and academic niceties, and as a consequence they are creating new centres of excellence and alliances of their own. The same is true of governments in most leading economies. Meanwhile, ordinary citizens are also becoming a bigger and bigger part of the equation. There is a growing sense that modern life is subject to ever more worrying risks – from nuclear accidents and environmental despoilation, to new forms of disease and everyday hazard.[12] Events such as Three Mile Island, the pollution catastrophe at Bhopal (with its hundreds of thousands of victims) and the British BSE farrago are taken to be indicative. The result is a decline of trust in science and scientists, vigorous demands for accountability and the rise of a new kind of popular activism – concerned centrally with forging fresh insights into just what is going on and then producing practical solutions. The bottom line is that knowledge itself is increasingly becoming 'contextualised' – that is, removed from purely intellectual or academic receptacles, and placed within much broader social bounds.

The recent development of environmental science provides an interesting example of how these trends are working out on the ground. The widely shared perception that the world is facing a mounting series of major environmental threats has triggered a novel response. Scientists from traditional subject areas have come together, and reached outside the academy, to create a knowledge – together with a way of knowing – in which debate about the key issues can take place in a more inclusive and effective manner. As time has passed, more and more organisations and individuals have become involved – from politicians, company and industry representatives, and non-governmental agencies to virtual activist networks and citizens' pressure groups, as well as the media and a range of public commentators. The point is that the fulcrum of discussion has moved away from a conversation between accredited experts behind closed doors, and that, in this process, the way in which knowledge is conceived has inevitably developed and changed.

Accurately conceptualising these transformations is far from easy, because they are obviously quite protean and complicated, but the social scientist Michael Gibbons and his colleagues have suggested that they can best be imagined in terms of a shift from what they call Mode One to Mode Two knowledge production. Mode One is the traditional approach, which is discipline-based – in other words, clearly structured into a well-defined array of separate, largely isolated, compartments. By contrast, Mode Two takes place in an almost endless space, where disciplines are transcended, and where nothing stands still. Mode One exists in a context largely governed by the interests of an essentially academic-dominated community. Mode Two is carried out in the context of application. There are also important differences in organisation. Mode One is resolutely hierarchical in its definition of expertise and relevance, and resistant to change, while Mode Two is more heterarchical, open and liable to ongoing metamorphosis. Finally, as regards quality control, Mode One refers back to the authority of academic tradition, essentially the established canon, but Mode Two is more socially accountable and reflexive, given to self-questioning, less sure of its assumptions, and embracing a comparatively fluid and varied set of practitioners.[13]

FUTURE SCENARIOS: GOING WITH THE FLOW

What does all this mean for the future of the business school? Our argument, in a nutshell, is that the context we have outlined in the previous pages presages great dangers for the schools but also great opportunities. To explain what we mean by this, we need to look in detail at some possible scenarios about how the sector may develop in the next few years.

To begin with, we consider a range of possibilities in which the schools simply go with the flow – that is, essentially, carry on with the way that both they and higher education as a whole are currently evolving. As we have shown, the key watchwords nowadays are competition and economic value. If the schools continue to accept this logic, they will inevitably place great emphasis on safeguarding their own position, either by the traditional route of increasing income and reducing costs or by developing some kind of fresh orientation to the market. No doubt such strategies will win immediate applause from many university administrators and politicians, since the former always naturally welcome cash cows, and the latter inevitably dislike subsidies. In our view, however, going down this road will in fact be neither as simple nor as ultimately rewarding as it might at first sight appear.

Let us begin by assuming that business schools simply continue operating exactly as they are. We can immediately see that there are several major clouds on the horizon. First, it is becoming evident that demand for the MBA in much of the world will probably soon peak. Indeed, some of the deans whom we talked with suggested that this was already happening. The basic fact is that the saturation point is in sight. Rapidly expanding economies such as China and India may keep the ball rolling in the coming years, but even their requirements have limits. The big question, therefore, is what the schools will do next. As we noted in chapter 3, some have already reacted by promoting new kinds of degree – for example, a growing range of MScs. But it is difficult to envisage that anything they attempt will really generate adequate replacement income flows. The MBA was a killer product in its day, the kind that comes along only very rarely, and as a consequence supplanting it will be extremely difficult, if not impossible. This whole situation is made all the more difficult because a range of 'for-profit' players, which by definition have a much more aggressive stance on provision, are hovering in the background, eager to increase their share of whatever markets develop.

Meanwhile, schools may find that other methods of increasing income prove equally sticky. Many deans and administrators told us of their plans to harness alumni groups, and, quite clearly, often saw them as relatively easily mobilised guarantors of a secure financial future. Such aspirations are probably realistic in the top-tier American schools, where there is a history of such things. Elsewhere, though, it will certainly not be so easy. At present, according to a recent survey, only 4.7 per cent of British alumni 'have provided financial support in an appeal or by way of a donation to their business school after graduating'.[14] Moreover, those in the know predict that attitudes will be hard to transform, even with resources and guile. An experienced UK business school administrator told us as follows:

> I think there are still people who are our sort of generation who
> think 'No, education's a public good, it's funded through the state
> and that's how it should be', and there's still that view around.
> I think people who are more connected to the higher education
> world, and the issues now, are probably going to become more
> receptive to knowing this is becoming a personal investment
> decision by students; universities are having to stand on their
> own feet financially. So, yes, I do see the different world we're
> living in and they may well take a different view but we need to

inculcate that from scratch now. It is tough going amongst people who weren't educated in that set of values and then say 'Please give us some money now you're earning more than £30,000' . . . So it's probably a twenty- or thirty-year plan . . . You need to build the sense that each generation kind of has an obligation of some sort to the following one . . .[15]

The prospects in the rest of Europe, Australia, Japan and the developing countries appear to be, for the most part, even less propitious.

On the other side of the balance sheet, the room for manoeuvre is also constrained. Cutting staff costs is always an option, and using innovative teaching methods linked to new information technologies may also offer economies, but, again, there are obvious downsides. Staff morale is already a problem in some places. We were surprised, as we have already noted, by the number of conversations that we had with faculty that swiftly turned into a litany of complaints. Put bluntly, those who consider themselves 'intellectuals' sometimes baulk at the prospect of 'production line teaching', where class sizes run into the hundreds. This is not, as they frequently told us, 'what they signed up to do'. Furthermore, many students who enrol for a postgraduate degree – and a comparatively *expensive* postgraduate degree at that – expect a certain amount of face-to-face contact time, and not just disembowelled interaction on a computer screen. Playing with the cost structure therefore definitely has its limits.

Of course, we have been proceeding so far as if the largely positive popular aura that currently exists around business schools will remain stable, but there are plenty of reasons for thinking that this, too, may be unrealistic. Criticism of the schools is nothing new, but it has certainly grown in intensity during the past few years, and also (as we have remarked) penetrated into the everyday media. Increasing dissatisfaction with globalisation, and anxiety about terrorism, Third World poverty, climate change and pollution, might provoke a tipping point. We have emphasised that the business school bubble is of recent origin. The current configuration is by no means guaranteed.

In ten years' time it could be courses in Mandarin, Arabic and environmental studies that pull in the numbers. It is a common but foolish conceit to assume that the existing zeitgeist will remain unaltered for ever. Nemesis often beckons. Interestingly, surveys in some countries already show that significant numbers of young people share a profound unease about aspects of the corporate world. In the United Kingdom only about a quarter of the population as a whole 'generally trust' business leaders to tell the truth, with no other professional group less trusted.[16] In the United States 'big business and related institutions', it is reported, enjoy 'little public support': surveys conducted by Within Worldwide, for example, show 'few Americans to have a "great deal" of confidence in any of their major institutions . . . but at the bottom of the league came big business, accountancy firms and financial markets'. Pollsters have made similar observations about other countries.[17] It might not take much for such attitudes to snowball out of control.

If the business schools continue along the same pathway, therefore, it seems that there will almost certainly be trouble in store. We imagine that the most prestigious institutions – Harvard, Chicago, London Business School, INSEAD, and so on – will continue to prosper. No doubt, as time passes, there will be rising stars in places such as India and China. Elsewhere, some of those with local monopolies may be able to hold there own. For the many hundreds of other players, however, the prospects look rather grim. One seductive option is 'the low road' – recruitment at any cost, reducing educational standards, squeezing staff for greater outputs and cutting corners wherever possible. By adopting such methods, schools may well struggle and survive, but the experience is unlikely to be a pleasant one, and nor will it be in any way socially desirable.

THE DEBATE ABOUT ALTERNATIVES

Of course, we are by no means the first to identify these potential problems, and in the last few years there has been a developing debate about alternative models.[18] A variety of different solutions have been mooted. But the choices really boil down to two basic approaches: getting closer to real-world managers, or getting closer to the academy. In the following paragraphs we briefly examine these options in turn, and evaluate their merits.

Proponents of creating a closer link with management normally invoke some kind of version of the long-established professional schools that are the cornerstones of much civic life. For example, in a recent *Harvard Business Review* article, Warren Bennis and James O'Toole contend that 'business schools would reap the greatest benefit from emulating the most innovative law schools', and justify themselves as follows:

> The law is a broad-based activity drawing upon many of the same disciplines relevant to business . . . Law schools, however, have not succumbed to physics envy and the scientism it spawns. Instead, they tend to reward excellence in teaching and in pragmatic writing. Research is an important component of legal practice and education, but most of it is applied research, and its validity is not equated with the presence of a scientific patina . . . When assessing the work of law school faculty members, evaluators ask questions such as, Is the research important? Is it useful? Is it interesting or original? Is it well thought-out, well argued, and well designed? All of these queries seem more appropriate as standards for appraising the work of business school faculties than the narrowly defined standard of scientific rigor.[19]

There is much to agree with here. There *is* something questionable about business school faculty who argue and write in abstruse jargon, and many of the topics that they research *do* seem arcane, sometimes even perversely so. If Bennis and O'Toole's piece is read as a plea for greater relevance, for remembering that academics have duties to the rest of society and not just a limited group of their immediate peers, we heartily concur. With that accepted, however, we are not convinced that this is actually the general panacea that its authors clearly intend. The professional school exemplar sounds good in theory, but in fact suffers from several significant difficulties and drawbacks.

It is important to be clear, first of all, about what the professional schools do. Their essential purpose is to turn out individuals who are well versed in the kind of knowledge that will directly help them practise their calling in later life. This is not static knowledge, because ideas about, for example, the law and medicine are of course constantly evolving. But it is knowledge that those who work in these fields at any given time will recognise as useful, and in most cases actually essential. Indeed, as we know, the schools and the professions that they serve commonly have very strong links precisely because they share a common conception of what the qualified practitioner must know. This happy fit is, of course, far from accidental. Senior faculty who teach in the schools also often simultaneously practise – for example, treating patients or appearing in court. Moreover, the professions concerned are highly organised, represented by long-standing associations that are able to speak with unchallenged authority. All this ensures a high degree of symbiosis. Could the business schools be revamped along similar lines? We remain doubtful.

There are obvious organisational difficulties. If business schools looked around today for partners who could truly represent management, they would struggle. Sectional interest groups, it is true, abound: the accountants have their own qualifying associations, and so on. But there is, and always has been, a dearth of umbrella bodies, and certainly nothing like the encompassing type that represents doctors and lawyers. The United Kingdom's Chartered Management Institute, for example, has a membership of 100,000, which sounds impressive on paper but is, in fact, only 2.5 per cent of the current management cohort in the country as a whole. Moreover, the schools could not necessarily call upon their own faculty to help plug the gap. Deans and administrators rarely seem to rate field experience highly. Selection committees usually prioritise research and academic expertise. Many faculty do consultancy work, but only a small minority actually run companies. Adjunct professors, brought in from outside, are relatively few in number, and sometimes treated as second-class citizens. In short, there is neither an obvious 'voice of management' nor an easy surrogate.

This, in turn, reflects a more fundamental problem, however, which is that there is little real consensus, anyway, about what management actually entails. It is quite possible to catalogue all the competencies that a doctor or lawyer must have in order to practise. It is far less easy to do the same for a manager. No doubt, some gurus and business school theorists will argue differently, and insist that they have produced comprehensive checklists. The 'airport lounge' literature on how to manage is certainly extensive. The facts tell their own story. When asked to define management essentials, academics disagree amongst themselves. There are in fact quite diverse, even competing, interpretations and traditions. On the ground, managers approach their work in radically different ways. Some techniques are acclaimed by everyone concerned as best practice, but are actually applied infrequently. Conversely, in other cases, fads and fashions sweep through countries and continents, even though the more enlightened vocally reject them. There is even considerable disagreement about basic values. For example, both faculty and managers are explicitly divided about the key question of whether firms should be run for stakeholders or shareholders. The inescapable conclusion is that management cannot be considered a profession in the same sense as medicine or law, and this in turn plainly raises strong doubts about whether the ideal of the professional school is in fact a realistic model to follow.

It is also necessary to point out that, even if all these problems were solved overnight, a strategy of getting close to management practitioners would still be problematic for another reason. Much discussion about how academics might cooperate more effectively with managers occurs without any consideration of power. The apparent assumption is that each side acts in good faith, and has an equal desire to reach the optimum solution. We wonder whether this is wholly realistic. Exemplary interactions do undoubtedly occur. But it is equally true that they are by no means necessarily guaranteed. Managers often have prime loyalty to their businesses, and quite specific kinds of agenda. Their desire for quick-fix solutions can loom large. They will also almost certainly be able to bring more resources to the table. In an increasingly competitive environment, academics may seize upon any chance to advance their careers, regardless of the implications. Collaboration can, therefore, easily end up being less about the search for truth and more about expediency, the advancement of a particular interest or even, perhaps, the deliberate marginalising of alternatives.

Recent explorations of the academy–business interface are not comforting. The investigative journalist Jennifer Washburn has impressively documented the ways in which US drug companies routinely use their extensive wealth to influence the scientific investigation of both illness and cures.[20] Her thesis is all the more striking because doctors and medical researchers are theoretically supposed to uphold the most exacting ethical codes. Surveying the issues more generally in 2003, Derek Bok, a former president of Harvard University, concluded: 'Universities have paid a price for industry support through excessive secrecy, periodic exposés of financial conflict, and corporate efforts to manipulate or suppress research results.'[21] As we have already remarked, how business schools currently cope with corporate influence is difficult to measure and assess. But it is surely not too far-fetched to suggest that, should the schools in future *deliberately* try to develop stronger relationships with 'the profession', they may well find themselves pitched into a world in which traditional academic values increasingly lose their purchase. And where integrity goes, needless to say, reputation often quickly follows.

What about the other suggested option – getting closer to the academy? Does this hold greater promise? Those who promote such a strategy argue that the business schools have been seduced by easy pickings.[22] They believe that the MBA, though lucrative, is essentially a degree that lacks real intellectual merit, and suggest that, by concentrating on it, the schools have deviated from the path of true scholarship. What is needed, they argue, is a reorientation towards traditional goals. The obsession with student recruitment, and thus media rankings, must be swiftly ditched. In place of gimmicks and fashion, faculty should concentrate on real research. This means new PhD programmes, and more applications to bona fide academic funding sources – primarily, the kind that already support projects in the social sciences. In this conception, then, if the business schools are to survive into the future, they will have to reinvent themselves as something akin to the time-honoured university department – teaching, certainly, but focused above all on the university's historic mission of unfettered knowledge creation. Does all this stand up?

There are, once again, some obvious practical difficulties. In the United States AACSB International figures demonstrate that the 'annual production of business school doctorates' is currently shrinking rather rapidly. Elsewhere, the numbers seem to be so small that it is difficult to identify trends. There are few studies that look at exactly why students undertake PhDs in business schools, but it is widely believed that opportunity cost plays a significant part in decision-making. The plain fact is that a newly graduated MBA, for example, can expect to make a great deal more in initial earnings by taking a job outside the academy than by continuing to do research within it. Organisations such as AACSB International might be able to persuade schools to reform their reward structures so radically that this problem can be overcome, but the chances look rather slim, not least because PhD teaching – at least as the degree regulations are currently formulated – tends to be relatively labour-intensive and therefore costly.[23]

There is also a danger that, by going down this route, the schools might end up in effect institutionalising their own irrelevance. Proponents of the 'return to scholarship' approach contend that 'basic theoretical research' precedes 'applied research', but that the two are inextricably linked by some kind of 'trickle down' mechanism.

Consequently, they believe, if the schools re-prioritised, their usefulness to the outside world need not suffer.[24] We have our doubts. We
recognise that there will always be a need for a certain amount of 'blue
skies' thinking, and we also understand there may be time lags
between advances in theory and everyday applications. But we are
aware, too, that the historical evidence regarding business schools in
this context is not reassuring. The truth is that the schools have to
varying extents always pursued fundamental research, but that this
has only ever brought fairly meagre returns in terms of everyday practice. Indeed, as we have already underlined, employers and managers
– the major potential end users – have been constantly critical for precisely this reason. In fact, more open-minded scholars are themselves
becoming increasingly aware of their own limitations, and the weakness of their work in real-life situations.

An example is telling. Social scientists within business schools
have long been concerned with allegedly rigorous modes of enquiry
geared to generating general rules and predictability. This is particularly so in relation to the discipline of strategy, because the widespread assumption is that 'what can be predicted can then be
controlled'. As many of those in the field now recognise, however, it
is far from clear what managers can really be taught about control,
and, in particular, about control in an uncertain future. One suggestion is that good strategy might in fact be 'non-predictive'.[25] More
damningly, it is also asserted that the very concept of 'strategy' may
be no more than an artifice created by researchers, something that has
little or no meaning outside the classroom.[26] Interestingly, this
chimes in with wider eddies of disenchantment about the allegedly
'scientific' status of management research as a whole. One or two
recent critics have persuasively identified cases in which unrealistic
assumptions have led to mechanistic and reductionist explanations,
and thence flawed theories – a situation that has, in turn, helped to
produce damaging practical applications in the outside world.[27] More
commonly, the charge against this kind of 'theory' is that it is manifestly useless. Addressing the American Academy of Management in

2003, the then president, Jone Pearce, reflected on her recent spell as interim business school dean, and reported that, in approaching her new role, she had found 'shared folk wisdom' far more helpful than anything she had previously learnt from the world of scholarship, in particular management journals.[28]

Our conclusion, therefore, is that all the possible strategies that we have looked at seem rather undesirable. Each *might* work, to a greater or lesser extent, for individual schools, but none offers a satisfactory way out for the sector as a whole – that is, a comprehensive solution to the existing maladies where there are no substantial downsides. We now examine a completely different approach, which we believe, speculative though it admittedly is, may just hold the key.

OPENING UP A SPACE FOR NEW KNOWLEDGE: THE BUSINESS SCHOOL AS *AGORA*

We remarked earlier that there were two relevant contextual changes going on at present, concerning, on the one hand, the university and, on the other, knowledge production. What we have discussed so far is strategies that are congruent with, or even inspired by, the former. What we want to do now is explore the potential that appears to be offered by the latter. Our supposition is that, if business schools are to survive and prosper meaningfully, then it is in this direction that they must reorientate. In essence, we suggest that the business school will need to go against the flow: the flow of the university's current use of business schools, the flow of those tendencies and critiques that would tend to move it either towards the Scylla of the academic model or towards the Charybdis of the professional model, and the flow of market responsiveness as the key touchstone of strategy.

It is time for the business school to define what it stands for in a new way that will position it centrally in the evolving world of knowledge. Indeed, it is our contention that the business school must clearly live the principle that the business of the business school *is* knowledge. We want to argue for an idea of the business school that is rooted less in 'marketing-speak' and more in a framework that transcends disciplinary boundaries and that bridges the profound gap that divides it from its stakeholders and users, actual and potential. Looking at this more closely, we believe that there must be new links between the business school and society; new links between research and practice; new links between business school research and research in other areas of social science, science, the arts and humanities; and changing relations between the business school and business itself, in order to provide knowledge for and about managers as they traverse an increasingly complex world. Cumulatively, this in turn demands that the business school transform itself into no less than a new and innovative kind of knowledge space.

How can we best describe what we have in mind? We have discussed this long and hard and conclude that the most apposite concept is the *agora*, an ancient Greek term first used to describe a centre of political, commercial, social and philosophical activity, a place of congregation, a forum for citizens, a religious and cultural focus and a seat of justice.[29] Obviously, we are not arguing for some direct transposition here; more an adaptation, the grasping of an essential spirit. What we particularly like about the notion of the *agora* is its democratic flavour, and its tolerance of dissent. The promise is of uninhibited discussion, the free exchange of ideas and the pursuit of truth. The contrast is with the *campus*, a field or pasture – a term that reflects the academy's location as a distant, sterile place, separate from the rest of the world.

From this starting point, we can move to broad practicalities. The challenge is to build something that reflects an acceptance of the reality that the academy can no longer claim its own autonomous separate space by right or tradition, that society is now talking back in a louder and more demanding voice than ever before, and that all of those involved need to become more cognisant of their responsibilities, in a context in which boundaries between state, market, science and culture are constantly being redefined. Such a design brief is, needless to say, quite taxing, but there are some important principles that will need to be respected. The *agora* must be an adaptable organisation composed of multiple stakeholders, running from the general to the rather specialised. It needs to be open and comprehensive, and, indeed, the more it is able to take on these characteristics the more 'socially robust' will be the knowledge it produces. It requires variety, so that it can constantly develop its assessments of the phenomena that it is studying. Finally, while the *agora* will continue to have aspirations about universalising understanding, it will also focus on local knowledge, tailored to purpose, and iconoclastic.[30]

If the business school is to transform itself in this kind of way then its organisational abilities will need to be enhanced. The only guaranteed method of making this happen is for those concerned to reflect upon and develop new management expertise, and simultaneously build the social capital and trust between partners that will allow the whole project to seed and grow. What this, in turn, means is that the business school will have to re-imagine itself, and become not just a 'knowledge carrier'[31] in its own right but also a key player in a new game, in which different stakeholders and a plethora of academic disciplines interact and evolve. In this respect, the schools can learn from those sciences in which innovative knowledge partnerships are already emerging. We have already referred to environmental sciences, but there are also interesting developments in physics. Here, some argue, the way science works is being comprehensively reorganised, with centralisation replaced by a scattering of production among multiple groups at multiple sites – as one account puts it, 'experiments are dispersed social-technical entities in which meaning is constructed at several peripheries and no single center can hold . . . [L]aboratories, factories . . . recombine in ways unimaginable half a century ago.' In this helter-skelter, the formerly separate worlds of applied and pure research cease to be clearly delineated as separate, and the management task is to organise networks of unprecedented spatial and 'authorial' complexity, in order to create an overarching sense of collective identity.[32] The important point about all these novel forms of collaboration is that they demand a kind of approach, not least from the academics involved, that is more reflexive, less certain of its own truth and more open to the truths of others than has ever been the case traditionally.

PARTNERS AND PARTICIPANTS

Who would be involved in the *agora*? In one sense, this is an irrelevant question, as the fundamental objective of what we are proposing is to widen access to the maximum degree possible, so that anyone with anything interesting to say will feel welcome. The objective is to open things up, not restrict them. With that acknowledged, however, it is clear that the contribution of some constituencies in the new endeavour will be crucial. As we have already indicated, we believe that links with the natural sciences may prove fruitful, not least because the relationship between the economy and the environment has obviously become a concern of worldwide importance. At the same time, we also believe that drawing in the full range of social sciences, together with the arts and humanities, will be vital. To explain why we have come to this conclusion, we need to look at some of the contributions that these disciplines might make.

To begin with, there is the important issue of scepticism. Much discussion of business today is relatively unquestioning. Fads and fashions are noted, and often enthusiastically gushed over, but they are rigorously interrogated much more rarely. There is little or no acknowledgement of history – the dimension of time. Conflicts and contradictions are frequently unrecognised. The discussion of consequences is circumscribed, often limited to a summation, in one version or another, of short-term profit and loss. Unfortunately, the business schools are sometimes just as culpable in these respects as anyone else. It is regrettable that much of the media, and some prominent consultants, failed to understand or report on what was occurring at Enron before its collapse.[33] But it is perhaps even more regrettable that, as we have seen, the schools, too, were sometimes equally blinkered. In our view, greater exposure to, say, political science, psychology and business history – to name but three – would help to overcome this problem by encouraging more balanced and rounded assessments. Once read, a book such as Geoffrey Tweedale's brilliant historical investigation of the asbestos industry, *Magic Mineral to Killer Dust*, stays in the mind for ever, and is an invaluable inoculation against corporate hype.[34] There are many other similar examples.

Beyond this, we believe that exposure to the broad array of these disciplines might also help in more substantive ways. It has been persuasively argued that much business education up to the present ultimately reflects one basic paradigm: what the British economist John Kay refers to as the American business model (ABM), an amalgam of unrestrained pursuit of self-interest, market fundamentalism and minimal state intervention.[35] It seems clear to many, including ourselves, that this situation is no longer tenable. Criticism of the ABM from inside and outside the business school is mounting. Some castigate the pervasive emphasis on immediate returns, and the over-reliance on 'slash and burn' tactics in corporate strategies.[36] Others wield a bigger club. The dystopian view of current trends is that the neoliberal free market model is inextricably producing increasingly serious problems across much of the world – maladies that range from declining wages, falling employment, growing inequality and social exclusion, to endemic insecurity for most if not all, the fracturing of societies, individualisation and ecological crisis.[37] In this context, there is growing interest in generating alternative models – organisations, processes and systems that do not share the ABM's increasingly obvious defects.

Shaping this quest is the key insight that markets function effectively only if they are embedded in social institutions that are themselves grounded in trust and community. Indeed, if balance is lost, and too much emphasis is placed on free markets, that may well – ironically – be destructive of the very social habitat that makes a successful, regulated system possible.[38] In this context, the urgent need is for a language that is relational rather than just transactional (that is, based purely on price)[39] and skills that range beyond the purely analytical, to include emotional intelligence and personal competence (self-awareness, self-regulation and motivation) but also social competence (empathy, awareness of others' feelings, needs and concerns, social skills and adeptness in relating to others).[40]

It is not easy to summarise all the different conversations that are occurring here, because they are so disparate, but a few examples will give some idea of the variety of new directions that are being taken. Jim March's pioneering Stanford course is a good starting point. It uses *Don Quixote, War and Peace* and other classic works of literature to challenge simplistic views of leadership, in order to make students more critical of existing management theory and improve everyday practice. March's perspective is grounded in the view that it is literature that is the best 'tool' available for making ethical and aesthetic sense of life, and that its study contributes to 'the poetry of leadership' – finding new meanings and new possibilities for collective action. March contrasts this 'poetry' with 'the plumbing of leadership', which is geared only to organisational efficiency.

Peter Senge's Society for Organizational Learning (SoL), based at the Massachusetts Institute of Technology, is another intriguing development.[41] This is a network of communities of enquiry and practice focused upon creating knowledge to enhance capacity for change. It brings together individuals (academics and business people), university departments, companies (such as AT&T, Boeing, Ford, Intel and the Shell Group) and public sector organisations, and draws on knowledge from science, social science, the arts and the humanities, with a particular focus on management issues such as knowledge and innovation, sustainability, and the integration of business and spirituality. The driving force behind Senge and SoL's work is a vision of 'capitalism with a conscience', a rethinking of growth in ways that are more congruent with the resource limits of the natural environment, global citizenship and ethical responsibility. The key methods used to foster learning are reflection and dialogue, the origins of which lie in ancient Greek philosophy. The SoL credo is set out in the Marblehead Letter of October 2001:

Complex, interdependent issues [such as social and economic divisions, the redefinition of growth, and the role of the corporation] are increasingly shaping the context for strategy. Yet the pressures created by these issues tend to keep leaders in a continual doing rather than reflecting mode. We believe that the tools and methods, and as important the quality of relationships and common concerns within the SoL community, can create unique opportunities for leaders to meet and genuinely 'think together', the real meaning of dialogue. Sustaining this opportunity may be vital in developing new capacities for shared understanding and coordinated action.

We, the sponsors and stewards of the SoL global organizing process, continue to want to develop SoL as a global enabling network where dialogue, research, collaborative action, and learning around such issues takes place at many levels . . . We believe that SoL's diverse membership and the commitment of members to creating and maintaining a reflective and action-oriented learning environment can be of enormous value as major global enterprises are faced with decisions that not only affect our own performance but have consequences felt around the world.

Senge, one of the world's most influential management thinkers, sees a main part of the challenge facing reformers as the deconstruction of dysfunctional folklore, not least that promoted by the business school. 'The problem has come in the last 50 to 75 years with the growth of business schools and large consulting firms,' he writes, and explains: 'The dominant mythology has become that the purpose of the company is to maximize return on investors' capital . . . Unfortunately business is run today by many people who went through MBA programs where they all learned the financial theory of the firm. It's simply a mythology, but mythologies often become reality for people.'[42]

Elsewhere, the emphasis has been on broader goals, the development of alternative overarching models and approaches. For some,

critical management studies (CMS) and critical management education seem to offer the best way forward. The premise here is that management is an exercise in power and control, a tool of capitalist
oppression, and that therefore the job of the business schools is to
provide a corrective, an education in which the drive for profitability
is explicitly balanced by other values, such as justice and ecological
well-being. For others, the most hopeful approach is to search for
whole new paradigms, which can then be used to supplant the ABM.
We have noted that the European Foundation for Management
Development on occasion speaks of developing and championing
'European values', and in our conversations with faculty in several
different schools we have been reminded that these ambitions res-
onate quite widely. There appear to be echoes, driven by similar
desires, in India and China. Interestingly, the pre-publicity for an
upcoming conference on African management asks 'How should
management and leadership theories be taught in sub-Saharan Africa?
Are there certain non-Western pedagogies that might be of relevance
to curriculum and program development in sub-Saharan Africa? What
about Western pedagogies?'[43] Of course, much of this thinking
remains controversial. Critics of CMS wonder, amongst other things,
whether it throws the baby out with the bathwater – in other words,
whether it offers any real guidance to those who actually have to run
organisations on a day-to-day basis.[44] The search for 'European values'
appears straightforward, but when operationalised, quickly runs into
difficulties, not least because on examination, the continent is of
course clearly rather diverse. Nevertheless, each of these lines of
thinking is provocative, and shows how wider perspectives can help
break the current logjam.

Finally, we think that contributions from the arts and the
humanities, in particular, are also highly desirable for a third reason,
which has to do with fundamental values. Business schools, whether
transformed into *agoras* or not, will always have to focus much of their
attention on the hard and unforgiving facts of life – the hurly-burly of
making money. The unarguable fact, however, is that immersion in the

commercial world has, in the past, produced cripplingly narrow visions of life. We have already referred extensively to the film *Wall Street*, and Gordon Gekko's 'Greed is good' speech. Quite clearly, this touched – and goes on touching – a major contemporary nerve. Wikipedia claims that 'Gekko became a source of inspiration for countless number of investment bankers around the world'.[45] On the other hand, it is clear that many in the academy and elsewhere found the speech repulsive, and viewed Gekko as an anti-hero. It is unlikely, to say the least, that intellectuals, whether in combination with each other or with wider groups of stakeholders, will be ever able to abolish what is, after all, one of Christianity's seven deadly sins. Clearly, however, many will believe that it is incumbent on them to continue trying. And, in this connection, great literature and art, for example, with their celebrations of very different values, may prove indispensable. In a ringing endorsement of what she terms 'humanistic values', the Chicago philosopher Martha Nussbaum writes as follows:

> People who have never learned to use reason and imagination to enter a broader world of cultures, groups, and ideas are impoverished personally and politically, however successful their vocational preparation . . . It would be catastrophic to become a nation of technically competent people who have lost the ability to think critically, to examine themselves, and to respect the humanity and diversity of others.[46]

We heartily endorse this viewpoint, and suggest that the *agora*, from the very start, should hold it dear.

PRACTICAL CHALLENGES, CATALYSTS AND 'GREEN SHOOTS'

We readily concede that the ideas we have laid out in the previous pages are very challenging in terms of practicalities. In discussing the *agora* with our colleagues, we have often been reminded that open systems of this type face many barriers, not least problems arising from salient and deep-rooted differences in culture. We cannot help but share their concerns, since the evidence is all around us. Many business schools have their own ways of doing things, their own informal understandings about what education is supposed to be about, and these frequently persist down through the years, even under different deans, giving institutions idiosyncratic characteristics, recognisable to staff and students alike. This, alone, is a formidable force for conservatism.[47] Moreover, within the schools, there are obvious gradations and hierarchies. Economists and finance specialists, for example, often view themselves as the academic elite, purveyors of solid, quantifiable data, and far superior to their colleagues in allegedly 'softer' qualitative disciplines. At the bottom of the pyramid, disdained widely to a greater or lesser extent (as we have noted), are those who deal in what is perceived as the mundane world of practice. Looking at academia as a whole, it is apparent that here, too, similar patterns persist. Certainly, cooperation between academics from different subject and departmental backgrounds is often at a premium. Put bluntly, the various 'tribes' by no means necessarily mix.[48] The French philosopher and psychoanalyst Julia Kristeva has written perceptively of academic interdisciplinarity as a 'perilous enterprise':

> Interdisciplinarity is always a site where expressions of resistance are latent. Many academics are locked within the specificity of their field . . . Even if they demonstrate or manifest a desire to work with other disciplines, more often than not it turns out that, in fact, the work undertaken fails to break new ground. Thus, the first obstacle is often linked to individual competences coupled with a tendency to jealously protect one's own domain. Specialists are often too protective of their own prerogatives, do not actually work with other colleagues.[49]

Finally, it is abundantly clear that academics and non-academics also find it difficult to communicate freely and without tension. Assumptions, mores, language and time horizons can be very different. Shared socio-economic status apparently does little to help bridge the gap. The owner of an 'upmarket dating agency' recently observed:

'I wouldn't say academics are snobby, but they move in a world that is quite insulated from other professions. You don't very often get academics mixing with bankers.' As an outsider, she found socialising in university circles stimulating, but was well aware that 'if you can't keep up because you've had one glass too many, you have to drop out of the conversation'.[50]

We do not have any magic solutions to these problems. It is a fact of life that communication between those from different backgrounds always throws up complications. Changing entrenched attitudes will require fortitude and patience. Much will depend on the business school leaderships. Nevertheless, although we admit that creating the *agora* will be very difficult, we also note that the situation is far from hopeless. The bigger picture is constantly evolving, and to some extent providing catalysts for the changes that we desire. To begin with, it is clear that the corporate world is taking the whole business of knowledge, and knowledge creation, much more seriously.[51] Firms view knowledge increasingly as a primary source of competitive strength, and intellectual capital as a key strategic weapon. The dominant rhetoric of strategy currently is about 'knowledge resources' and 'core competences', based upon unique configurations of 'knowledge assets'.

Moreover, these attitudes are partly mirrored at government level. A major debate in economic and social policy circles concerns the hypothesis that developed nations can no longer compete on cost and therefore need to develop superior knowledge. In the United Kingdom the Department of Trade and Industry talks about 'the knowledge driven economy', one in which the exploitation of knowledge has come to play a predominant part in the creation of wealth, and urges that it should encompass the exploitation and use of knowledge in all production and service activities, not just those sometimes classified as high-tech or knowledge-intensive.[52] Successive British government initiatives and policy documents have put the university at the heart of the knowledge-driven economy, envisaging it as a prime knowledge producer, linked to networks and regional clusters of competence in specific industrial domains. The logic is to drive up levels of creativity and skill in order to encourage innovation, and this has led to an increasing emphasis on the contribution of research and education to wealth creation.

Significantly, several higher education institutions are responding to the same agenda, and introducing new courses that work in a similar direction. At Nottingham the Institute for Enterprise and Innovation offers master's programmes for those initially trained in science, with a particular focus on bioscience. Similar developments are under way at the Open University, the Said Business School in Oxford and (as we have already described) the University of California, San Diego. In the United States there is much interest in the 'responsive Ph.D.', premised on the argument that 'the doctorate in totality and in every discipline will benefit enormously by a continuing interchange with the worlds beyond academia'.[53] The aim here is to promote new research paradigms and more adventurous scholarship, and to build partnerships between those who create the doctoral process and those whom it impacts upon – for example, employers who might benefit from the contributions to knowledge it creates. Themes running through 'responsive Ph.D.' programmes include connections to the community, professional development and the incorporation of a business perspective wherever it is appropriate. As regards the latter, the University of Texas at Austin offers postgraduates a credit-bearing course in entrepreneurship, designed to serve as a catalyst for innovations, based on the transfer of knowledge between the academy and society, and the integration of entrepreneurial thinking with scholarship, so that it has 'a meaningful impact on communities important to students'. The driving ambition of the course is to help students 'envision creative ways to apply intellectual training and expertise to scholarship, the community, the corporate world, and other arenas'.[54]

Lastly, we also believe that there are some current developments *within* business schools that gesture to the kind of future that we desire, and might even be thought of as 'green shoots'. In chapter 6, we spent some time looking at the Financial Services Research Forum. We can also point to SoL (mentioned above) and the Fenix programme, a collaboration between the Stockholm School of Economics and Chalmers University, funded by leading Swedish companies such as Volvo and Astra, which gives executives the chance to complete doctoral-level research on their own companies, but in a setting that constantly exposes them to leading-edge academic debate.[55] Of course, we concede that none of these conforms, in our sense, to an *agora*. Typically, knowledge is shared by the different participating constituencies, but it is less common for it to be actively co-produced: membership is restricted and there are financial barriers to entry; and academics essentially remain in control, shaping the agenda. That accepted, however, all these examples are interesting departures, and together they demonstrate that cooperation within the academy, and between the academy and the outside world, is achievable. Indeed, their very existence perhaps provides an antidote of a sort to the pessimist's seductive refrain that nothing can ever alter for the better.

THE CHALLENGE

In our view, therefore, the business schools stand at some kind of crossroads. With an unhappy past behind them, the schools today exhibit many debilitating maladies. They may decide to proceed into the future essentially unchanged, but that, we believe, would lead only to further pain. Their better option, we have argued, is to countenance a real change of direction. The notion that 'the business of the business school is business' needs to be firmly ditched, in favour of a much broader and more generous vision. Our suggestion is that the *agora* provides a suitable model, which will re-establish the social bond between the schools and the outside world.

We recognise that some will see our suggestions as idealistic and impractical. We do not underestimate the difficulties of moving 'from here to there'. Clearly, a good deal depends on the political choices of those who run universities. The attraction of short-term gains will have to be set aside, and replaced by a more thoughtful and longer-term strategy. Power will have to be ceded, as linkages with emerging outside bodies and social forces are first brokered and then deepened. None of this will be easy. We take heart, however, from the fact that some senior university administrators are also now calling for a major rethink. Harvard's Derek Bok, who we have already quoted, is a case in point. In a measured polemic, he argues that it is high time to combat the excessive commercialisation of higher education and the insidious 'marketisation' of teaching and research by ensuring that academic principles – informed by 'ideals that give meaning to the scholarly community and win respect from the public' – become the touchstone of university policy.[56] In essence, what we are recommending puts the business school and its 'bottom line', actual and potential, firmly at the heart of this agenda.

NOTES

1 Seymour E. Harris, *The Economics of Harvard* (New York: McGraw-Hill, 1970), 491.

2 Melvin T. Copeland, *And Mark and Era: The Story of the Harvard Business School* (Boston: Little, Brown and Company, 1958).

3 Daniel J. T. Schuker, 'Summers named Eliot Univ. prof', *Harvard Crimson, Online Edition*, 7 July 2006.

4 This chapter draws upon, and expands, points made in Ken Starkey, Armand Hatchuel and Sue Tempest, 'Rethinking the business school', *Journal of Management Studies*, 41(8) (2004), 1521–31.

5 Gerard Delanty, *Challenging Knowledge: The University in the Knowledge Society* (Buckingham: Society for Research into Higher Education/Open University Press, 2001), 22; Jean-François Lyotard, *The Postmodern Condition: A Report on Knowledge* (Manchester: Manchester University Press, 1984), 33.

6 Clark Kerr, *The Uses of the University* (Cambridge, MA: Harvard University Press, 1963).

7 Talcott Parsons and Gerald M. Platt, *The American University* (Cambridge, MA: Harvard University Press, 1973).

8 Lyotard, *The Postmodern Condition*, 4–5.

9 Bill Readings, *The University in Ruins* (Cambridge, MA: Harvard University Press, 1996), 19, 46.

10 See pp. 7–8 above and Alison Utley, 'Outbreak of "new managerialism" infects faculties', *Times Higher Education Supplement*, 20 July 2001. On this subject, see also Birnbaum, *Management Fads in Higher Education*.

11 Michael Gibbons, Camille Limoges, Helga Nowotny, Simon Schwartzman, Peter Scott and Martin Trow, *The New Production of Knowledge: The Dynamics of Science and Research in Contemporary Societies* (London: Sage, 1994); and Helga Nowotny, Peter Scott and Michael Gibbons, *Re-Thinking Science: Knowledge and the Public in an Age of Uncertainty* (Cambridge: Polity Press, 2001).

12 Ulrich Beck, *Risk Society: Towards a New Modernity* (London: Sage, 1992).

13 Gibbons et al., *The New Production of Knowledge*, 3.

14 Survey details at www.the-abs.org.uk/ABS_PR_25.html.

15 Interview, 11 March 2004.

16 Ipsos Mori finding as at 2005: see www.ipsos-mori.com/polls/trends/truth.shtml.

17 Allan Hyde and Brian Grosschalk, 'The business world will never be the same again', 16 September 2003, at www.mori.com.

18 For a useful short introduction to current thinking, see Chris Ivory, Peter Miskell, Helen Shipton, Andrew White, Kathrin Moeslein and Andy Neely, *The Future of Business Schools in the UK* (London: Advanced Institute of Management Research, 2006).

19 Bennis and O'Toole, 'How business schools lost their way', 103.

20 Washburn, *University, Inc.*

21 Derek Bok, *Universities in the Marketplace: The Commercialization of Higher Education* (Princeton, NJ, and London: Princeton University Press, 2003), 77.

22 Zimmerman, *Can American Business Schools Survive?*

23 For relevant discussion, see AACSB International Management Education Task Force, *Management Education at Risk*, esp. 13, and Ivory et al., *The Future of Business Schools in the UK*, 16–18.

24 Zimmerman, *Can American Business Schools Survive?*, 6–7.

25 Robert Wiltbank, Nicholas Dew, Stuart Read and Saras S. Sarasvathy, 'What to do next? The case for non-predictive strategy', *Strategic Management Journal*, 27(10) (2006), 981–96.

26 Andrew Inkpen and Nandan Choudhury, 'The seeking of strategy where it is not: towards a theory of strategy absence', *Strategic Management Journal*, 16(4) (1995), 313–32; Jay B. Barney and Robert E. Hoskisson,

'Strategic groups: untested assertions and research proposals', *Managerial and Decision Economics*, 11(3) (1990), 187–98.

27 Eric W. K. Tsang, 'Behavioral assumptions and theory development: the case of transaction cost economics', *Strategic Management Journal*, 27(11) (2006), 999–1011. See also Ghoshal, 'Bad management theories are destroying good management practice', 75–91.

28 Jone Pearce, 'What do we know and how do we really know it?', *Academy of Management Review*, 29(2) (2003),175–9.

29 We have borrowed this idea from Nowotny, Scott and Gibbons, *Re-Thinking Science*.

30 Nowotny, Scott and Gibbons, *Re-Thinking Science*, 262.

31 Kerstin Sahlin-Andersson and Lars Engwall (eds.), *The Expansion of Management Knowledge: Carriers, Flows and Sources* (Stanford, CA: Stanford University Press, 2002).

32 Peter Galison and Caroline A. Jones, 'Factory, laboratory, studio: dispersing sites of production', in Peter Galison and Emily Thompson (eds.), *The Architecture of Science* (Cambridge, MA: MIT Press, 1999), 497–533.

33 See, for example, Stefan Stern, 'Red faces on the City desks', *Independent*, 19 March 2003, and Matthew Beard, 'Bosses gather for audience with Enron admirer', *Independent*, 29 March 2003.

34 Geoffrey Tweedale, *Magic Mineral to Killer Dust: Turner and Newell and the Asbestos Hazard* (Oxford: Oxford University Press, 2000).

35 John Kay, *The Truth About Markets* (London: Penguin Books, 2004).

36 See, for example, Will Hutton, *The State We're In* (London: Jonathan Cape, 1995).

37 Ulrich Beck, *The Brave New World of Work* (Cambridge: Polity Press, 2001).

38 Will Hutton, *The World We're In* (London: Little, Brown, 2002).

39 Carrie R. Leana and Denise M. Rousseau, *Relational Wealth: The Advantages of Stability in a Changing Economy* (New York: Oxford University Press, 2000).

40 Daniel Goleman, *Working with Emotional Intelligence* (London: Bloomsbury Publishing, 1999).

41 What follows is based upon material at www.solonline.org.

42 Peter Senge, 'Better business', *SGI Quarterly – A Buddhist Forum for Peace, Culture and Education* (October 2006), at www.solonline.org/news/item?item_id=9000239.

43 Pre-publicity for conference on 'Leadership and management studies in sub-Saharan Africa', to be held in Accra, Ghana, during 2008.

44 Ken Starkey, 'Critical management education – a step not far enough?', unpublished working paper.

45 See http://en.wikipedia.org/wiki/Gordon_Gekko.

46 Martha Nussbaum, *Cultivating Humanity: A Classical Defense of Reform in Liberal Education* (Cambridge, MA: Harvard University Press, 1997), 297, 300.

47 See, for example, Simon Kragh and Sven Bislev, 'The globalisation of business schools: international business school students share many common values, but those values are not always reflected in the cultures of the institutions where they study', *European Business Forum*, 22 March 2005.

48 See Hazard Adams, *The Academic Tribes* (Urbana and Chicago: University of Illinois Press, 1988), and Tony Belcher and Paul R. Trowler, *Academic Tribes and Territories* (Buckingham and Philadelphia: Society for Research into Higher Education/Open University Press, 2001).

49 Julia Kristeva, 'Institutional interdisciplinarity in theory and in practice', *de-, dis-, ex-*, 2, 5–6.

50 Harriet Swain, 'Come-hither eyes . . . and some impressive publications', *Times Higher Education Supplement*, 20 October 2006.

51 Nancy M. Dixon, *Common Knowledge: How Companies Thrive by Sharing What They Know* (Boston: Harvard Business School Press, 2000); Thomas H. Davenport and Laurence Prusak, *Working Knowledge* (Boston: Harvard Business School Press, 1998).

52 Department of Trade and Industry, *Our Competitive Future: Building the Knowledge Driven Economy* (London: Department of Trade and Industry, 1998).

53 Anon. *The Responsive Ph.D.: Innovations in U.S. Doctoral Education* (Princeton, NJ: Woodrow Wilson National Fellowship Foundation, 2005), 5.

54 See www.utexas.edu/ogs/development.html.

55 Bengt Stymne, 'Travels in the borderland of academy and industry', in Niclas Adler, A. B. (Rami) Shani and Alexander Styhre (eds.), *Collaborative Research in Organizations: Foundations for Learning, Change, and Theoretical Development* (Thousand Oaks, CA: Sage Publications, 2004), 49–50.

56 Bok, *Universities in the Marketplace*, 206.

Epilogue

There is a story to be found on the internet in various versions. Set in a South American country, it describes a boat arriving in the harbour of a tiny village. A US tourist disembarks and compliments a local fisherman on the quality of the fish he is selling. Then the tourist asks the fisherman how long it took him to catch them. 'Not very long,' the fisherman answers. The American spots a business opportunity. 'Why don't you stay out longer, and then you can catch more?' he asks. The fisherman explains that the size of the catch is perfectly adequate for his needs. It is enough to feed himself and his family. The American asks him what he does with the rest of his time. The fisherman answers that, once his needs are met, he spends his time sleeping late, playing with his children, taking a siesta with his wife. He spends his evenings in the village meeting with friends, playing his guitar, singing songs. He has a full life, he tells the tourist.

The tourist gets excited. 'I have an MBA from Harvard Business School and I can help you. What you need to do is to start fishing longer every day. You should then sell the extra fish that you catch, and with the extra income you earn you can buy a bigger boat, and catch more fish.' The fisherman asks, 'And what then?' The tourist warms to his theme with missionary zeal. 'The larger boat will enable you to earn extra money. You can then buy a second boat, a third boat. Why, soon you will have enough money to own a whole fleet. You won't need a middleman to sell your fish on. You will be a big player, who can negotiate directly with the processing plants. The sky's the limit! You could even buy your own plant. Then you could leave this small village and move to the capital, or Los Angeles, or New York. You could become the chief executive of a major international corporation.'

The fisherman asks how long all this will take. 'Twenty to twenty-five years maximum,' answers the tourist.

'And after that?' enquires the fisherman. 'Well,' says the tourist, 'then it gets really good. When your business is really big you can start playing the stock market and make really serious money – millions and millions.'

'And after that?' the fisherman wonders.

'After that you'll be able to take it easy – retire, even. Relocate to a small village near the sea, sleep late, play with your children, go fishing for fun, take a siesta with your wife, spend your evenings playing the guitar, singing with friends.'

Index